THE AGE OF CHARLES MARTEL

THE MEDIEVAL WORLD

Editor: David Bates

THE AGE OF
CHARLES MARTEL

PAUL FOURACRE

An imprint of **Pearson Education**

Harlow, England · London · New York · Reading, Massachusetts · San Francisco
Toronto · Don Mills, Ontario · Sydney · Tokyo · Singapore · Hong Kong · Seoul
Taipei · Cape Town · Madrid · Mexico City · Amsterdam · Munich · Paris · Milan

Pearson Education Limited
Edinburgh Gate
Harlow
Essex CM20 2JE
England
and Associated Companies throughout the world

Visit us on the world wide web at:
http://www.pearsoneduc.com

First published 2000

ISBN 0 582 06475 9 CSD
ISBN 0 582 06476 7 PPR

British Library Cataloguing-in-Publication Data
A catalogue record for this book is available from the British Library

Typeset by 35 in 11/13pt Baskerville MT
Produced by Addison Wesley Longman Singapore (Pte) Ltd.
Printed in Singapore

To my family.

CONTENTS

EDITOR'S PREFACE

Charles Martel (*c.* 688–741) is a figure of well-night heroic proportions in much twentieth-century historiography. At the heart of this reputation are the famous victory over an Islamic army at the battle of Poitiers in 732 or 733 and his contribution to the eventual establishment of his Carolingian descendants as the ruling family over the Frankish lands. He can be portrayed not only as saving Christendom in what is often seen as one of the decisive battles of world history, but as preparing the ground for the enormously important reign of his even better known grandson, Charlemagne. Since achievements on this scale would appear to demand special explanations, Charles has been identified not only as a great warrior, but as someone who prepared the way for the final deposition of the Merovingian kings in 751 by his son Pippin and who revolutionised the military organisation of the Frankish state. His patronage of missionary activities amongst the pagans to the east is seen as making the Carolingians into the papacy's favourite family, thereby explaining papal support for Pippin's removal of the Merovingians.

Paul Fouracre's new treatment of Charles and his times examines critically each element of this reputation and places Charles securely within the social, political and cultural setting of the eighth century. In order to do this, the book supplies a panoramic appraisal of power, kingship and aristocratic values, which leads to a reassessment of most aspects of Charles's career. The great warrior remains at the centre of the picture, but the long-term goals and innovative policies frequently attributed to him are for the most part rejected in favour of an analysis which sees him as an extremely able embodiment of the norms and values of contemporary politics. Thus, for example, while Charles's attitudes were certainly motivated by a family-centred drive to keep the Carolingians at the heart of the politics of the Frankish world, his success in regaining his father's position as mayor of the palace to the Merovingian kings was based on immediate personal concerns over status and power. The brief period at the end of his life when he did not install a new Merovingian king was an episode which his sons speedily brought to an end and which did not therefore lead inexorably to the disappearance of the Merovingians. Even the victory at Poitiers was one event in a broader struggle against Islamic attacks and should not be seen as the *one* decisive moment. The cooperation of missionaries, papacy and Franks largely conformed to already existing patterns.

Paul Fouracre's extensive research and publications on the history of the early medieval Frankish kingdoms make him a superbly qualified author to contribute this latest book to the Medieval World series. His skilful reinterpretation of key sources allows him to reassess many key later eighth- and ninth-century narratives whose prime purpose was to present Carolingian triumph as a logical and legitimate process. By stripping away this misleading veneer, he is able to give Charles Martel's life a much more realistic context and to use it for a wide-ranging reappraisal of the political life of the Frankish kingdom in the seventh and eighth centuries. The result is a book which illuminates the forces which both threatened and sustained the geographically vast kingdom of the Franks. Accessibly written and presenting every historical controversy clearly, the book fulfils magnificently the series' aim of using an individual's life to illuminate a wider subject.

David Bates

PREFACE

This book has been more than a decade in the making, or, rather, eight years of inaction followed the signing of a contract to write it, and then came two years of fitful writing. I must therefore thank David Bates, the series editor, and Longman, for their patience. I hope that I am wiser than I was when I first thought of writing a book about Charles Martel, and that the delay has allowed me to develop a more subtle understanding of this subject. The intervening period has certainly seen some excellent work on the subject of Frankish history, much to my benefit.

In keeping with the series guidelines I have tried to keep the notes to a minimum, and to refer the reader to English translations of the sources and to secondary works in English. It is a reflection of the liveliness of scholarship in the field of early medieval history in Britain and North America that there is so much to read on this subject in English, but very many works on early Carolingian history are in German, and this preponderance is reflected in the notes and bibliography. Although I have studied the Franks for over twenty years, I was genuinely surprised to find how little there was to read on the subject of Charles Martel in French. This is a great pity, as it is in France that Charles Martel's place in history is most in need of re-evaluation.

I am indebted to the kindness of colleagues who have helped this work on its way. My colleagues at Goldsmiths College have always been encouraging and supportive. Jennifer Ward in particular has been a valued sounding board over many years. Elsewhere in London, I thank John Gillingham for some very useful advice on how to structure a book of this nature. Jinty Nelson read all of it, Guy Halsall very nearly all of it, and Susan Reynolds the chapter which deals with the question of 'feudalism'. All three of them not only made valuable suggestions and made face-saving interventions, they also often provided me with new material and put the books and articles I should have read into my hands. Jinty Nelson has never ceased to be my intellectual mentor, even though she discharged her duty as my Ph.D. supervisor nearly twenty years ago. Ian Wood was typically generous with his thoughts and unpublished work, and Andrew Weir used his journalistic skills to track down material on the 'groupe Charles Martel'.

Finally, David Ganz used his encyclopaedic knowledge of manuscripts to think of, and find, a suitable illustration for the cover of this book. The help of such colleagues and friends made it often a pleasure to write *The Age of Charles Martel*, and reminded me of how lucky I am to study early medieval history in London. They are not, of course, responsible for any of its deficiencies or for the large number of errors I am sure to have made.

Paul Fouracre
Goldsmiths College, London
July 1999

ABBREVIATIONS

AMP — *Annales Mettenses Priores*

Fredegar/ — *The Fourth Book of the Chronicle of Fredegar with its*
Fred. Contin. — *Continuations*

LHF — *Liber Historiae Francorum*

MGH — *Monumenta Germaniae Historica*

MGH DD — *Monumenta Germaniae Historica, Diplomata Imperii*

MGH SRG — *Monumenta Germaniae Historica, Scriptores Rerum Germanicum in usu scholarum*

MGH SRM — *Monumenta Germaniae Historica, Scriptores Rerum Merovingicarum*

MGH SS — *Monumenta Germaniae Historica, Scriptores*

INTRODUCTION

Charles Martel was born about the year 688, and he died in 741. His contemporaries remembered him first of all as a supremely successful military leader. They were particularly impressed by his victory over an Arab force in 732 or 733 in the encounter known as the battle of Poitiers. The fame of this victory spread quickly and widely. In England, for instance, there may be a reference to it at the very end of Bede's *Ecclesiastical History*.[1] Bede, or a very early copyist of his work, spoke of a Frankish triumph which turned the tide of war against the 'dreadful plague of Saracens'. This assessment of the victory would in fact be handed down to modern times, elevating the battle of Poitiers to a place amongst the supposedly decisive battles of history and Charles Martel to a place among the heroes of France. It is a measure of the extent to which this view of Charles Martel as the saviour of France from the Arabs has affected the modern imagination that an extreme right-wing terror group in France has named itself after him. Between 1973 and 1991 this 'groupe Charles Martel' was responsible for a series of attacks on people of North African origin. It is most unfortunate that post-war French scholarship has done so little to challenge a national myth capable of inspiring such outrageous behaviour. As we shall see in the course of this study, there is every reason to question the significance traditionally attached to the battle of Poitiers, and Charles Martel is long overdue for removal as a 'French' national hero. Most recent work in this area has in fact been done by German-speaking scholars.[2]

Charles, therefore, was, and sometimes still is, regarded as a heroic warrior who defended Christ's people from unbelievers. His nickname, Martellus, 'the Hammer', which was first recorded in the ninth century, invited comparison

---

1 *Bede's Ecclesiastical History of the English People*, ed. and trans. B. Colgrave and R. Mynors (Oxford 1969), V, ch. 23, pp. 556–7.
2 There is only one fairly recent French biography of Charles: J. Deviosse, *Charles Martel* (Paris 1978), but this is hardly a scholarly work. Deviosse's bibliography lists only seven works published after 1950, only four works in German, and none in English. The battle of Poitiers is treated as a massive set-piece clash between civilisations, which would decide the fate of Europe. See pp. 159–78.

with the Old Testament hero Joshua.[3] This analogy was already being made explicit in the later eighth century when the author of the *Continuations of the Chronicle of Fredegar* likened Charles's assault on the city of Avignon to Joshua's capture of Jericho. Joshua, who with divine assistance crushed the enemies of the Lord throughout the land of Israel, was a telling role model for Charles Martel, for the comparison pointed to the absolute right of the Franks to conquer other peoples and to expect God's help in their task. The portrayal of the Franks as God's people would gather strength in the generations after Charles Martel, and as the Franks became more and more powerful, Charles Martel's reputation would likewise grow as he came to be seen as the progenitor of the later Frankish successes. By the late eighth century it was claimed that the Franks had killed 375,000 Arabs at Poitiers, a figure which would be widely quoted for the rest of the Middle Ages.

Given his heroic stature as the saviour of Christendom against the Arabs, it is at first sight surprising to learn that Charles Martel also came to be regarded as an enemy of the church. This view developed in the ninth century and found expression in a vision in which the great warrior's tomb in the monastery of St Denis was opened and found to be empty. What could be seen, however, were scorch marks which indicated that Charles had been dragged off to hell by a dragon. The reason for his grisly fate was that he had plundered the lands of the church. We shall see later how the picture of Martel as a despoiler of the church was crafted, and also what purpose that image was meant to serve, but the point to be made here is that it was in the attempt to reconcile these two contrasting reputations that the modern view of the age of Charles Martel was generated. The age was seen as a watershed period of European history which would witness the birth of medieval society, no less. The solution to what one might term the 'hero/villain problem' was cogent, for it argued that the contradictions apparent in the sources were in fact different sides of the same coin, namely, Charles Martel's reorganisation of society for war. The reorganisation resulted not only in military success for Charles Martel himself, but it also determined the shape European society would take in the longer term. Like all clear and simple explanations of supposedly crucial moments of history, this view was, and indeed still is, attractive.

It was the great German legal historian Heinrich Brunner who in 1887 thus formulated the thesis that Charles Martel was an outstanding warrior

---

3 *Vita Rigoberti*, ed. W. Levison, *MGH SRM* VII (Hanover and Leipzig 1920), ch. 8, p. 66: '[Charles] . . . who was later known as "Martellus" on account of his fierce spirit and because from an early age he was a warlike man, most brave in his strength'.

who saved Christendom precisely because of (rather than despite) his spoliation, or secularisation, of church lands. Martel, Brunner argued, had taken land from the church in order to lease it out to his warriors in return for their military service. This new step was necessary to provide extra resources for a military machine which was becoming more expensive to maintain as it developed into a predominantly cavalry force. It was cavalry, argued Brunner, which gave Charles Martel the edge over his enemies, and in particular over the Arabs, hitherto unstoppable by an ill-equipped and slow-moving European infantry. According to the Brunner thesis, the social and economic implications of this military change were immense. For as the new style cavalrymen were dispersed over the sequestered church lands they became masters of the countryside, the ancestors, as it were, of the knightly class of the High Middle Ages, around whom the political institutions and economic structures of medieval society would be built.[4] In this view, therefore, the military needs of Charles Martel gave birth to 'feudal society', that is, a society based upon the tenure of land in return for military service.

Brunner's arguments gained ready acceptance and other historians went on to elaborate the institutional and economic aspects of his thesis. They also drew out the importance of the Arab invasions as a prime factor in the ending of Antiquity and the birth of the Middle Ages. Finally, a mid-twentieth-century version of the Brunner thesis offered a technological explanation for the change to cavalry warfare: that it was the introduction of the stirrup into Martel's armies which allowed the cavalrymen to become proper shock troops, that is to say, riders who could charge the enemy and would be able to stand the shock of impact, thus staying in the saddle after knocking down the opponent with a lance. The stirrup, in other words, allowed the cavalry to become fully effective for the first time in European history.[5] Now, so much cold water has been poured on these ideas that one might have expected them to have sunk out of sight decades ago, but they remain topical because they actually address the central questions about the career of Charles Martel: why was he so successful? What were the effects of his success? To what extent did he foster military, social and economic change? Or was he rather the beneficiary of changes already in motion? These fundamental questions remain open because although we know enough about Charles Martel to see that he was indeed a figure of massive historical stature, there is surprisingly little evidence which bears directly

---

4   The seminal article is H. Brunner, 'Der Reiterdienst und die Anfänge des Lehnwesens', *Zeitschrift der Savigny-Stiftung für Rechtsgeschichte, Germanistische Abteilung*, 8 (1887), 1–38.

5   Lynn White Junior, *Medieval Technology and Social Change* (Oxford 1962), pp. 1–28.

upon Charles himself. So when we come to explain his career and its significance, we must draw on a wide range of background information. Any study of the career of Charles Martel will thus spend rather more time discussing the historical background than examining the man himself. It is bound, therefore, to become a work on the age of Charles Martel, rather than a biography.

Recent work on this subject has continued to grapple with the problems first addressed in Brunner's generation, albeit to play down the element of change in the period by demonstrating that Charles did not secularise church lands, that he was not the master of a new form of warfare, that society was not reorganised around cavalrymen, and so on. Similarly, much work has been done showing how earlier historians misinterpreted, or mis-understood, the sources when they saw in them elements of great change. In particular, the partisan nature of the narrative sources has been well documented, and the steps in the construction of Martel's reputation, as both hero and villain, have been illuminated. I too shall address these issues because they are concerned with the central, and still very much unre-solved, question of the historical significance of the age of Charles Martel. The result, it is to be hoped, will be a fresh interpretation of his career which takes on board the advances of recent scholarship. The particular purpose of this volume, therefore, is to bring the specialist studies of the different aspects of the age to bear upon a general account of Charles's career. For despite all the scholarly attention this subject has received, there is still no study in English devoted to the sum of Charles's career rather than to its various parts. And where this study hopes to gain new insights is in adding a cultural dimension to the more familiar aspects of military and political history. Instead of beginning with the assumption that Charles Martel was the architect of a qualitatively different and new political order, we will start with an examination of the nature of the previous Merovingian regime which was the platform for Frankish expansion in the eighth cen-tury. For if we are to identify areas of change, this must start with a proper understanding of what went before. A sense of the basis of power and of how power was mediated through custom and religion should also make us more alive to the cultural echoes of the political and military events which are the principal concern of our sources.

The first half of the eighth century was ostensibly a period of great pol-itical and military change as an old and allegedly ailing Merovingian dynasty gave way to a new and vigorous Carolingian regime. The Merovingian kingdom had been made up of three parts or sub-kingdoms. These were: Austrasia, the eastern part which included lands on either side of the River Rhine, and stretched as far west as the Champagne in present-day France; Neustria, which was made up of a great arc of lands that ran from

Champagne, through the Paris basin round to the Loire mouth; and Burgundy, which bordered Austrasia and Neustria in the Champagne and stretched southwards down into the Rhône valley and towards the Alps. To the south and south-east of these core regions lay Aquitaine and Provence, the different 'counties' (*civitates* or *pagus*) of which were attached to either Austrasia or Neustria in a complex of local arrangements. In the east, the duchies of Thuringia, Bavaria and Alemannia owed allegiance to the Merovingian rulers of Austrasia.

Over the course of the seventh century, Neustria and Burgundy had coalesced into a single kingdom, and much of the history of the later seventh century is taken up with Austrasia's struggle to resist absorption into a Frankish kingdom unified under Neustrian leadership. The struggle was fought out in the outlying regions too, and it provides a setting for the career of Charles Martel. His rise to power can be seen as marking the resolution of this struggle with the triumph of Austrasia over all the other regions. Under his descendants, the Carolingians, the old Merovingian regional identities, and the politics based on them, would fade away.[6] The other main feature in the background to Charles Martel's career was the Franks' relationships with other peoples. Francia and its dependent duchies shared borders with Frisians, Saxons, Slavs, Lombards and Visigoths, with the latter being replaced by Arabs in the time of Charles's father Pippin. We have already seen that of these neighbours and enemies it is traditionally the Arabs who have been seen as the most dangerous. This is highly debatable, but the arrival of a people from the Middle East on Francia's borders does require a word of explanation.

Following the death of the Prophet Mohammed in the year 632, Arab forces under the banner of Islam had spread from Arabia northwards into Palestine and Syria, north-eastwards into Iraq and Iran, and north-westwards into Egypt and the rest of North Africa. By the end of the seventh century they had reached the Atlantic coast of North Africa and in 711 they crossed over into Spain where they overwhelmed the forces of the Visigothic regime. Although the Pyrenees formed a natural barrier against a further permanent expansion northwards, the Arabs were raiding across the mountains into Aquitaine in the early 720s. It is against this history of an apparently inexorable advance that Charles Martel's victory against the Arabs at Poitiers in 732 or 733 has been judged so important. He was, in other words, the only person capable of turning the Arab tide. As we have

---

6 For the transformation and demise of Neustrian identity, see the Introduction by K-F. Werner, 'Faire Revivre le Souvenir d'un Pays Oublié', in H. Atsma (ed.), *La Neustrie. Les Pays au Nord de la Loire de 650 à 850*, Beihefte der Francia, 16 (2 vols, Sigmaringen 1989), pp. xiii–xxxi.

already hinted, the significance of his victory has been greatly exaggerated, but the Arabs were nevertheless one of the major forces in Charles Martel's world. The final element of this world to be introduced here is the papacy. Though not a 'people', nor a neighbour or an enemy, the papacy never lay beyond the mental horizons of the Franks. From the later seventh century onwards, the popes in Rome were becoming more proactive among the peoples north of the Alps (including, of course, the English). In the age of Charles Martel this activity had important consequences in Aquitaine, Bavaria and Thuringia. If any Frankish ruler wished to control these regions, they too had to deal with the popes.

The Carolingian dynasty, which replaced the Merovingians and reshaped Frankish history, took its name from Charles (Carolus) Martel, though he himself, of course, ruled as only the leading royal official (mayor of the palace), never as king, even though in the later Middle Ages he might be portrayed as wearing a crown (see the frontispiece to this volume). The first Carolingian king was his son, Pippin I, who was consecrated in the year 751, and the regime is generally considered to have reached its apogee under Pippin's successor, the legendary Charlemagne (d. 814). In this context the age of Charles Martel is seen as a decisive phase in the rise of the Carolingians, in which the family (known to historians as 'Arnulfings' or, more often, 'Pippinids' in the pre-Martel period) broke out of their Austrasian homeland and imposed themselves on all of Francia. The political and military steps by which this breakthrough happened are revealed in narrative sources which are with one exception all solidly pro-Carolingian. The effect of this kind of reportage was to magnify the triumph of the family, and it was the apparent magnitude of their success which encouraged Brunner's generation to explain it in terms of phenomenal change. Modern scholarship has picked away at this picture of unqualified Carolingian success by taking on board the fact that the sources reveal only one point of view, and that late-eighth- and early-ninth-century writers were, in the main, working under the patronage of the Carolingian family itself. But though challenged on many points, the narrative of Merovingian decline and Carolingian rise still forms the basic framework for the history of this period because it is a history so firmly and consistently supported by sources close to events. That narrative we must therefore basically accept, but where we must differ is on points of interpretation.

The four main sources which outline the events of this period are the *Liber Historiae Francorum*, the *Continuations of the Chronicle of Fredegar*, the early Carolingian annals and the so-called *Earlier Annals of Metz*. Their narratives can be supplemented by the retrospective comments of Einhard's *Life of Charlemagne*, by a range of hagiographic sources, by letters and charters, and by narratives composed outside Francia in Italy, England and Spain.

Comment will be made on the nature and reliability of each of these sources as information is drawn from them, but it will be helpful at the outset to put our main narrative sources into context. The *Liber Historiae Francorum* (*LHF* for short) is the one source which is not obviously pro-Carolingian, for the simple reason that it was composed around the year 727 and thus predates the period of unchallenged Carolingian leadership.[7] For the same reason, its view of events in the early eighth century provides some alternative to those later Carolingian accounts written with the benefit of hindsight and with the justification of their patrons in mind. It is not clear who wrote the *LHF* or exactly for whom it was written, but the chronicle can be said to express the point of view of what it terms the *Franci*, meaning the Frankish leaders of the Neustrian heartlands in the Seine–Oise region.[8] The value of this text is that it shows the history of Martel's family in the context of politics which still revolved around the Merovingian kings and the Neustrian court. Towards the end of the work the family does become more prominent, and in fact Charles Martel emerges as one of the author's heroes, but equally it emphasises both the fragility of Pippinid success and the continuing importance of the *Franci*.

The *Continuations of the Chronicle of Fredegar* are based on the *LHF* up to the year 721 when the latter's account effectively breaks off. Thereafter the chronicle was continued up to the year 751 on the orders of Charles Martel's half-brother, Count Childebrand, and then Nibelung, Childebrand's son, had the work carried on to 768 when it ends.[9] It has recently been argued that the work was in fact written up in two stages rather than added to piecemeal over the period 721–68, and that Childebrand commissioned the first section to present to his nephew King Pippin upon his elevation to the throne in 751. The second section, it is argued, was similarly a *pièce d'occasion*, to be presented to Pippin's son Carloman at the time of his accession to the throne in 768. Whatever the exact circumstances in which the work was put together, it is clear that it is strongly pro-Carolingian in sentiment. Its narrative is the earliest and most detailed account of the whole career of Charles Martel that we possess, but because of its partisan

---

7   *Liber Historiae Francorum*, ed. B. Krusch, *MGH SRM* II (Hanover 1888), pp. 215–328, chs 43–54, trans. with commentary, in P. Fouracre and R. Gerberding, *Late Merovingian France. History and Hagiography 640–720* (Manchester 1996), pp. 87–96. In subsequent notes the work will be referred to as *LHF*.

8   R. Gerberding *The Rise of the Carolingians and the Liber Historiae Francorum* (Oxford 1987), pp. 146–72.

9   *The Fourth Book of the Chronicle of Fredegar with its Continuations*, ed. and trans. J.M. Wallace-Hadrill (London 1960). The *Continuations* will be referred to in the plural, even though specific passages were the work of a single continuator. In notes the work will be referred to in the short form *Fredegar* (for the main chronicle) or *Fred. Contin.* (for the Continuations).

nature we must think carefully about possible distortion in each and every detail. For example, the *Continuations* distort the account of events leading up to the battle of Poitiers in order to vilify Charles Martel's opponents in Aquitaine, and Roger Collins has recently demonstrated just how inaccurate the information about Aquitaine is, despite the fact that the author was describing events which were both recent and famous.[10]

The *Earlier Annals of Metz* take the Carolingian view of history a great deal further. Written in 805, this much more sophisticated work reflects the intellectual advances of the late eighth century.[11] The language of the *Earlier Annals of Metz* is much more clearly marked by classical usage than that of the *LHF* or the *Continuations of Fredegar*. The author wrote history in a more nuanced fashion than our earlier authors, being able to employ a much richer vocabulary. But for our purposes, the most important point to note is that the author of the *Annals* had a very clear and coherent picture of the rise of the Carolingians which at the same time justified their actions in terms of piety and duty. The work is in fact hagiographical in tone in that it portrays the Carolingians following a path of justice which leads towards salvation both for themselves and for the Franks, their subjects. The *Earlier Annals of Metz* thus rewrote history at every turn. Not only did the author backdate Merovingian decadence and Carolingian pre-eminence by half a century, he (or, possibly, she) also in effect damned the memory of all but Charles Martel's branch of the Carolingian family itself. Nevertheless the work contains details found in no other sources, and its highly coloured interpretations of events are always of great interest.

The fourth in our set of key narrative sources, the early Carolingian annals, is quite different. They consist of sparse yearly entries in eight slightly different versions.[12] Annals, as their name suggests, are the accounts of events organised on a year by year basis, each year being given a single entry.[13] The earliest annals of the eighth century give only the briefest of entries for each year, and since the annals copy each other, many of the

---

10 R. Collins, 'Deception and Misrepresentation in Early Eighth-Century Frankish Historiography: Two Case Studies', in J. Jarnut, U. Nonn and M. Richter (eds), *Karl Martell in Seiner Zeit*, Beihefte der Francia, 37 (Sigmaringen 1994), pp. 227–47; R. Collins, *Fredegar*, Authors of the Middle Ages, 13 (Aldershot 1996), pp. 112–17.

11 *Annales Mettenses Priores*, ed. B. von Simson, *MGH SRG* (Hanover and Leipzig 1905). In subsequent notes the *Earlier Annals of Metz* will be referred to as *AMP*.

12 These are the *Annales Sancti Amandi, Annales Tiliani, Annales Laubacenses, Annales Petaviani, Annales Laureshamenses, Annales Alamannici, Annales Guelferbtytani* and *Annales Nazariani*, ed. G. Pertz, *MGH SS* I (Hanover 1826), pp. 6–12, 22–30.

13 On how the annalistic form of writing developed, see R. McKitterick, 'Constructing the Past in the Early Middle Ages: The Case of the Royal Frankish Annals', *Transactions of the Royal Historical Society*, 6th series, 7 (1997), 101–29.

entries are identical in all eight versions. By the ninth century the entries had become much fuller as events were recorded in more detail and as authors began to offer more judgement on what they recorded. The *Earlier Annals of Metz* are thus technically annals because they are arranged year by year, but since the author makes a running commentary on events, and since there is an argument which runs throughout the work, the source looks much more like a chronicle, that is, a work of history unified by consistent themes and ideas. The earliest Carolingian annals are, by contrast, brief and laconic, but they do contain unique information of a nominal kind. They are obviously 'pro-Carolingian' in that the little that they do say invariably concerns the successful military activity of Carolingian leaders, and for this very reason they are an indispensable source for the campaigns waged by Charles Martel's father Pippin, by Charles himself, and by his sons. They tell us, for instance, about some campaigns in Germany about which we would otherwise be quite ignorant.[14]

The strongly common feature of all of these narrative sources is the way in which they all emphasised Charles Martel's success in war, first against the Neustrians and then against various non-Frankish peoples. They also furnish a rough context in which to understand that success, namely, the weakness of the Merovingian kings and the poor leadership of the Neustrians as opposed to the excellence of Martel's generalship. Clear too is their impression that the peoples on the periphery of the Frankish realm who had once been subject to the Merovingians resisted Charles Martel and had to be subdued by force. From the letters of the Anglo-Saxon missionary Boniface, it is equally obvious that military success was consolidated through the establishment of the Frankish church, which subjected native churches to its own authority and at the same time acquired landed resources in the conquered areas. Martel's family built up their spiritual prestige as patrons and protectors of an expanding church, a role which was greatly enhanced when the papacy made efforts to seek Charles Martel's support.

We may rightly seek to reinterpret what the sources have to say on some or all of these matters, but we must accept that they were what contemporaries or near contemporaries thought were the most important issues of the day. What modern scholarship attempts to achieve by re-evaluating the concerns of the sources is to find alternative explanations for Martel's success, and to reassess its significance. As we have seen, historians of Brunner's

---

14 An example is a reference in the *Annales Sancti Amandi, Annales Tiliani* and *Annales Petaviani* (pp. 6–7) to a campaign against the Aleman leader Willeharius in the year 712. This campaign is not mentioned in the *LHF, Fred. Contin.,* or *AMP. The Annales Sancti Amandi* and *Annales Tiliani* have the interesting detail that the campaign was led by a bishop. See below, ch. 2, p. 51.

generation did this by highlighting later complaints about the loss of church land and treating them as evidence that Charles Martel built his power on lands taken from the church. Today we would reject that line of argument on the basis that the evidence for it is too late, too flimsy, and too partial. Nor would scholars now think it sensible to search for a single overriding explanation of all the changes apparent in the age of Charles Martel. Similarly we can see that underlying the brusque narrative of conflict and conquest there were highly complex political relationships and shifting alliances. In fact modern historians would now agree that what appears in the narrative as straightforward conquest might more sensibly be described as a process of cultural assimilation and development.

This approach is especially important with regard to the relationship between the core areas of Francia and those surrounding territories which had somewhat separate identities. It is often supposed that the latter regions, such as Aquitaine, Alemannia and Bavaria, were involved in attempts to make themselves independent of Frankish rule and that it was the Carolingians who forced them back into line. This view, however, is concerned with only one aspect of the relations between core and periphery. Another way of analysing the relations would be in terms of a growing cultural integration right across Western Europe, with the outlying regions becoming rivals to the Franks as they developed comparable power based on similar religious and social institutions. This reappraisal starts from the observation that the Franks had always ruled over a massive territory (larger than modern-day France, even under the weakest rulers), and yet their governmental machinery was always crude and the resources at their disposal were always meagre. We must assume, therefore, that there were forces other than mere coercion which bound their polity together. How this pull towards integration was manipulated and shaped in the age of Charles Martel will be one of the themes running through this study, for it provides the essential complement to the history of military conquest. Where the Franks could not work with the grain of cultural integration, in Saxony, and, to a lesser extent, in Aquitaine, they faced a massive uphill struggle to insert their people and their institutions into the region. Even the mighty Charlemagne had to wage war for over thirty years in order to subdue the Saxons. It is therefore important to look carefully at the social and cultural development of each region in order to understand its relations with other areas.

As a preliminary we must start with the Merovingian regime, for if the later Merovingians were neither so weak nor so friendless as Carolingian writers proclaimed, we must reconsider the story that presents their decline as the explanation of the rise of the Carolingians. The next chapter will therefore be devoted to an understanding of the strengths and weaknesses of the later Merovingian regime, that is to say, it will sketch out the political environment which shaped the age of Charles Martel. Next we will explain the somewhat chequered rise to power of Charles's family, the Pippinids, and see that Charles himself was actually a rather insignificant member of this family. We will then look at how a crisis in the family propelled Charles to the forefront, and at how he was then able to stamp his authority all over Francia, bringing the outlying peoples into his orbit. We shall then continue the story into the decade after Charles Martel's death in order to get a fuller picture of developments. It is indeed necessary to think hard about Martel's legacy as a way of assessing his career. Finally, we shall draw the study to a close by measuring back to our point of departure, the later Merovingian period, and also by looking forward to the apogee of Carolingian power, for this will allow us to see the age of Charles Martel in full perspective. It is at this point that we can come to some conclusions on the issues first broached just over a century ago by Heinrich Brunner. Of course, we have in sum little more information at our disposal than had the historians of Brunner's generation, but what we do have is a more subtle and better informed understanding of how all the parts might fit together.

CHAPTER ONE

The Merovingian Background

In the year 613 the Merovingian king, Clothar II, united all of the Frankish lands under his rule. A year later he issued an edict, the so-called Edict of Paris, in which he stressed his authority over all parts of Francia, but also pledged to respect the privileges and customs of the 'provinces'.[1] At the same time he convened a church council, also held in Paris, in which he addressed the church in similar terms.[2] Given that much of the Edict of Paris was concerned with the affairs of the clergy, there is considerable overlap between the texts of the Council and the Edict on matters such as the election of bishops, on disputes between clergy and bishops or on whether or not clergy should be judged in lay courts. Secular and ecclesiastical interests here converged on a single focus: the desire to uphold a divinely sanctioned social and religious order, with the intended result being that God would continue to ensure good fortune for Clothar's kingdom.

These documents would not have looked out of place in the Carolingian world in which kings, even victorious ones, likewise feared that unless they propitiated God their luck would soon begin to run out. In Carolingian legislation too there would be a convergence of ecclesiastical and secular interests, and just like the Edict of Paris, many Carolingian edicts or 'capitularies' would open with an exortation to respect the ancient canons of the church. But at one time historians went much further than this in seeing links between the Edict of Paris and the Carolingians, for they thought that provisions in the Edict actually made possible, or even caused, that

---

1 *Clotharii Edictum, Capitularia Regum Francorum* I, ed. A. Boretius, *MGH Legum*, sectio II, vol. 1 (Hanover 1883), pp. 20–3.
2 *Concilium Parisiense*, ed. C. de Clercq, *Concilia Galliae a 511–695, Corpus Christianorum*, series Latina 148A (Turnhout 1963), pp. 275–82.

development of non-royal power which led to the rise of the Carolingians, and in particular to the rise of Charles Martel, a non-royal leader who had supreme power. Let us follow this argument as a way into thinking about the nature of Frankish political culture which is the setting for the career of Charles Martel.

In 612 it must have seemed totally against the odds that the Neustrian king Clothar II would emerge as sole ruler of the Franks. He had been on the point of defeat by his cousin's children, Theuderic king of Burgundy and Theudebert king of Austrasia, but then Theuderic killed his brother Theudebert and then died himself just as he was on his way to finish off Clothar. In these circumstances, it is argued, Clothar was peculiarly dependent upon the support of his more powerful subjects, especially when it came to trying to rule the regions of Burgundy and Austrasia which had so suddenly and unexpectedly come under his sway. The Edict of Paris has been read in this context as Clothar's deal with the nobility. In return for their support, it is said, he guaranteed their privileges and, by agreeing that only local men should hold provincial power, he effectively resigned control over outlying areas and in these parts allowed the development of hereditary office holding. This move has been seen as a *faux pas* which had consequences unforeseen by the hapless Merovingians but all too familiar to modern connoisseurs of constitutional history. In these historians' view, any nobility worth its salt would snap up a golden opportunity such as this to gorge itself at the expense of royal resources and prerogatives. In this case, supposedly, the concession of regional privileges steadily bled the Merovingian kings of their wealth, power and prestige. Eventually, as the ninth-century writer Einhard put it, the Merovingians would have no more vigour, possessing only the empty title of king, their resources amounting to a single estate.[3]

According to Einhard, and to many a modern textbook, the ultimate beneficiaries of the Merovingians' retreat into the shadows were, of course, the family of Charles Martel. The Pippinids emerged in the course of the seventh century as the leaders of the nobility in Austrasia. They worked themselves into a position from which they could control the royal palace, and through the royal palace they exercised the king's powers, always in his name, but ever in their hands. Eventually, under Charles Martel they were kings in all but name, and in the time of Martel's son Pippin, they took the name as well, relegating the last Merovingian to a monastery, tonsured as a monk, or possibly even scalped. Now this story, which is one of the grandest

---

3 Einhard, *The Life of Charlemagne*, ed. and trans. P. Dutton, *Charlemagne's Courtier. The Complete Einhard* (Ontario 1998), ch. 1, pp. 16–17.

narratives of early medieval political history, takes the partisan Carolingian viewpoint at face value. It is anachronistic in that it expects the Frankish nobility to have behaved as if reacting against a much more powerful monarchy (the Edict of Paris has even been termed the 'Magna Carta of the Frankish aristocracy'),[4] and it tells us nothing about the culture of power which would help us understand how or why, or indeed if, the Carolingians were any more successful than their Merovingian predecessors.

To arrive at a more realistic understanding of the Merovingian background to Carolingian power, let us begin again with the observation that the Edict of Paris was essentially similar to later Carolingian legislation. One good reason for the similarity is that legislation in both periods drew on the same stock of Roman and Canon law. But another explanation is that in many respects the conditions in which rulers operated changed little over the whole period. This we can see with the very clause of the Edict which is supposed to have opened the floodgates to noble power. Clause twelve stated that no judge from one region or province should be appointed in any other region. This has often been taken to mean that judges, these typically being counts, should be chosen only from amongst local people, and since local government basically resided in the hands of the counts, the chief representatives of royal power in each area would now be local men, with local interests, but with little incentive to carry out orders sent out from the royal palace. The clause went on to say, however, that the reason that judges should be local men was that they should have hereditary property in the region in which they held office, so that if they acted unlawfully in taking away the property of others, they could have their own property taken in return.[5] So, this measure was actually aimed at restraining and controlling local officials, not at giving them their head. It was a measure which may have had Roman precedent, and certainly did have precedent in earlier Merovingian legislation put forward by Clothar's father, King Chilperic (d. 584).[6] The provision would also be found in Carolingian legislation.

In each district the count was the figure chiefly responsible for the maintenance of law and order. The term 'district', from the Latin *districtum*, reflects this role. In classical Latin the term meant 'punishment', but in the Merovingian period *districtum* also came to mean the area in which an official exercised jurisdiction, that is, the area in which he had the right and duty to punish people. Punishment usually involved fining or distraining those with property. Those without property, and especially unfree people,

---

4   H. Mitteis, *The State in the Middle Ages*, trans. H. Orton (Amsterdam 1975), p. 50.
5   E. James, *The Origins of France* (London 1982), p. 141, seems to have been the first modern historian to draw attention to this second part of clause twelve.
6   *Edictus Chilperici*, ch. 8, *Capitularia Regum Francorum* I, p. 9.

could be punished by loss of life or limb, or, if they were free people who were too poor to pay fines, by enslavement. In both later-Merovingian and Carolingian Francia, the 'state' (meaning the collection of institutions and officials whose power was in theory derived from royal authority) was essentially weak.[7] Counts and other royal officials could only exercise powers for which there was a degree of consensus amongst those with property, and in practice this meant exercising powers which protected the latter group's wealth and status. Hence the vicious treatment of people of lesser status, and hence that legislation which allowed redress against officials who took property 'illegally'.

In documents which were concerned with property, that is, which recorded the transfer, gift or sale of land, or which recorded the settlement of disputes over land, we see what looks like an impressive level of bureaucratic competence. The legal machinery involved looks rather effective. But the appearance of efficiency may be misleading because the documents in question, which provide our evidence, were produced at the request of those who benefited from them and because here the involvement of royal officials, or even of the king himself, was actively sought by the beneficiaries. The evidence is thus one-sided, largely reflecting the successful use of what bureaucratic machinery there was. There were, however, few mechanisms to compel people to use bureaucratic and formal legal procedures if they were unwilling to do so, and alongside the machinery of royal government there were alternative customary and informal ways of maintaining order and privilege and of settling disputes. These measures relied on self-help, drew on networks of social support and need not have involved the officers of the king at all. Such customary procedures sometimes figure in narrative sources, but are rarely mentioned in formal documents.[8] They could include the use of violence to protect honour or to take revenge for insult or injury. Furthermore, when it came to policing the countryside, the 'state' seems to have been largely ineffective against outlaws and brigands. It is significant here that in 864 when the ruler Charles the Bald legislated to bring such criminals to justice, he largely repeated the measures first announced in the Edict of Paris two and a half centuries earlier, namely,

---

7 For the argument that the 'state' may actually have been stronger in the sixth century, a period of elite formation in which the nobles were more dependent upon the ruler to help them secure positions of power and privilege, than in the seventh when the elite was better established and more independent, see G. Halsall, *Settlement and Social Organization. The Merovingian Region of Metz* (Cambridge 1995), pp. 33–53.

8 P. Geary, 'Extra-judicial Means of Conflict Resolution', *La Giustizia nell 'alto Medioevo (Secole V–VIII)*, Settimane di Studio del Centro Italiano di Studi sull'alto Medioevo, 42 (Spoleto 1995), pp. 569–601, argues that an informal settlement of disputes would have been far more common than settlement using formal legal procedures.

that it was the duty of the 'powerful' in the countryside to deliver notorious wrongdoers to court.[9] In relation to law and order, not much had changed. Charlemagne too could do little more than plead with the powerful not to shelter criminals but to deliver them up for punishment. Charlemagne, in fact, is often said to have tackled the issue of law and order more effectively than any other Frankish ruler, but in his legislation too there is much about the principles of justice, but little about how criminals might actually be brought to book.[10] This coexistence of law and custom in a world in which the ruler's power was practically rather limited, is the proper background to the 614 Edict of Paris, and rather than stress elements of very dubious constitutional significance it is more helpful to be aware of the deeper continuities in Frankish political culture.

The career of Charles Martel shows how even a successful leader could not break with custom nor invent new institutions in order to strengthen the machinery of government. But it also shows that social and political consensus might be manipulated to build up power on a personal basis. One avenue open to rulers was to invoke supernatural support for their power, as we saw in the Edict and in the Council of Paris where Clothar II called the church to order so that he might strengthen his authority over all of Francia. That leaders should increasingly stress this aspect was to rule in line with a growing sense of religious duty and piety throughout society. It is also true that ecclesiastical organisation had preserved the skeleton of late Roman provincial government, and this organisation could be used to support royal authority when rulers made it their priority to defend the faith. As we saw in the Introduction, Charles Martel would be compared to the biblical hero Joshua, and it is inconceivable that he could have built up his power without presenting himself as the foremost protector of the church and of the faithful. We should therefore include religion as another factor in that consensus which underpinned (as well as limited) the authority of rulers. Authority was in these terms as much a cultural phenomenon as it was the product of bureaucratic organisation and fiscal resources. Let us look at this in more detail to see how Francia under the Merovingians and Carolingians could have governing institutions which were in many ways weak but could be nevertheless a very large and successful kingdom, and one which exercised upon its neighbours a very strong pull towards cultural integration.

---

9 *Edictum Pistense*, ch. 18, *Capitularia Regum Francorum* II, ed. A. Boretius and M. Krause, *MGH Legum*, sectio II, vol. 2 (Hanover 1897), p. 317.
10 P. Fouracre, 'Carolingian Justice: The Rhetoric of Improvement and Contexts of Abuse', *La Giustizia nell 'alto Medioevo*, pp. 771–803, at p. 798.

The roots of what one might term 'the Frankish system', that is, consensual rule over a very extensive territory, based on the protection of property and social status, lay on the one hand in the history and geography of the later Roman Empire, and on the other in the confederate nature of the Franks themselves. The Franks were a west German people who first appeared in the Rhineland area in the third century. In the course of the fourth and fifth centuries they developed their identity as troops who served the Roman authorities and in the process acquired a growing degree of control over north-east Gaul. When Roman authority collapsed throughout Gaul in the later fifth century, the Franks moved south and west as military rulers, and in the early sixth century they defeated first the Visigoths and then the Burgundians, which meant that they now controlled Gaul as far as the Pyrenees to the south. To the south-east their rule stretched into the southern Alps and Provence. At the same time they retained control over the Rhineland, and once they had defeated the Alamans and Thuringians, they extended their influence into central and southern Germany too. Thus by the mid-sixth century the Franks had influence over a massive swathe of territory which included the area of modern-day France and most of what would become Germany. It has even been argued that in this early period the Franks controlled southern England too, although for this there is only circumstantial evidence.[11] Apart from England, if indeed it really had been under Frankish control, no part of this massive territory would sucessfully break away from Frankish control for many centuries to come, nor would the Franks add much in the way of new lands to their empire until the time of Charlemagne.

One reason for the impressive stability of this huge bloc of territories was their fortunate strategic position. They lay outside the range of Byzantine intervention, and beyond the reach of the Arabs, the two groups who would destroy the Franks' Gothic neighbours in Italy and Spain. To the east, Saxons, Thuringians and Bavarians, the last two peoples under leaders appointed by the Franks, provided a buffer against Slavonic settlers and Asiatic invaders. Thus throughout the entire period of Frankish rule, that is, from the sixth to the tenth centuries, the existence of this massive political entity was never under serious threat from invaders. Nor was it ever seriously threatened by disintegration from within, that is to say, no one region ever broke away to form a separate non-Merovingian kingdom, even though civil wars and dynastic crises afforded plenty of opportunities to do this. It seems, therefore, that in this large area of Europe north of the Pyrenees and Alps, no satisfactory alternative to Frankish rule could be envisaged.

---

11 I. Wood, *The Merovingian North Sea* (Alsingås 1983), pp. 12–13.

As we have seen, the Frankish rulers worked with the grain of social power by protecting property and preserving status and privilege. Leaders everywhere had something to gain from being part of a Frankish regime, and much to lose if other leaders could be mobilised against them. But a rather more subtle explanation of why leaders should have been willing to support Frankish rulers, be these Merovingians or Carolingians, is to be sought in the development of a common culture of power through which leaders from a variety of different ethnic backgrounds would acquire a Frankish identity, or at least seek to be part of a wider political community based on the Frankish court. This cultural phenomenon needs to be examined in more detail, as it is the key to understanding how Francia did not disintegrate but was actually welded together more firmly under the hammer blows of Charles Martel.

When the Franks occupied western and southern Gaul in the late fifth and early sixth centuries, they did little to disturb the power and privileges of the Gallo-Roman ruling elite. The latter had secured their status through the control of land and the exercise of public office, and increasingly they maintained it by holding the leading positions in the Catholic Church. This they could continue to do under the Franks. South of the River Loire, for instance, it is clear that most of the counts, and virtually all the bishops, thus the leaders in each community, continued to bear Gallo-Roman names. Towards the end of the sixth century, more and more Frankish names are to be found in Aquitaine, Burgundy and Provence. Partly this indicates that Franks were replacing the native aristocracies in these areas. But intermarriage between incoming Franks and locals was a strong factor in the formation of an elite which was of mixed origins but identified itself as Frankish. Women were therefore important in this cultural fusion. The change in naming fashion also shows the locals adopting Frankish names, and thus taking on elements of a Frankish identity even where intermarriage did not take place.

The word 'aristocracy' is of Greek origin and it was unknown to the Franks, or, for that matter, to the Gallo-Romans. Both groups used the Latin term 'noble' to designate those of high social status, but this term could apply to a wide spectrum of people, ranging from better-off freemen to those members of the elite who took part in what might be termed 'national' politics. This latter group (whom historians often call simply 'magnates') could be distinguished by special terms or titles of mostly Roman origin, which reflected their power and status. They were thus referred to as 'the powerful' or 'the more-powerful' (*potentes/potentiores*), 'the illustrious' (*illustres*), 'the best' (*optimates*), or 'the near' (*proceres*) (meaning, 'near to the king'). Our modern term 'excellency' retains something of the flavour of this kind of address. In addition there was a host of official titles such as 'duke', 'count', 'seneschal', or *domesticus*, which were held only by those of the highest status. All these terms are strongly masculine. The status of important women was usually described in relation to males, that is, fathers or spouses, or it was expressed by the general term 'noble'. Whatever its origins,[12] we can say that by the seventh century the nobility in Francia as a whole was effectively hereditary, although it expected to hold office from the king, and in many areas it was of mixed ethnic descent.[13] As we know from clause twelve of the Edict of Paris, Clothar II expected his counts to be hereditary property owners in the area in which they held office, and in many areas such people would have been descended from Gallo-Roman or mixed race families.

It is thus clear that the more powerful in society derived their power from the conjunction of family wealth and royal office holding. The former gave the office holder the resources and social clout to carry out his duties. Office in turn helped to protect his wealth and status, to legitimise his actions, and provided opportunities to increase his wealth and authority. It was above all the desire to grasp such opportunities which drew local leaders into supporting the Frankish kings and which cemented the vast territories ruled by those kings into a single political entity. To explain further this urge to be part of a supra-regional political community we must understand that the social hierarchy in Francia was essentially derived from that of Late Antiquity. But to maintain this hierarchy, great concentrations of wealth were required. The *potentiores* of the fifth century had drawn their wealth from vast landed estates, which were often spread over several regions in order to supply their needs by taking produce from different ecological zones. This pattern of exploitation continued, as we can see from an extraordinary document, the Will of Bishop Bertramn of Le Mans, drawn up around the year 616, which shows Bertramn holding estates scattered throughout most of modern-day France.[14] The widespread distribution of estates was one reason why the most powerful families would have an interest in more than

---

12 There has been vigorous debate about the origins of the Frankish nobility, prompted by the work of A. Bergengruen, *Adel und Grundherrschaft im Merrowingerreich* (Wiesbaden 1958), who argued that the nobility had its origins in service to the kings (*Dienstadel*) rather than in blood and birth (*Geburtsadel*). For reaction to this position, see F. Irsigler, *Untersuchungen zur Geschichte des frühfränkischen Adels* (Bonn 1969), and H. Grahn-Hoek, *Die fränkische Oberschicht im 6 Jahrhundert. Studien über ihre rechtliche und politische Stellung* (Sigmaringen 1976). For an excellent summary of the debate, T. Reuter, *The Early Medieval Nobility* (Amsterdam 1978), Introduction.

13 R. Le Jan, *Famille et Pouvoir dans le Monde Franc (VIIe–Xe siècle). Essai d'Anthropologie Sociale* (Paris 1995), p. 249.

14 M. Weidemann, *Das Testament des Bischofs Bertramn von Le Mans von 27 März 616* (Mainz 1986), pp. 79–81.

one region, and thus a vested interest in keeping all regions under a single authority. In order to maintain their wealth and status they thus had to operate on a supra-regional level. Another factor which encouraged contact across the regions was the desire of leaders to associate with others of equally high status. Where this led to marriage alliances, families could become spread over massive distances.[15] Even Charles Martel, an Austrasian to the core, had a Neustrian nephew. It is also generally accepted that in the period 400–650 Europe was becoming poorer as its population declined or dispersed and agrarian production fell.[16] These conditions reinforced the pressure upon the magnates to look for the extra resources that participation in kingdom-wide politics might bring, and of course the larger the kingdom, the greater the rewards for those at the top. In short, a massive territory was required to sustain the hierarchy in the form inherited from Roman society.

Many of the magnate families which were spread over extensive territory in this way were of course very large, and, as we have just seen, women played an important role in their formation. Consequently it has been argued that the form of the typical magnate family was extended, and that it was also loosely structured, with membership of the family being the chief way in which individuals identified themselves as being part of a group. This kind of family, in which both male and female kindred were included, is described as 'cognatic'. Another term often used is the German *Sippe*, the equivalent term in English being 'clan'. Although this is technically an incorrect use of 'clan' (all those descended from a common ancestor), the term does capture the sense of a large group of related people with a common family identity. Examples of *Sippen* which were prominent in the later Merovingian period are the Agilolfings, the 'Faronids' (or 'Gundoinings' as the south-west Austrasian branch of the family are known) and the Pippinids themselves. As we shall see later, the term 'cognatic' is itself rather a loose one, and all members of the family were not equal, for cognatic families discriminated against more distant members when it came to inheritance. Each family thus had a core of close relatives, usually no bigger than all of those descended from the same grandparents, through whom the bulk of the family wealth would be passed down. The Pippinid family is typical in this respect. It nevertheless remains true that in this period women appear to have had greater opportunities to inherit wealth than they would have later.

15   For the longer-term effect of such exogamous marriage practices on the *Regnum Francorum*, see Le Jan, *Famille et Pouvoir*, pp. 306–7.
16   For an overview of economic history see R. Hodges and D. Whitehouse, *Mohammed, Charlemagne and the Origins of Europe* (London 1983), and on the economy of Francia, G. Depeyrot, *Richesse et Société chez les Mérovingiens et Carolingiens* (Paris 1994), esp. pp. 145–54.

It has been argued that it was the church which was responsible for improving the position of women, successfully pioneering women's rights of inheritance, through which it hoped to receive endowments from women with the right to dispose of their land as they wished.[17] But it is wishful thinking on the part of social historians to imagine that the church had a coherent strategy in this manner. It seems more sensible to consider enhanced opportunities for female inheritance in the light of the growing wealth and power which some families enjoyed, hence the possibility of important heiresses. Wealthy daughters, like wealthy sons, reflected a family's social standing and could bring great influence through marriage alliances, just as giving to the church brought prestige and influence as well as spiritual benefits. The questions of family structure and female wealth and power have an important bearing upon the career of Charles Martel. Much of the wealth of his father Pippin came from his marriage to an heiress, Plectrude. Plectrude was not, however, Charles's mother, and as a widow she would make strenuous efforts to exclude Charles Martel from the core of the family's inheritance. Charles, in turn, established a new core by excluding Plectrude's grandchildren.

A brief examination of the resources of power is the prerequisite to considering power in the wider cultural context. In the late Roman period income from land was an essential state resource which provided the bulk of taxation, in addition to the rent paid to landlords. In the early medieval period, direct taxes levied on land on behalf of the state gradually declined, but many of the dues and services once paid to the state now went to the landlords.[18] Although there is very little evidence predating the great estate surveys or 'polyptychs' of the Carolingian period, it is clear from Merovingian charters that land was described in terms of those resources which provided income in this way. What is striking in the terminology of both charters and 'polyptychs' is that land of every kind, from waste and woodland to the most intensively farmed areas, could be assessed for its productive value. An essential precondition for the conversion of potential resource into actual income was the existence of a tied peasantry, both free and unfree, whose labour could be directed at will by the landlord. Research into the way in which the relationship between peasantry and landlords produced wealth has often focused on the great estates of the Paris basin. The reason is that this area is better documented than most as it contained great stretches of

---

17 This is the argument put forward by J. Goody, *The Family and Marriage in Europe* (Cambridge 1982).
18 W. Goffart, 'From Roman Taxation to Medieval Seigneurie: Three Notes', *Speculum*, 47 (1972), 165–87 and 373–94, and W. Goffart, 'Old and New in Merovingian Taxation', *Past and Present*, 96 (1982), 3–21.

church land, and one monastery based there, St Germain des Prés, on the west bank of the Seine in the suburbs of the old Roman city of Paris, produced the most extensive estate survey of them all. It is in this area that historians have traced the development of so-called 'bi-partite' estates on which lords had an inner reserve of land farmed by their direct labour force, greatly augmented by the work of tenants settled on outlying farms who provided extra labour as part of their rent. There is great interest in this arrangement partly because it is seen as the ancestor of the manorial system of the central Middle Ages, and partly because it is seen as a more productive system of agrarian exploitation which began to generate that increase in wealth which would very, very slowly lift Francia out of the economic recession it had been in since the late Roman period.

The early phase of this development, which can plausibly be placed at the end of the seventh century, is of undoubted importance for an understanding of the age of Charles Martel, as it helps to explain the strategic importance of the Paris basin in Charles's campaigns. But perhaps more revealing is the observation that in other areas too landlords organised their holdings in a more systematic manner to increase their income from the land. This is particularly striking in areas east of the Rhine which did not share the Roman legacy of great estates. The development of this form of social and economic organisation in the east would erase one of the most characteristic differences which had once distinguished those areas within the bounds of the former Roman Empire from those which lay outside it. The process was one which would strengthen the position of the nobility east of the Rhine and prepare the way for their integration into the Frankish elite. From their point of view, one can see how 'Frankification' might seem a rather attractive prospect. As we shall see in Chapter 4 when we examine affairs in this area in more detail, this analysis does present serious problems because written evidence surfaces only in the eighth century when the nobility east of the Rhine began to draw up charters and to dispose of land in Roman/Frankish fashion. We thus cannot be sure how they were organised before this. Nevertheless, we can extrapolate from other forms of evidence, and judging from the fact that the Christian Church was less organised in these areas, we can be confident that 'Frankification' did go hand in hand with the development of noble power and landholding. The process was most dramatic, and traumatic, in Saxony in the wars of Charlemagne's reign, where a fledgling Saxon nobility sheltered behind Frankish arms while the local population was violently subdued and landholding reorganised around the newly founded churches.

So far we have seen how the need to garner wealth led the most powerful in society to support distant rulers and to become their representatives in different regions. It has also been argued that desire to maximise landed resources encouraged the nobility east of the Rhine to imitate Frankish practices, and that this process was a very important factor in opening up the eastern regions to Frankish influence. Early medieval society, like most pre-modern societies, was violently competitive, with competition for power being sharpened by lack of resources. Over several generations families would tend to sink in social status as growing numbers in successive generations ate into the family inheritance. Leaders faced pressure from below from their own family members as well as from other clients and followers to provide that wealth which would protect or, better, enhance the status of their dependants. This very basic point about a social dynamic which pushed clients to seek lords, and lords to seek power, is one we should always bear in mind when considering the behaviour of the nobility in any medieval period, but especially in the age of Charles Martel, in which there was large-scale conflict and a reordering of loyalties.

Having looked at the links between wealth, office and power we turn now to the cultural and religious factors that helped form an integrated elite which increasingly identified itself as Frankish. As we have already noted, the Franks' origins lay in a confederation of groups. They were thus a heterogenous people with an identity which was always evolving, and the elite in Francia was a relatively open one which recruited members from what had originally been separate ethnic groups. This we saw with those of Gallo-Roman descent taking on Frankish names and becoming part of the wider Frankish political and religious establishment. Frankish culture was marked by a degree of flexibility which allowed people to retain specific identities within a single political community. This phenomenon is most clearly visible in the field of law, in which the different peoples of Francia each had their own law-code. Historians refer to this as the 'personality' of the law, meaning that each person was entitled to be judged according to his or her 'own' law. The Franks were actually rather proud of this principle, for it implied that they ruled an empire which was made up of many different peoples.

Rulers issued law-codes for their subject peoples, and in 802 in response to his coronation as emperor, Charlemagne is said to have called the dukes, counts and people together and 'had all the laws in his realm read out, each man's law expounded to him and emended wherever necessary, and the emended law written down'.[19] But despite evidence that such laws were

---

19 *Lorsch Annal s.a.* 802, trans. P.D. King, *Charlemagne. Translated Sources* (Lambrigg 1986), p. 145.

indeed written down, and even that some laymen owned law books, the use of law was in practice pragmatic and paid little or no attention to written texts.[20] The dividing line between law and unwritten custom was always thin, and far from there being a sense of opposition between the formal use of law in court and the informal procedures of local custom, the two were complementary and could be used in tandem. This open-ended approach to the use of law allowed the accommodation of different traditions within a single legal system, and was perfectly suited to a society with overlapping identities and regional variations in law and custom. Each law case could in theory be discussed quite rationally according to a host of variables such as local custom, personal or institutional status, and, not least, the evidence of witnesses and documents. It was this flexibility which made law a vehicle for mediation between people of different backgrounds.[21] The provision of a common forum for the settlement of disputes, and for the recording of gifts and transactions, was a cornerstone of social consensus. The different peoples of Francia continued to identify themselves by their own laws, and individuals also identified themselves as being descended from this or that ethnic group, and this included those descended from the early conquerors of Gaul, the *Franci* themselves. Nevertheless, by the end of the seventh century outsiders were coming to look on all the inhabitants of Francia as 'Franks'. Centuries later, when West Europeans entered the lands of the Middle East in the course of the Crusades, the inhabitants there would call all Westerners 'Franks', the term being a portmanteau for people who were greedy, warlike, 'Latin' speaking and Catholic. It was the history of the Franks, as an inclusive rather than exclusive people, and their enduring capacity for cultural assimilation (and colonisation), which made their very name both elastic and durable.

The church was, of course, central to the development of a common culture and integrated elite in Francia. The Catholic Church was, as we have seen, responsible for preserving much of Roman culture and many of the institutions of Late Antiquity. Bishops, and, increasingly, abbots, were figures of great political and social, as well as religious, importance. It has often been said that many of the towns of Gaul would not have survived in the harsh economic conditions of the early Middle Ages if they had not been the centres of episcopal power and ecclesiastical administration. Indeed, by

---

20 H. Nehlsen, 'Zur Aktualität und Effectivität germanische Rechtsaufzeichnungen', in
    P. Classen (ed.), *Recht und Schrift im Mittelalter*, Vorträge und Forschungen, 23 (Sigmaringen 1977), pp. 451–83.
21 P. Fouracre, 'The Nature of Frankish Political Institutions in the Seventh Century', in
    I. Wood (ed.), *Franks and Alemanni in the Merovingian Period. An Ethnographic Perspective* (Woodbridge 1998), pp. 285–316, at pp. 286–91.

the seventh century, the bishop was in many towns a much more important figure than the count.[22]

A single church was a prerequisite for a single kingdom, and the list of the seventy-nine bishops and one abbot who attended the Council of Paris in 614 is impressive testimony to the way in which representatives from all regions (including, incidentally, Kent in south-eastern England) could be brought together to follow a common programme. The church was a unique body in that everywhere, at least in theory, its members were subject to the same body of rules and governed by a single, formally constituted hierarchy. No wonder that rulers like Clothar II used the machinery of church councils to articulate notions of universal authority, nor is it surprising that these notions would increasingly be coloured by biblical examples and moral concerns. As the Carolingians rose to power, they would go further down this road, sponsoring a reform of the church which would make it yet more responsive to the needs of rulers. In the process they constructed a regime which can be fairly described as theocratic.

As important as providing a framework of universal institutions and a model of centralised authority, was Catholicism's role as a common cultural denominator. Francia, unlike Ostrogothic Italy or Visigothic Spain, faced no religious divisions which would hamper the formation of a single ruling elite made up of the incoming barbarian and the native nobilities. Although divisions between Catholics and Arians in Italy and Spain have often been exaggerated, it remains true that in Francia adherence to the same form of Christianity made both for more rapid intermarriage between natives and newcomers and also for the speedier transfer of cultural traditions from Gallo-Romans to Franks. The best evidence for this comes from hagiography, which was the most prolific form of writing in our period. Writing about saints reflected the aristocratic culture of Late Antiquity. Specifically, one can see how the ideal qualities of the great man of the Roman world were transformed into the virtues of the saint. This was done via the figure of the bishop, who was usually, like the great man, of noble birth, well educated, and in a position of civic as well as religious leadership. Thus the style of the pagan and secular epitaph became the framework for the description of the career of the bishop. The term 'virtue', which had conveyed the ideal qualities, or 'manliness', of the nobleman, came to refer to religious excellence, and eventually it would mean 'miracle', as God acknowledged such excellence by making manifest His power on earth.[23] When in the

---

22   F. Prinz, 'Die Bischöfliche Stadtherrschaft im Frankenreich vom 5 bis 7 Jahrhundert', *Historische Zeitschrift*, 217 (1974), 1–35.

23   M. Heinzelmann, ' "Sanctitas" und "Tugendadel". Zur Konzeptionen von "Heiligkeit" in 5 und 10 Jahrhundert', *Francia*, 5 (1977), 741–52.

seventh century more and more people of Frankish origins became bishops, and became saints too, they were described in the same terms. In other words, Franks and Romans now shared the same cultural and religious values, and because these were ideal values, credited with the ability to cause supernatural power to manifest itself, they exercised a very strong pull on the elite in general. The result was a growing culture of sanctity in which many new saints were created and many new monasteries were founded.

Given the importance of women in family structures (noted above) it is unsurprising that saintly virtues were not restricted to males, so that females could, and did, play an important role in securing the reputation and high religious status of the family. In fact, so many noble families acquired saints in the period 600–750 that historians have spoken of sanctity as a normal attribute of high noble status, referring to the process by which this holiness was acquired as one of 'aristocratic-self-sanctification'.[24] But this goes too far, as the process was never so self-conscious, nor so systematic. Nevertheless, at the same time older cult centres responded to the invention of new saints and the establishment of new monasteries by finding a few more saints of their own, either by the discovery of the remains of old martyrs, or via the sanctification of recently dead leaders. In this atmosphere, where leaders had died violently, it was natural to proclaim them martyrs. Since bishops were political leaders of importance, and since politics in this age could be very violent, we see the creation of bishop-martyrs and a growing connection between sanctity, politics and power.[25] For not only did leading families rally around saintly ancestors who could deliver supernatural support, the institutions which grew up around cult centres also became powerful landowners and the source of great wealth. Their influence upon the way in which landed resources were organised and exploited has already been mentioned in this chapter. Another rather important connection between sanctity and power was made through hagiography itself, and it would spill over into the writing of history. That is, where the saint had been a figure active in politics, the 'saint's life' tended to describe his or her career in highly polarised terms. He or she could do no wrong, his or her opponents could do no right. Political history was thus presented as a struggle between good and evil, between heroes and villains. Carolingian writers would apply this convention to their heroes, the family of Charles Martel, and they would portray the rise of the Carolingians to power as a struggle for justice. Opposition to them was simply unjust.[26]

---

24   It was F. Prinz who first formulated the concept (*Adelsselbstheiligung* in German) in his *Frühes Mönchtum im Frankenreich* (Munich 1965), pp. 489–93.
25   P. Fouracre, 'Merovingian History and Merovingian Hagiography', *Past and Present*, 127 (1990), 3–38, at 9–13.
26   Fouracre, 'Carolingian Justice', 772–7.

The culture of sanctity was not evenly spread across the Frankish kingdom. It spread from the towns to the countryside during the seventh century, but the density of cult sites was noticeably thinner in the Austrasian north and east. The areas to the east and north of the River Moselle had been on the periphery of the Roman Empire and few Roman martyrs were associated with them. There were likewise fewer new monastic foundations here, and consequently fewer Austrasian noble families produced saints. Although the Pippinids themselves had founded the monastery of Nivelles in present-day Belgium, and the family had a saint in Gertrude, the first abbess of Nivelles, the stamping-grounds of the saints were more typically in Neustria and Burgundy. The Austrasians did have Cologne, a once-important Roman town in which there were the relics of ancient martyrs, but in the early 680s these relics were removed by the bishop, and future saint, Audoin of Rouen. Neustria, at this stage the dominant partner in an unhappily united kingdom, not only possessed the premier cult sites, it also had the power to acquire yet more relics, and Audoin's stature as a holy man was unrivalled.

Neustrian saints, both ancient and modern, and the monasteries and basilicas which housed them, were centres of power and memory which Charles Martel's father Pippin, and Charles himself, found hard to control. They could not prevent some of their opponents in Neustria and in Burgundy from being hailed as saints, and an anti-Pippinid or anti-Carolingian strain emerged in hagiography which ran counter to the Carolingian view of history mentioned earlier. Faced with a Neustrian establishment imbued with spiritual prestige, Pippin and Charles Martel turned to an alternative source of sanctity, Anglo-Saxon missionaries who were keen to foster the church amongst the Germanic peoples of the east. Another response, at a later date, would be to prefer the cults of long-dead martyrs over those of the more recently dead, thus putting an end to the sanctification of opponents.[27] The politics of the age of Charles Martel would therefore bring to a close the phase of 'aristocratic-self-sanctification' amongst the Frankish elite. But the culture of sanctity remained as strong as ever, and it would be proudly presented as a defining feature of Frankish identity. This is clearly expressed (in its Carolingian form) in the Prologue to a revision of Frankish law (*Lex Salica*) made in the reign of the first Carolingian king, Pippin. The Franks, it said, were superior not only in battle but also because they had honoured and made rich gifts to those martyrs whom the Romans had persecuted.[28]

---

27 P. Fouracre, 'The Origins of the Carolingian Attempt to Regulate the Cult of Saints', in J. Howard-Johnston and P. Hayward (eds), *The Cult of Saints in Late Antiquity and the Early Middle Ages* (Oxford 2000), pp. 143–65.

28 *The Laws of the Salian Franks*, trans. K. Fischer-Drew (Philadelphia 1991), p. 171.

So far we have looked at those common cultural characteristics which helped to integrate leaders from different backgrounds into a single elite. We have also examined the social and economic forces which led that elite to participate in the political community through which the massive Frankish kingdom was constituted. Let us now turn briefly to the royal court where that community actually met, and look at the role of the kings in maintaining peace amongst the nobility. We should also note how that competition and rivalry which made the nobility eminently biddable could turn into feuding and fighting which could dislocate the political structure of the kingdom. We shall then be able to draw together all of these background features to show their bearing upon the career of Charles Martel.

The Frankish royal court consisted of a permanent establishment of household officials who were drawn from the magnates. The court revolved around the king, and it was held wherever the king was, which was usually in one of a half a dozen or so favoured palaces situated on royal estates. In the period of Neustrian dominance, that is, for most of the seventh century, this meant that the court usually gathered in the Seine–Oise area. At other times, rulers would favour other areas: Charlemagne, for instance, rarely visited Neustria. It is nevertheless striking to see how little the structure of the royal court changed over the entire Frankish period, and also to note how the courts in different West European societies were organised along very similar lines. This was not only because they derived their officials from the same late Roman traditions of bureaucratic organisation and household management,[29] but also because in each society courts played the same role as centres of negotiation between rulers and subjects, and between different groups of magnates. In Merovingian Francia the key figure here was the mayor of the palace, for he controlled access to the king and effectively he was the broker between the interests of the magnates and those of the ruler. The mayor of the palace was regarded as the most important non-royal person in the kingdom, and it was, of course, as mayor that Charles Martel exercised power.

The royal court was not just a talking shop and writing office, it was also a leading cultural centre, and to spend time at court was a mark of high social status. Young males of the higher nobility were educated at court, and this experience was vital not only in encouraging those bonds of association through which a single political community was constructed, but also in forming the shared culture and values which gave that community a common language of power. This phenomenon is revealed in letters between

---

29 P. Barnwell, *Kings, Courtiers and Imperium. The Barbarian West, 565–725* (London 1997), pp. 23–40.

former colleagues at court who kept in touch throughout their later careers. One can indeed say that in the mid-seventh century, Francia was dominated by a friendship network that had been built up in the courts of kings Clothar II (d. 628) and Dagobert I (d. 639). Audoin of Rouen was at the centre of this network, and as we have just seen, it was a group whose influence was strengthened by its identification with sanctity.[30] As we shall see in the next chapter, Charles Martel's father had to come to terms with the Neustrian court circle, even after he had beaten them in battle.

A wider group of magnates was drawn to the court on the occasion of annual assemblies or at times of royal succession. The importance of the assemblies in binding the kingdom together must be emphasised very strongly. It seems likely that these meetings, which were held in spring, originated in the parade ground inspections that the Franks had had when they were the Roman Empire's federate troops back in the fifth century. In the sixth century it can be seen that important legislation was issued in spring, at the time of the assemblies, and throughout the Frankish period the assemblies would retain their dual function as a military gathering and a decision-making (or better, perhaps, 'decision-announcing') body. From royal charters of the late seventh and early eighth centuries we can also see that this gathering of the powerful provided an opportunity to hear court cases before a tribunal made up of the leaders from all over the kingdom, and one late-seventh-century narrative source, the *Passio Praejecti*, describes such a tribunal in operation at an assembly held at Easter 675 in the town of Autun. It is this description which is in fact the best illustration we have of the interplay between rights derived from a participant's 'personal law', and the merits of a case in practical, procedural and political terms.[31] This particular case shows a defendant summoned unwillingly to court. It is clear that magnates could not refuse such a summons without putting themselves at great risk. The assemblies could mobilise massive force through the collective power of the elite, and rulers could use the occasion to punish those they deemed unfaithful. The punishment here was likely to be death, and the context was a ritual affirmation of loyalty to the king.

There was, therefore, a coercive side to the assemblies, but it was a coercion possible only with the support of the majority. A glance at the list of those who made up the tribunal at cases heard in the late seventh and early eighth centuries shows magnates coming to assemblies in the Paris

30   P. Fouracre and R. Gerberding, *Late Merovingian France. History and Hagiography 640–720* (Manchester 1996), pp. 136–52.

31   *Passio Praejecti*, ed. B. Krusch, *MGH SRM* V (Hanover 1910), pp. 225–48, trans. with commentary in Fouracre and Gerberding, *Late Merovingian France*, pp. 254–300, here chs 23–25, pp. 288–91.

region from as far away as Marseilles, thus making a round trip of over 1,500 kilometres. These cases include judgements made against the Pippinid family. It is obvious that the Pippinids had to gain control of the assemblies, but that at the same time they could not dispense with them as they were the very axis around which the political community revolved. They were also occasions at which loyalty to the Merovingian kings was expressed, so they were points of potentially great embarrassment, or even danger. For if the Pippinids, or even Charles Martel himself, were perceived to be disloyal or to be challenging the right of the assembly to express their traditional loyalties, their rule could be judged 'tyrannical', that is, rule without consent and without a proper legal basis. This potential danger may be one reason why the Carolingians seemed to hesitate for a whole generation before they made themselves kings, and why, right up to the moment at which they deposed the Merovingian kings, they observed the formalities of obeisance to them. In the *Earlier Annals of Metz* and in Einhard's *Life of Charlemagne* there are apparently awkward explanations of why the Carolingians continued to join in the ritual profession of loyalty to the Merovingians, even when they themselves were the real rulers of Francia. For the authors of these works the solution was to ridicule the Merovingians, and to show Pippin as a sensitive and selfless figure who protected them by stage-managing the assemblies so that the Franks would continue to make obeisance, while the mayor did the real work of government and covered up the king's essential weakness. It is striking that the conduct of the spring assemblies and the Carolingians' respect for Frankish traditions remained such delicate issues as late as the early ninth century, when these works were written. Sensitivity turned on the fact that whatever his personal standing, the king personified Frankish tradition and gave legitimacy to the whole political edifice.

Royal office was, as we saw earlier in this chapter, an important source of power, and royal authority legitimated power. The figure of the king stood for impartiality and the defence of right through due process. These were not abstract ideas but concrete necessities in a society tense with competition and rivalry. This we saw at comital level in the Edict of Paris where counts ('judges') were required to have hereditary property in the area in which they held office as a guarantee of a source of compensation in case they should illegally take the property of others. Here, the king was the ultimate guarantor against the abuse of power. There is no case-evidence of any king intervening against counts in this way, but we do have later evidence of peasants who sought to defend their rights against landlords in the king's court.[32]

---

32 For two ninth-century cases, see J. Nelson, 'Dispute Settlement in Carolingian West Francia', in W. Davies and P. Fouracre (eds), *The Settlement of Disputes in Early Medieval Europe* (Cambridge 1986), pp. 45–64, at pp. 48–53.

It is the accessibility of royal justice, and the widespread belief, however naïve, in its impartiality, that encourages historians to contrast the 'public' justice of the Frankish period with the 'private' or 'seigneurial' justice of the tenth and eleventh centuries. This contrast is in some ways misleading, but it is useful in pointing up the way in which people from all over Francia saw the king as a figure of final appeal.

Among the magnates recourse to royal judgement was a favoured way of settling disputes, for the highest court in the land was a suitable place in which to discuss the affairs of those of highest social status. Kings thus kept the peace between the powerful, and sometimes this meant intervening to prevent actual fighting. They in fact intervened in magnate affairs a great deal, making use of local rivalries to advance their own interests. As we shall see in the next chapter, the Pippinids themselves were far from immune to this kind of interference. As already stated, the royal court was the place where deals were brokered and the politics of reward and punishment were worked out. The leaders were understandably nervous about any one group having too much influence upon the king, and they were particularly aware of the way in which the mayor of the palace could dominate the king. Their fear was articulated in a late-seventh-century narrative, the *Passio Leudegarii*, which spoke of how when the king, Clothar III, died in 673, the magnates were afraid because the mayor Ebroin had prevented them from assembling to raise up the new king. If they could not get access to him, they would be in great danger, 'because as long as he kept the king, whom he ought to have raised up before the people to the glory of the royal fatherland, in the background and just used his name, Ebroin would be able to do harm to whomsoever he wished, with impunity'.[33]

The context of this episode was a growing factionalism in the political community, which was the result of two generations of political unity and relative peace. When factionalism developed into feuding and fighting, then the political community scattered. People no longer dared to attend the royal court, nor did they gather for assemblies. The unity of the kingdom thus instantly dissolved, although a settlement of the disputes could bring it all back together again. We shall see in the next chapter what part factionalism played in the rise to power of the family of Charles Martel, but the point to be made here is that as the competition between different magnate groups became keener, there was more than ever a need for a royal umpire, so that far from fading from the political scene in the generations after 614, the king remained at its centre. The king was at its apex; he was its *culmen*. As

---

33   *Passio Leudegarii*, ed. B. Krusch, *MGH SRM* V, pp. 282–322, trans. with commentary in Fouracre and Gerberding, *Late Merovingian France*, pp. 191–253, here ch. 5, p. 222.

the *Passio Leudegarii* put it when describing an interregnum, 'since no king sat firmly on the throne, each [of the rulers of the provinces] saw as right whatever he himself wished to do, and that is how they began to act, without fear of discipline'.[34]

The sense that it was impossible to live without a king went hand in hand with the Franks' extraordinary attachment to a single, narrow royal bloodline, the descendants of Clovis. Keeping to the bloodline was a way of reinforcing the special separate status of the king, which was needed if he was to be seen to be above the rivalries of his mightier subjects. The result of allowing such a restricted group to hold royal power was, famously, the advent of child kings. That it was possible for a child to occupy the throne shows just how coherent this political community had become, and just how far it had developed stable institutions in which the king was the focus of political consensus. The consensus was that there should be kings, and that they should be Merovingians. It would be difficult to get rid of the Merovingians without risking unpicking the Frankish kingdom itself.

Against this background we can see that it was no easy task for the Carolingians to bring about that reordering of loyalties which would allow them to replace the Merovingians as kings. As we shall see, the political reorientation began when the influence of the Neustrian *Franci* waned, and the old political consensus based on the Neustrian court collapsed. The political community was then divided into winners and losers, as what had been a prolonged period of peace was replaced by what seems to have been almost continual warfare: from the early eighth century onwards the narrative sources mark as exceptional those years in which there was no war. But if the background helps us understand why it took such violence to shake the Franks from their traditional loyalties, it also allows us to see that that dislocation has as its context great underlying social and cultural stability. As we saw when looking at the Edict of Paris, Frankish society would change little in the age of Charles Martel. The same pull towards integration which had enabled Clothar II to unite the Frankish kingdom in the years after 613 would aid Charles Martel and his sons to rebuild a consensus around themselves. And the same desire to profit from participation in Frankish success would continue to draw nobility from the periphery towards the centre. But first, the family of Charles Martel had to be firmly identified as winners before the social, religious and economic forces we have examined in this chapter would run in their favour. How they emerged as winners is the subject of the next chapter.

---

34 *Passio Leudegarii*, ch. 15, pp. 231–2.

CHAPTER TWO

The Rise of the Pippinids

Beginnings

In the year 613 when King Clothar II's luck changed so suddenly for the better, it was, said the *Chronicle of Fredegar*, the faction of Arnulf bishop of Metz and of Pippin which invited the king to come and rule in Austrasia.[1] This is the first appearance of the Pippinids in history. Later in the eighth century this reference to Arnulf and Pippin acting together would become the cornerstone of a tradition that the two formed such a close alliance that Pippin's daughter Begga married Arnulf's son Ansegisel. Their child would be Pippin II, who was Charles Martel's father. The Carolingians would thus claim to be descended from the most noble of ancestors, one of whom, Arnulf, had come to be venerated as a saint. Writing at the end of the seventh century, the author of the *Life of St Gertrude* (the life, that is, of Pippin's daughter Gertrude, abbess of Nivelles) asked: 'who living in Europe does not know the loftiness, the names, and the localities of her lineage?'[2] Hindsight may persuade us that this lineage was destined for great things from the start, and that it started most auspiciously with a marriage alliance that could almost have been made in heaven. But contemporary evidence, not least from the *Life of Gertrude* itself, argues otherwise. There is no real proof that Ansegisel was Arnulf's son, and it is a fair guess that anyone hearing or reading Gertrude's *Life* in the generation after it was written would have

---

1 *Fredegar*, ed. and trans. J.M. Wallace-Hadrill (London 1960), ch. 40, pp. 32–3.
2 *Vita Geretrudis*, ed. B. Krusch, *MGH SRM* II (Hanover 1888), pp. 464–71, trans. with commentary in P. Fouracre and R. Gerberding, *Late Merovingian France. History and Hagiography 640–720* (Manchester 1996), pp. 301–26, here Prologue, p. 320.

judged that her lineage contained rather more losers than winners, and that her family was heading for disaster.[3] It is essential to grasp this point, not simply to correct the defective vision that comes with hindsight, but also to explain the family's behaviour in terms of its persistent political insecurity. The Pippinids did indeed 'rise' in the course of the seventh and early eighth centuries, but they rose in the teeth of opposition, and they could not be secure until all of their opponents had been crushed. What we see in the age of Charles Martel is a decisive and bloody phase of this struggle. For the Pippinids and early Carolingians, the fight for supremacy was the engine of survival.

Pippin was a leading Austrasian magnate, rich in land in the Moselle valley and to the north around Liège.[4] Arnulf was equally rich. But despite their support for Clothar II in 613, the king gave the position of mayor of the palace in Austrasia to a man named Rado who may well have been their opponent. Clothar, it seems, favoured a group of western Austrasians who had strong family ties with the Neustrians. Rado was probably a member of a family group which historians have called the 'Faronids' or 'Gundoinings'. This group of highly privileged people, who held land and power in the area in which Burgundy, Neustria and Austrasia met, were well placed to serve Clothar II as a link between his three kingdoms. Members of the family would continue to be prominent throughout the seventh century. The great Audoin, bishop of Rouen in the later seventh century, and an acclaimed holy man, was connected to them, for instance. Another of the leading family groups under Clothar was the Agilolfings, who were in fact related to the Faronids. The Agilolfings were even more widely spread across Francia, and the rulers of Bavaria were Agilolfings. There was even a line of Agilolfing kings in Lombardy. The Agilolfings and Faronids together dominated southern Austrasia, and they seem to have been rivals to the Pippinids. The Merovingian kings, past masters at dividing in order to rule, most probably stimulated this rivalry, hence the appointment of Rado, rather than Pippin, as mayor of the palace in Austrasia, and the same tactic would be used against three generations of Pippinids. At the same time, the Pippinids

---

3 For circumstantial evidence that Arnulf was an ancestor of the family see G. Halsall, *Settlement and Social Organization. The Merovingian Region of Metz* (Cambridge 1995), pp. 15, n. 7, 263, n. 1.

4 R. Gerberding, *The Rise of the Carolingians and the Liber Historiae Francorum* (Oxford 1987) pp. 120–30, argues that the Pippinids acquired land in the Liège area through Pippin's marriage to Charles Martel's mother Alpaida, although he admits that the family of Plectrude, Pippin's other wife, held land at Süsteren near Liège. M. Werner, *Der Lütticher Raum in frühkarolingischer Zeit*, Veröffentlichungen des Max-Planck Instituts für Geschichte, 62 (Göttingen 1980), pp. 419–84 makes out a good case for extensive Pippinid landholding in the area. It must be stressed that none of Alpaida's family or lands can be firmly identified.

and their allies, whose power was confined to Austrasia (unlike that of the Faronids or Agilolfings), were put at a further disadvantage as Austrasia began to be treated as a subordinate kingdom.

After Rado's death, in about 617, Pippin was finally made mayor,[5] and in 623 Austrasia did once again have a king of its own, Clothar's young son Dagobert, but the fact that Clothar kept for himself parts of western Austrasia shows its subordinate status. Pippin and Arnulf were Dagobert's chief advisers. Fredegar tells us that they persuaded Dagobert to order the death of one of their enemies, an Agilolfing lord called Chrodoald. In 629, however, Dagobert succeeded Clothar as king of all Francia and Fredegar reported with some bitterness that he then began to discriminate against the Austrasians.[6] This in turn led to Pippin's loss of influence in Austrasia, as the Austrasians seem to have blamed him for their misfortunes, and some of them wanted Dagobert to have Pippin killed, rather as Pippin had engineered Chrodoald's death. As the Austrasians became more and more dispirited, the Slavonic Wends began to make serious inroads into Frankish territory in the east, and in 632 Dagobert installed his son Sigibert as king of Austrasia, but, it seems, on condition that Pippin's influence on the young king be limited. The key position of tutor to Sigibert was given to a magnate called Otto,[7] whose name suggests that he was a Faronid.

Only on Dagobert's death in 639 did Pippin re-emerge as leader of the Austrasian magnates, in alliance with Bishop Cunibert of Cologne. But when Pippin himself died in 640 it was Otto, not Pippin's son Grimoald, who took over as leader. Grimoald and Cunibert of Cologne began to manoeuvre against Otto, at which point another Faronid, Radulf duke of Thuringian, rose in revolt. Grimoald, King Sigibert and a force of Austrasians crossed the Rhine and marched east against him. En route they met and killed Chrodoald's son Fara and 'his people', who were, presumably, supporters of Radulf. Radulf, however, successfully resisted them from his stronghold on the River Unstrut, and in one of the wonderfully evocative passages which distinguishes the *Chronicle of Fredegar* we hear of the young king, Sigibert, aged about ten, sitting on his horse with tears pouring down his cheeks because he had lost so many of his faithful followers in the battle against Radulf.[8] Fredegar added that the men of Mainz did not support the king in this battle.

---

5 *Fredegar*, ch. 45, p. 35 mentions a man called Chuc who may have been mayor of Austrasia 614–17.
6 *Fredegar*, chs 58, 60, pp. 49, 50.
7 *Fredegar*, ch. 86, p. 72. The Latin might just mean that it was Otto's father Uro who was the tutor.
8 *Fredegar*, ch. 87, pp. 73–4.

The whole incident is a revealing one. First, if we take it that the men of Mainz and Fara and his people were supporting Radulf, then we should conclude that the Pippinids enjoyed little or no support along the Main river, which was the key route into central Germany. Nor could they have had much influence in Radulf's base, Thuringia. It is interesting in this light to note that the eighth-century Carolingians, Charlemagne amongst them, also had problems with these areas, despite all of St Boniface's work in the region of Hesse, which lies between the Rhine and Thuringia.[9] This point reinforces the observation that the bedrock of Pippinid and early Carolingian political support lay to the north of this area, in between the rivers Rhine and Meuse, stretching from Cologne in the east to the so-called *Silva Carbonaria* just west of Liège, and down to Trier in the south. It would be in this area that a beleaguered Charles Martel would find support when all other regions were hostile towards him.

Second, the Radulf incident shows the importance of kings, even child kings, as army leaders. Kings seem to have been necessary for the raising of large armies. Sigibert had been made king at the demand of the Austrasians, who were facing attack from the Wends, and though he could have been little more than two years old at the time, it was reported that the Austrasian armies were more effective after his arrival. This could have been to do with the treasure that Sigibert brought with him, and also because demands for military service were harder to resist when a king was present. But Fredegar's image of Sigibert ten years later below Radulf's fort, sitting upon his horse and crying his eyes out, points up the paradox of later Merovingian kingship: as kings they were so valued that mere babes in arms could command respect and obedience, but when small children were kings they could not be other than figureheads and ciphers for regent mothers and mayors of the palace, so that eventually it would become more and more difficult for the kings to exercise independent power. Under Charles Martel we reach the point at which the mayor was so powerful that he could rule without a king, but before this, early in his career when he was under military pressure and fighting against the Neustrian king, Charles had to find and crown his own Merovingian. His sons would be forced to do the same when they in turn were faced with a military crisis.

Back in the 640s, Radulf, for his part, crowed about his victory, acted like a king, and made his own treaties with neighbouring peoples, but, Fredegar

---

9   In 785–86 Charlemagne faced a serious revolt in the areas east of the Rhine. According to the *Annales Nazariani*, s.a. 786, trans. P.D. King, *Charlemagne. Translated Sources* (Lambrigg 1986), pp. 154–5, one of the rebel leaders told Charlemagne that if the revolt had had more support, 'never would you have been seen alive crossing to this side of the Rhine again'.

admitted, he did not go so far as to renounce Merovingian overlordship altogether. Again this is a pattern we shall see later, when leaders of border regions used their military power to resist the early Carolingians, but defended themselves from charges of infidelity by claiming that they were loyal to the Merovingians. It is interesting to note that none of them, not even the mighty Agilolfings in Bavaria, took the alternative course of declaring themselves kings. Perhaps all of them, like Radulf, had too many family ties with other Frankish magnates to envisage life outside a Frankish polity, even one led by Carolingians. This is an important factor in understanding why this kingdom did not fall apart in the later Merovingian period.

The final observation to be drawn from the Radulf affair is that some participants travelled huge distances to reach the Unstrut. Fredegar told of how the count of Saintes was there with the men from his county. From Saintes in western France to the Unstrut in eastern Germany it is well over 1,200 kilometres as the crow flies, and many more than that as the men of Saintes must have ridden. The willingness of counts and dukes to march such extraordinary distances is what made the Carolingian Empire possible, but the Radulf affair shows that such behaviour was rooted in the Merovingian past. The ability to generate this kind of willingness is what lies behind the unity of the Frankish kingdom.

After returning from Unstrut, Grimoald and Cunibert managed to have their rival Otto killed, and Grimoald became mayor in his place. Over the next decade Grimoald became more and more powerful, and even had his son adopted by Sigibert, giving him the Merovingian name Childebert. This 'Childebert the adopted' was destined to follow Sigibert as king of Austrasia. What followed when Sigibert died in 656 was what historians refer to as 'the Grimoald coup'.[10] Sigibert did have a son of his own, called Dagobert, perhaps born rather late in the reign, and possibly not the son of his queen, the powerful Himnechild. Upon Sigibert's death, Grimoald seized Dagobert and had him exiled to Ireland, possibly with Himnechild's connivance. 'Childebert the adopted' then became king, but either in 657, or in 661/62 when Childebert died, the Neustrians, presumably with the help of Grimoald's Austrasian enemies, captured the mayor and executed him for treason. A king from Neustria, Childeric II, was now installed in Austrasia and married to Himnechild's daughter Bilichild. If politics thus far had been something of a roller-coaster ride for the Pippinids, their fortunes now were in free fall.

---

10   Few political events in early medieval history have attracted as much scholarly attention as the 'Grimoald coup'. This is because it is seen as of great importance, in line with the view that the history of the period turned around the rise of the Carolingians, and also because contradictions between the different sources, uncertain chronology, and great gaps

Obscurity

For the next fifteen or so years the Pippinids more or less disappear from history. Wulfoald, a magnate from the Verdun region, became mayor of the palace to Childeric. The *Life of Gertrude* tells of how 'out of hatred for her father' attempts were made to drive Grimoald's daughter Wulfetrude out of Nivelles, the Pippinid family monastery, with the aim of taking it over.[11] There are also indications from charter material that Grimoald was, as it were, air-brushed out of the history of his homeland. He had, according to early charters of the double monastery of Stablo-Malmedy, played the leading role in the foundation of this prestigious institution and had given it the estate of Germigny in the region of Rheims. But in charters from Childeric's reign it was said that Sigibert had founded Stablo-Malmedy, and that it was he who had given it Germigny:[12] Grimoald had become a non-person. The *Chronicle of Fredegar*, which can be shown to have been put together in the early 660s, had not one word to say on 'the Grimoald coup'. The *Earlier Annals of Metz* would later effectively deny that Pippin I had even had a son.

This is all that is known for certain about the family in these years of crisis, but there is a story in the *Earlier Annals of Metz* which some historians accept, though others reject it as legend.[13] According to these *Annals*, Ansegisel, who was married to Grimoald's sister Begga, and was the father of Pippin II, was killed by a man named Gundoin. When Pippin grew up, he hunted Gundoin down and killed him, along with his followers. Thereafter

---

in information mean that events can be reconstructed and interpreted in several different ways. For the range of positions taken on these events, see B. Krusch, 'Der Staatsstreich des fränkischen Hausmeiers Grimoald', in *Festgäbe für Karl Hampe* (Weimar 1910), pp. 411–38; L. Levillain, 'Encore la Succession d'Austrasie', *Bibliothèque de l'Ecole des Chartes*, 106 (1945–46), 5–63; E. Ewig, 'Noch einmal zum "Staatsstreich" Grimoalds', in C. Bauer, L. Böhm and M. Müller (eds), *Speculum Historiale: Geschichte im Spiegel von Geschichtsschreibung und Geschichtsdenkung* (Freiburg and Munich 1965), pp. 454–7, reprinted in E. Ewig, *Spätantikes und Fränkisches Gallien. Gesammelten Schriften (1952–1973)*, I (Zurich and Munich 1976), pp. 573–7; Gerberding, *Rise*, pp. 47–66; I. Wood, *The Merovingian Kingdoms* (London 1994), pp. 222–4; and M. Becher, 'Der sogenannte Staatsstreich Grimoalds. Versuch einer Neubewertung', in J. Jarnut, U. Nonn and M. Richter (eds), *Karl Martell in Seiner Zeit*, Beihefte der Francia, 37 (Sigmaringen 1994), pp. 119–47.

11 *Vita Geretrudis*, ch. 6, p. 324.
12 J. Halkin and C. Roland, *Recueil des Chartes de l'Abbaye de Stavelot-Malmedy* (Brussels 1909), charters nos 3, 4 and 6, pp. 8–10, 10–14, 18–23. Charter no. 6 is often said to show the monasteries' endowment being halved as a way of punishing Grimoald. It is more likely that the halving was meant to reduce and redefine the sacred space surrounding the monasteries in the light of increasing settlement in the Ardennes forest.
13 I. Haselbach, 'Aufstieg und Herrschaft der Karolinger in der Darstellung des sogenannten *Annales Mettenses Priores*', *Historischen Studien*, 406 (1970), 1–208, at 45–6 rejects the story as unfounded legend. Werner, *Lütticher Raum*, pp. 100–11, accepts it.

Pippin took power in Austrasia. The author of the *Earlier Annals of Metz* certainly distorted information, or as we have just seen, left it out, but he or she did not otherwise invent stories at will, nor is any other part of the work obviously influenced by 'legend', so there is reason to think that this story may have some basis in fact. Ansegisel was certainly dead by the later 670s.[14] One of the Stablo-Malmedy charters, dated to 669, was addressed to a Duke Gundoin, and the historian of the Lombards, Paul the Deacon, writing in the late eighth century also spoke of Pippin II crossing the Rhine to kill an enemy.[15] The historian Matthias Werner, who is inclined to believe the Gundoin story,[16] has advanced the following reconstruction of events: after the Grimoald coup, Ansegisel was also killed. Gundoin was appointed duke in the Pippinid heartland, and a magnate called Hodo, to whom the Stablo-Malmedy charter was also addressed, was made *domesticus* (the officer who administered the lands of the fisc) in the crown lands which the Pippinids once held. A charter of 699 from the monastery of Wissembourg refers to Hodo as Gundoin's son, and a Wissembourg charter of 705/6 shows that his mother, Wolfgunde, was none other than the daughter of Wulfoald.[17] In other words, Gundoin was married to Wulfoald's daughter, and since the name he gave his son was a variant of the name Otto, it seems likely that Gundoin was in some way also related to the Austrasian mayor Otto who had been killed in the wake of the Radulf affair. The *Earlier Annals of Metz's* story that Gundoin and Pippin II were deadly enemies is thus highly plausible. The killing of Gundoin would therefore have been round three of a feud which stretched back over a generation. At the same time, King Childeric appointed Theodard bishop of Maastricht, which lay right in the centre of the Pippinid lands. When Theodard was murdered, Childeric appointed Lambert to succeed him.

That the Pippinids were able to make a comeback was due to events elsewhere, as factional violence engulfed Neustria and Burgundy. In 673 Childeric, like Clothar II and Dagobert I before him, became king of all three Frankish kingdoms, and, like Dagobert, moved to Neustria, taking Wulfoald with him. But Childeric so alienated the Neustrians and Burgundians that in 675 they killed him, along with his pregnant wife, Bilichild. Wulfoald fled back to Austrasia and disappeared from view. It was now, argued Werner,

---

14   *LHF*, ch. 46, trans. with commentary in Fouracre and Gerberding, *Late Merovingian France*, p. 91, he is referred to as 'the late Ansegisel'.
15   Paul the Deacon, *Historia Langobardorum*, ed. G. Waitz, *MGH SRG* (Hanover 1878), IV, ch. 37.
16   See above, note 13.
17   *Traditiones Wizenburgenses*, ed. L. Glöckner and A. Doll (Darmstadt 1979), nos 223 and 228, pp. 441–4, 455–6.

that Pippin killed Gundoin. Lambert was ejected from Maastricht and exiled to Stablo-Malmedy, which once again came under Pippinid control. The Austrasians now, amazingly, retrieved Sigibert's son Dagobert from his exile in Ireland and made him king in Austrasia. This was done probably to counter Neustrian aggression towards Austrasia. The most powerful man in Neustria was the mayor Ebroin, who had re-established his ascendance following Childeric's murder. Ebroin was a fearsome military leader who had scores to settle and allies to support, and among the latter were people from western Austrasia.

According to the *Liber Historiae Francorum* (*LHF*), from about 676, Austrasia was led by 'Pippin and Martin'. Who Martin was is a mystery, but it is usually assumed that he was a close relative[18] of Pippin. Pippin and Martin gathered a large force (which suggests that they might have had King Dagobert with them) and attacked Ebroin. Ebroin met them on Austrasian territory and routed their army at the battle of Bois du Fays. Pippin escaped, but Martin took refuge in the nearby fortress of Laon. Ebroin induced him to emerge and then killed him. In 679 King Dagobert II was murdered (by whom is uncertain), and again Austrasia, and the Pippinids, looked extremely vulnerable within a theoretically reunited kingdom. Once more events in Neustria saved them: in 680 Ebroin was himself murdered, and his successor, Waratto, favoured a policy of peace. But Waratto was then displaced by his son Ghislemar, who attacked Pippin at the stronghold of Namur, well into Austrasian territory. Yet again luck was on Pippin's side: Ghislemar died suddenly, Waratto resumed his position as mayor and Audoin of Rouen made peace. This was in fact the occasion on which Audoin visited Cologne and removed martyr relics to Rouen. In 686 Waratto died and was replaced by his son-in-law Berchar, but the choice of Berchar as mayor divided the Neustrians and some of them went over to Pippin. This seems to have tipped the balance in Pippin's favour, and in 687 he invaded Neustria and fought with Berchar at the battle of Tertry, near the River Somme. He won. In the following year Ansfled, Waratto's widow, had her son-in-law Berchar killed, and the way was now open for a marriage alliance between her family and that of Pippin. In the same year, 688 that is, another marriage bore fruit: by his wife Alpaida, the *LHF* tells us, Pippin 'had a son named Charles, a warrior who was uncommonly well educated and effective in battle'.[19] The age of Charles Martel had indeed begun.

---

18 On the chronology of the *LHF* for the 670s, Gerberding, *Rise*, pp. 78–84.
19 *LHF*, ch. 49, p. 93 and n. 68. 'Well educated' translates the Latin *elegans*. An alternative meaning could be simply 'fine' or 'handsome'.

Family

Victory at the battle of Tertry was not quite the moment at which the Pippinids became for ever the unchallenged leaders of the Franks, as the *Earlier Annals of Metz* claimed, for as we shall see, the family's greatest crisis was still yet to come. Nevertheless this is an appropriate point at which to reflect upon the kind of resources which enabled the family to survive and to prosper in the violent world of late Merovingian factional politics. In the last chapter it was said that power was derived from a conjunction of family wealth and office holding. On this basis historians generally assume that all the males named in the narrative sources were magnates who had much land and held mighty office.

If the holding of wealth and office were the constants of political history, a more variable factor was the possible relationships these people might have had with each other. Sometimes we are told of such links, as in the case of Pippin I and Arnulf, who were said by the *Chronicle of Fredegar* to have been part of the same 'faction' (*factio* is the term used). But where no such clear indication is given, factions and alliances can be deduced from circumstantial evidence. It is assumed here that people who were related to each other by blood or through marriage would have been on the same side in politics. Where other information is lacking, the main method that modern historians have used to work out to which family group an individual belonged is inferring blood relationship from names, on the assumption that members of the same group tended to have similar or linked names. It was on this basis, remember, that Hodo, son of Gundoin, was thought to have been related to Otto, one-time mayor of the palace in Austrasia. This method of inquiry is known as *Namenforschung* ('name-research'), for the pioneering work in the field has been done by German-speaking scholars. *Namenforschung* has indeed proved useful in suggesting relationships that we might otherwise not identify: Hodo/Otto is a case in point. We must nevertheless ask whether people in the same family will always have borne linked names, or whether people with similar names must always have been members of the same family.[20] For instance, if Pippin and Martin were closely related, their names would not show this, or, conversely, Grimoald's daughter was called Wulftrude, but other evidence would make it seem unlikely

---

20 For a vigorous defence of *Namenforschung* methodology in the light of these problems, see W. Hartung, 'Tradition und Namengebung im frühen Mittelalter', in I. Eberl, W. Hartung and J. Jahn (eds), *Früh- und hochmittelalterlicher Adel in Schwaben und Bayern, Regio*, Forschungen zur schwäbischen Regionalgeschichte, 1 (Sigmaringen 1988), pp. 21–79.

that she was related to her father's successor Wulfoald or to the latter's daughter Wulfgonde. In addition, scholars sometimes disagree over whether two names are indeed linked, or even whether or not they are identical. Identification by name alone must therefore be treated with great caution. Equally, we cannot be sure that all the members of the same family would have been on the same side, for family members were actually quite likely to fight each other over matters of leadership and inheritance. Charles Martel would himself become a wicked uncle as he deprived his nephews of their inheritance, freedom, and, in one case, life. His son Pippin too would exclude his nephews, and his grandson Charlemagne would do the same.

This apparently uncharitable behaviour leads us to question the solidarity of the cognatic family. There is no doubt that there were some families which were large enough to be described as a 'tribe' or 'people' (*gens*), and that individuals were identified as belonging to that group. We saw an example of this with the Agilolfings, when Chrodoald, whom Pippin and Arnulf had had killed, was described by Fredegar as *de gente Agilolfingam*, 'being of the Agilolfing people'.[21] But most other family names and group identities are given by historians rather than expressed by contemporaries. The Faronids/Gundoinings are such a group, although in this case there is the evidence to distinguish a common characteristic: rivalry with the Pippinids. But we cannot attribute a consciousness of identity to the Faronids, nor to any other grouping made up by modern historians. It is also now understood that families identified and organised themselves in different ways for different purposes: in big groups in times of war or conflict, but as narrowly as the modern family at moments of inheritance.

For the first half of the seventh century it is the narrative sources which provide the names and tell us about the actions of the magnates. After about 650 we also have an increasing number of charters which become the main source of names, and by looking at the transactions in which people participated we can sometimes discern family groups or alliances. The common, and largely correct, assumption here is that people who donated land to the same ecclesiastical institution, or who witnessed such donations, must have had social as well as religious ties with each other. Charters, of course, also tell us who had land where, and it is thus through their charters that the Austrasian lands and allies (and therefore resources) of the Pippinids have been identified. In relation to the Pippinids, the charters which are most revealing are those which documented donations

---

21 *Fredegar*, ch. 52, p. 42.

to the monastery of Echternach, which lay just west of Trier.[22] Although the first of these documents is only from 697/98, the year of Echternach's effective foundation, where they mention a donor's parentage, they can provide information on the preceding generation.

The Echternach charters provide most of the evidence for the family of Plectrude, Pippin II's wife. They show her family holding extensive lands in an area stretching from northern Alsace to Cologne. It is clear that Plectrude was the source of much of Pippin's influence in this area, and it was Plectrude who would lead the family after Pippin's death in 714. Charles Martel was not, of course, Plectrude's son, and she would in fact imprison him in 714. He would, in turn, imprison her grandsons and even kill one of them. But it is also clear that descendants of Plectrude's sister, Adela, would later be counted as his supporters. As we shall see in Chapter 4, Charles might even have married into the family via the descendant of another sister, Regentrude. The Echternach charters show another circle of lands, relatives and associates to the north around Liège in Belgium. This is where Charles Martel's mother, Alpaida, came from, but Plectrude was active here too. The very last charter issued by Pippin was a grant of land to endow the monastery of Süsteren, which lay to the north of Liège.[23] Plectrude was there as the charter was drawn up, but Pippin was absent, already suffering from his final illness.

Another group of charters concerned with the monastery of Wissembourg, to the east of Metz, is often taken to show the reverse side of the Echternach charters, that is, opposition to, rather than support for, the Pippinids. We have already touched on this, when Wissembourg charters were cited as evidence of the links between Gundoin, Hodo, Wulfgonde and Wulfoald. Wissembourg seems to have been to the Gundoinings what Echternach was to the Pippinids, and it has recently been argued that when the descendants of this family were finally beaten by Charles Martel in the 720s, they gave all that was left of their lands to Wissembourg.[24] Many historians have observed that if the Wissembourg donors were indeed firmly anti-Pippinid, it then follows that the Pippinids could never have had much influence in the Metz region, despite the original alliance of Pippin I and Arnulf of Metz. Arnulf had indeed been bishop of Metz, but this does not necessarily

---

22 The most recent edition of these charters is in C. Wampach, *Geschichte der Grundherrschaft Echternach im Frühmittelalter* I, pt 2 (Luxembourg 1930), but for the sake of convenience the edition used here is that of J. Pardessus (ed.), *Diplomata, Chartae, Epistolae, Leges, Aliaque Instrumenta ad Res Gallo-Francicas Spectantia* (2 vols, Paris 1843, 1849, reprinted Aalen 1969).
23 Pardessus, *Diplomata, Chartae*, no. 490, pp. 298–9.
24 Halsall, *Settlement*, p. 14.

mean that his family were local landowners, and there are slight indications that they, like the Pippinids, had their lands in the north.[25] Associations between the Pippinids and Metz seem to have been made later, in the Carolingian period, and to have been the fruit of the Carolingians' desire to have Arnulf as the family's ancestor.

It may be going too far to say that the Wissembourg donations reveal an organised anti-Pippinid opposition group in southern Austrasia, for we simply do not know enough about the donors to determine their political views. The Gundoinings, as we have seen, did have a long track record of rivalry with the Pippinids, but they must have had other concerns too. Some Wissembourg donors may even have been Pippinid supporters. In fact one of them, Theotcharius (whose donation is the first ever recorded for Wissembourg), has been identified on the grounds of his name as none other than Plectrude's father. Nevertheless, if we imagine that southern Austrasia was indeed an area in which the Pippinids had little or no support, it makes Charles Martel's achievement all the greater in defeating the Neustrians in 717, that is, before he was master of all Austrasia. In that year the Neustrian king, Chilperic II, made a donation direct to the church of Metz, which might suggest that the old alliance between the magnates of south-west Austrasia and the Neustrian royal house was still in operation.[26]

As we have seen, the identification of families and factions relies upon a great deal of speculation, much of which is informed by assumptions which are in themselves questionable. The reconstruction of the Pippinid family relies on the further assumptions that all those holding land in one place were related, and that those with linked names must have been related. If we insist on hard evidence for the identification of its members, this family appears as a fairly narrow group based in its Austrasian heartland, and consists of the direct descendants of the principal males Pippin I, Pippin II and Charles Martel. If, however, we are prepared to accept linkage on the basis of name forms and landholding, we get a massively extended family, with branches in Aquitaine, Bavaria and Thuringia as well as in Austrasia.[27] The key figure here is the lady Irmina of Oeren, and at issue is the identity of her daughters. It seems highly probable that Plectrude was Irmina's

---

25 Werner, *Lütticher Raum*, pp. 465–77. Halsall, *Settlement*, pp. 14–16 argues that Arnulf may have been an outsider who faced resistance in Metz.

26 *MGH DD*, ed. G. Pertz (Hanover 1872), no. 89, pp. 78–9.

27 For the maximum possible extent of the family, counting those with similar or linked names as members, see E. Hlawitscha, 'Die Vorfahren Karls des Grossen', in W. Braunfels (ed.), *Karl der Grosse. Lebenswerk und Nachleben*, I (Düsseldorf 1965), pp. 51–82. For the minimal extent, accepting only hard evidence for family connections, M. Werner, *Adelsfamilien im Umkreis der frühen Karolinger. Die Verwandtschaft Irminas von Oeren und Adelas von Pfalzel*. Vorträge und Forschungen, 28 (Sigmaringen 1982).

daughter.[28] It is equally probable that another daughter was Adela of Pfalzel, but another three possible daughters have been identified, and from them grow three more branches of the family tree. In all three cases the identification of these women as the daughters of Irmina and the sisters of Plectrude has been contested. Nevertheless, even if many of these ties of blood and marriage did not exist, it still seems certain that those in the circle of Echternach should be counted as Pippinid supporters.[29] It must have been these landholders in the Moselle and Meuse regions who remained loyal to the family following the Grimoald disaster, and who would enable it to return to power after 675. Or, to put it another way, these people must have had much to fear, and little to gain, from the arrival of outsiders like Gundoin, or Wulfoald, in the region.

Land and power

It is of course important to try to identify all the members of Charles Martel's family in order to understand the politics of the age. If we accept that all those mentioned in the charters and chronicles were relatively wealthy landowners, then the identification of family and supporters does also give us an indication of the sources of the family's power and influence. We can, however, use the same evidence to say much more about the nature of the family's resources, and about power in general. The charters show us, for instance, that control over a dependent peasantry was necessary for the taking of income from land.[30] They also show us that land was generally held in fractions of larger units, usually expressed as 'portions' of a group of lands (*villa*, or *locum*). The charter of 706 in which Pippin and Plectrude took the monastery of Echternach under their protection shows both these features.[31] It also furnishes 'evidence' that Irmina of Oeren and Plectrude were close relatives, for the two women held land which appears to have

---

28 Werner's refusal to accept a link between Irmina and Plectrude on the basis that there is no hard evidence for it (*Adelsfamilien, passim*, but esp. pp. 120–39) seems unduly harsh given that there is good circumstantial evidence for a connection. Both women, for instance, held land which had been inherited from the same source.

29 M. Costambeys, 'An Aristocratic Community on the Northern Frankish Frontier 690–726', *Early Medieval Europe*, 3 (1994), 39–62, at 40–2, argues that people who donated land to Willibrord should not necessarily be counted as Pippin's supporters as that land only later came into the hands of Echternach. But given the close links between Pippin and Willibrord from the moment of the latter's arrival in Francia, it seems very likely that making a gift to Willibrord was a Pippinid-friendly action.

30 See above, ch. 1, pp. 21–2.

31 Pardessus, *Diplomata, Chartae*, no. 467, pp. 273–4.

been inherited from the same source: the duke Theotarius, who may well have been the same person as the duke Theotcharius who donated land to Wissembourg.[32] By 706 the estate of Echternach had been divided several times. Theotcharius had held only half of it, and this half was further divided between his son Theodardus and daughter Irmina. Pippin and Plectrude had acquired Theodardus's share. According to the formulae of the charters, what 'holding' land like this actually meant was having control over the cultivated lands and pastures, and having rights over everything on the land. This included people as well as livestock, buildings and any other facilities or 'appurtenances'. When land was divided and a portion given away, then the people who worked the land were often named. From this it is clear that land was valued in terms of rights and income. That these were divisible indicates that the cultivators remained in place. What the Austrasian charters show us are estates which must have been divided up like this over several generations, which likewise suggests that they had a labour force which had been in place, and subject to control, for at least several generations.

In the Introduction we looked briefly at the 'Brunner thesis', which argued that Charles Martel's power was based on the leasing out of church land to warriors. In elaboration of this idea it has also been argued that because the Pippinids held land at the periphery of Frankish territory they were able to benefit from the colonisation of new land which could likewise be given out to their followers. But the Echternach charters show that this area of Austrasia was certainly not a land of sod-busters, not even in Toxandria, the area to the north of Liège which was a frontier zone between Francia and Frisia: Toxandrian charters in which land was given to Echternach show the same pattern of fragmented landholding. Nor is there any reason to suppose that across the border into Frisian territory the pattern would have been any different. It has often been assumed that at least in Francia the land fragments had once been parts of single, unified estates which over the generations had been broken down into small portions by the process of partible inheritance. It is undeniable that portions were divided when they were passed on to more than one heir, just as Irmina and Theodardus had each received half of what had once been held by Theotcharius, but whether or not the starting point was indeed an undivided *villa* we simply cannot tell. What the charter evidence does make clear, however, is that division was matched by exchanges and purchases of land through which holdings were combined and rearranged to provide more effective units of exploitation. In our 706 charter, for instance, this seems to be precisely what Pippin and Plectrude had been doing in

---

32   This is the view of Glöckner and Doll, *Traditiones Wizenburgenses*, p. 428.

Echternach. There was therefore a dynamic aspect to landholding as land-ownership was divided and holdings shuffled, although, as we have seen, the actual cultivators who provided the income from the land remained in place. Female inheritance was another factor in the division and agglomeration of landholding. Indeed, the 'rise of the Pippinids' depended in large part on the acquisition of land from two heiresses, Begga and Plectrude. As Matthew Innes has recently observed, it was because people were used to landownership circulating in this way, and, one should add, used to the practicalities of imposing their control over different groups of cultivators, that land could be used as the payment for political support.[33]

There are two exceptions to the pattern of fragmentary holdings: estates held in integrity and perpetuity by the church, and fiscal land held in the name of the kings, for neither were subject to partible inheritance. It is not hard to see that holding church land or fiscal land was highly advantageous, which helps explain why people were so keen to associate with the church and to serve the kings. The Pippinids benefited on both counts. In the 706 charter to Echternach Pippin and Plectrude trumpeted their generosity to the monastery, but also stated that it should remain under their protection. In a second charter issued on the same day, they spelled this out again: when Willibrord the abbot of Echternach died, the monks could themselves choose another abbot, on condition that he remained faithful in all things to Pippin and Plectrude's descendants, and that the community remain under their protection and guardianship.[34] The family in effect now owned Echternach, and they were thus in control of a network of lands which need never be divided up.

Another strategy for keeping land undivided was to give it to a church and then to receive it back as a tenancy which could be inherited but not divided. As we shall see in Chapter 5, it is this practice, the granting of 'precarial tenures', which was mistaken by Brunner and others for the deliberate secularisation of church property under Charles Martel. In their capacity as dukes and mayors of the palace, the Pippinids also exercised control over fiscal lands. This control they seem to have lost following the fall of Grimoald. As we saw from the Stablo-Malmedy charter, it was their opponent Gundoin who was duke in the area during the reign of Childeric II and it was Gundoin's son Hodo who was the area's *domesticus*. After Gundoin's death, the Pippinids resumed control of the fiscal lands in this area, and in the period after the death of Dagobert II when Austrasia had

---

33 M. Innes, *State and Society in the Early Middle Ages: The Middle Rhine Valley 400–1000* (Cambridge 2000), ch. 2.
34 Pardessus, *Diplomata, Chartae*, no. 468, pp. 274–5.

no king, the family may have treated the fiscal land around Liège as its own: the estates of Herstal, Hemalle, Jupille and Chèvremont, which may all once have been part of the same block of fiscal land, appear later as family estates.[35] Finally, the Pippinids can be seen using three fortified sites: Chèvremont, Namur and Laon. Very little is known about Frankish fortifications in this period, but it seems likely that the leading aristocratic families had access to forts, just as Radulf had been able to take refuge in his fort on the Unstrut. The Gundoinings probably had a fort on the site which later became the monastery of St Mihiel. It does not, however, seem likely that leaders normally resided in forts.[36]

Consolidation

Victory at the battle of Tertry allowed the Pippinids to consolidate their resources in Austrasia and to extend their influence beyond it, but as already observed, the *Earlier Annals of Metz* exaggerated when they said that following the battle, 'Pippin took over sole leadership of the Franks'. What in fact followed Tertry was a compromise with the magnates of the Neustro-Burgundian kingdom. Pippin's son Drogo married Anstrude, the widow of the Neustrian mayor Berchar, after Berchar had been murdered at the instigation of his mother-in-law, Ansfled. Ansfled was the widow of another Neustrian mayor, Waratto, and marriage into this leading family allowed the Pippinids to gain influence in the all-important Rouen area. The first-fruits of this influence were the exile of Ansbert, Audoin's successor as bishop of Rouen, and his replacement by Gripho, a firm supporter of Pippin. In 701 we see the appointment of another ally, Bainus, as abbot of the prestigious monastery of St Wandrille near Rouen. Gifts to St Wandrille followed, and in 707 Pippin took St Wandrille and its daughter-house Fleury (founded by Pippin in 703) under his protection. It thus looks as if St Wandrille was becoming a Pippinid family monastery in the same way, and at roughly the same time, as Echternach. Later, in the time of his uncle Charles Martel, Hugo, the son of Drogo and Anstrude, would strengthen the family's influence in the Rouen area, being simultaneously the abbot of St Wandrille and of the nearby monastery of Jumièges, as well as bishop of Rouen, of

---

35 Werner, *Lütticher Raum*, pp. 419–25.
36 No forts from the seventh century have been excavated, but work has been done on sixth-century aristocratic residences: R. Samson, 'The Merovingian Nobleman's House: Castle or Villa?', *Journal of Medieval History*, 13 (1987), 287–315. Samson's view is that sixth-century residences were not fortified.

Bayeux and of Paris. Hugo was, however, brought up by his grandmother Ansfled, while Drogo his father was made duke in distant Champagne. St Wandrille would later join in a rising against the Pippinids and continue to harbour anti-Carolingian sentiments in the time of Charles Martel. So despite the marriage alliance with Ansfled, and despite Hugo's ascendancy, the family did not have it all their own way in the Rouen area. Ansfled and Anstrude may have been able to strike a hard bargain precisely because without their help Pippinid prospects in Neustria would have remained dim even after the victory at Tertry. Again we see the key role women played in the family's fortunes and in politics generally.

To the north of the Neustrian heartlands we can detect Pippin extending his influence westwards from his homeland into the area of the River Sambre, where he added Lobbes to the group of monasteries the family controlled in the Meuse region. This group included the houses of Nivelles, Fosses, Maubeuge, Mons and Andenne, and it marks the concentration of wealth and influence the family had in this area.[37] We have already discussed the way in which Pippin and Plectrude gained control of Echternach further to the south. At about the same time they founded the monastery of St Hubert in the Ardennes and that of Kaiserworth further to the east on the River Rhine, and in 714 they took Süsteren to the north of Liège under their control. We have seen, too, that Pippin's son Drogo became duke in Champagne, which was an important border area between Austrasia and Neustria. Here again influence was manifested through the control of monasteries, those of Moutier-en-Der and (less certainly) Hautvillers. It had also been the bishop of Rheims, Reolus, who in 687 had switched loyalties from Berchar to Pippin and had thus prepared the way to Tertry.

The significance of this active 'monastic policy' (*Klosterpolitik*) is hard to assess. Since the great bulk of our evidence comes from monastic sources, and since there is a general increase in the numbers of charters which survive from this period, it would be all too easy to exaggerate the importance of the Pippinid *Klosterpolitik*. The contrast between the family's activity in Austrasia and in Neustria in this respect is nevertheless illuminating. In Neustria, as we know, the family exercised influence in the Rouen area, but it failed to make much impact in the Seine–Oise region, which was the very heartland of the Neustrian elite. Crucially, the monasteries of St Denis and St Germain-des-Prés, the bishopric of Paris, and the other 'senior churches' privileged by the Merovingians, eluded their grasp until the next generation. Nineteen original charters, drawn up in the period 691–717, and preserved

---

37 Gerberding, *Rise*, pp. 98–9. See also A. Dierkens, *Abbayes et Chapitres entre Sambre et Meuse (VIIe–XIe siècles)*, Beihefte der Francia, 14 (Sigmaringen 1985), pp. 318–27.

in the monastery of St Denis, cast very interesting light on the situation at the Neustrian court. Comparing these charters with those issued by the Pippinids in Austrasia in roughly the same period, it is clear that after 688 Pippin did not pack the Neustrian court with his own followers.[38]

There are, indeed, slight indications that the Austrasian presence in Neustria was now actually less intrusive than it had been in the brief reign of Childeric II (673–75). Three royal *placita* (documents, which record the decisions of royal court cases) include extensive lists of those who participated in the court's judgement. Present at court were magnates from as far afield as Marseilles. One of these documents, and two other *placita*, record judgements made in the royal court against Drogo and Grimoald, Pippin's sons. At issue in all three cases were the interests of St Denis, and their message to the Pippinids was clear: 'hands off'. The apparent weakness of the family here demonstrates the paradox of their position in Neustria: to expand their influence they had to utilise the apparatus of government and the collective magnate power vested in the royal court, but in doing this they could not act independently of a consensus of magnate and royal interests which actually served to limit their power in Neustria. To square the circle they allowed the Neustrians to keep their privileges and lands. Drogo, as we saw, married into a leading Neustrian family, and when Grimoald became mayor of the palace sometime after 695 he appears in the *LHF* as a figure in sympathy with the Neustrians. Despite his run-in with St Denis, Grimoald was remembered by the author of the *LHF* as 'loyal, sober, cultured and just'.[39] At the same time, as we have also seen, the Pippinids consolidated their postion in Austrasia itself by extending their monastic empire. They also attacked various non-Frankish peoples beyond the borders of Austrasia. It was their successes in these campaigns which arguably did most to enhance the family's prestige and to make them acceptable as leaders of the Franks. This aggression against non-Franks would grow much fiercer under Charles Martel, sounding the rhythm of growing Carolingian power.

External enemies

According to the *Earlier Annals of Metz*, after his victory at Tertry, Pippin turned his attention to 'the various peoples who had once been subjected to

---

38 P. Fouracre, 'Observations on the Outgrowth of Pippinid Influence in the "Regnum Francorum" After the Battle of Tertry (687–715)', *Medieval Prosopography*, 5 (1984), 1–31.
39 *LHF*, ch. 50, p. 94.

the Franks, that is, the Saxons, Frisians, Alemans, Bavarians, Aquitanians, Gascons and Britons. For the leaders of those peoples, having turned into stubbornness, withdrew themselves in evil presumption from the rule of the Franks because of the idleness of former leaders.'[40] This Carolingian view, that the peoples on the periphery of Francia slipped into independence because the later Merovingians were too idle to stop them, has generally been accepted by modern historians. The situation was in fact much more complex than this, for each of these peoples had their separate history of relations with the Franks, and as was suggested in the Introduction, a degree of acculturation, competition and assimilation underlies the narratives of separatism and conquest.

As we observed with the rebellion of the Thuringian duke Radulf, what appears to be 'separatism' was more likely caused by feuding within the Frankish elite. Aquitaine presents a similar case: the dukedom was detached from the rest of Francia in that same bout of Neustro-Burgundian infighting which had given the Pippinids a chance to recover their fortunes, but as Charles Martel would find to his cost, the Aquitanians were quick to join up with the Neustrians again when they reckoned that together they might defeat and plunder the Austrasians. If we can believe the ninth-century *Breviary of Erchanbert*, the duke of the Alemans and neighbouring dukes stopped obeying the Franks because they were prevented from serving the Merovingian kings as they had always done.[41] This sounds as if they resented Pippin coming between them and the king. Of Pippin's actual campaigns against the Alemans or Sueves, as they are also termed, we know very little. There is a brief reference to a campaign against the Sueves in the *LHF*, a reference which is curiously omitted in the *Continuations of the Chronicle of Fredegar*. The early Carolingian annals, however, tell us a little more. In 709, after the death of Gottfried (the Aleman duke whom, as we have just seen, the *Breviary of Erchanbert* had presented as pro-Merovingian), Pippin attacked his son Willeharius. Further attacks followed in 710, 711 and 712.[42] The *Earlier Annals of Metz*, with what may well be wishful thinking, added that in 712 Pippin brought the whole region under his authority. After 712 Willeharius is never mentioned again. What exactly was going on here is a mystery, but it has been suggested that Pippin had intervened in a dispute between Gottfried's sons, supporting one Lantfrid against Willeharius, and

---

40 *AMP*, trans. Fouracre and Gerberding, *Late Merovingian France*, p. 359.
41 Erchanbert, *Breviarum Regum Francorum*, ed. G. Pertz, *MGH SS* II (Hanover 1829), a 715–827, p. 328.
42 The attack in 711 was led by one Walaric, that of 712 by 'a certain bishop'. In the later *Chronicle of Ado, ex Chronicon Adonis*, ed. G. Pertz, *MGH SS* II, p. 318, this bishop is identified as 'Anepos, a man of a secular way of life'. He is otherwise unknown.

it is certainly true that later there was an alliance between Charles Martel and Lantfrid.[43] Lantfrid's support would in fact be crucial to Charles's intervention in neighbouring Bavaria. Family politics rather than separatism thus seem to lie behind events in Alemannia.

For Pippinid involvement in either Bavaria or Brittany there is no direct evidence. The Frisians and Saxons, however, were proper enemies, although in the sixth and earlier seventh centuries the Saxons had been part of the wider Frankish confederation. Both peoples were non-Christian, and their expansion at this time posed a direct threat to the Franks. In the course of the seventh century the Frisians had expanded from their homelands to the north of the River Rhine in what is now Holland. During the reign of Dagobert I the Franks had controlled the area up to the Rhine and held a fort at Utrecht on the north bank of the river. Since there was a church dedicated to St Martin in Utrecht, it seems that the area was at least nominally Christian and under Frankish control, Martin being the Frankish saint *par excellence*. Thereafter the Franks lost Utrecht, the church there fell into ruin and the Frisians advanced to the River Maas.[44] Frisian traders at this time played a pivotal role in what has been termed 'the North Sea economy'. Their silver coins, known as 'sceattas', were the principal currency of North Sea trade, and the Frisians were particularly important in bringing overseas goods to eastern and southern England. It is in fact from an English source, the early-eighth-century *Life of St Wilfrid*, that we first hear the name of a Frisian leader. In 678 the English bishop and exile Wilfrid preached in Frisia before making his way to Rome. He was welcomed by the 'king' of the Frisians, Adalgisl, who also gave him protection against the Neustrian mayor Ebroin.[45] The emergence of a paramount leader, the welcoming of a Christian missionary and the confident rejection of Ebroin's demand that they hand over Wilfrid, all suggest that Frisia had become a power to be reckoned with. It was in a position to deny Frankish tutelage by developing an independent church, and given its dominance of North Sea trade and strong links with England, Frisia was a strong competitor for power and influence in an area over which the Franks had traditionally held sway. But above all else, Frisian advances pressed directly upon the homelands of the Frankish elite in both Austrasia and Neustria.

---

43 J. Jarnut, 'Untersuchungen zu den fränkisch-alemmanische Beziehungen in der ersten Hälfte des 8 Jahrhunderts', *Schweizerische Zeitschrift für Geschichte*, 30 (1980), 7–28.

44 The authoritative article on Frisian–Frankish relations in this period is W. Fritze, 'Zur Entstehungsgeschichte des Bistums Utrecht. Franken und Friesen 690–734', *Rheinische Vierteljahrsblätter*, 35 (1971), 107–51.

45 *The Life of St Wilfrid by Eddius Stephanus*, ed. and trans. B. Colgrave (Cambridge 1927, reprinted New York 1985), chs 26–7, pp. 52–5.

In campaigns mounted against Adalgisl's successor Radbod in 690 and 695, Pippin drove the Frisians back beyond Utrecht and thus regained control of the important trading centre of Dorestad which lay at the confluence of the rivers Lek and Rhine.[46] At the same time he took control of missionary activity by becoming the protector and patron of the English missionary Willibrord. We have already seen how Willibrord's foundation at Echternach was richly and widely endowed not just by Pippin and Plectrude but also by their associates and allies. Bede, in his *Ecclesiastical History*, told of how in 696 Pippin sent Willibrord to Rome to be consecrated archbishop of the Frisians.[47] This might be taken to suggest that Pippin wished the new Frisian church to have a measure of independence under the aegis of Roman authority, but in practice it seems that the bishopric of Cologne continued to claim authority over Utrecht, as it had done in Dagobert's day.[48] We shall discuss later in more detail the relationship between the Carolingians and the English missionaries in the light of the latter's peculiar links with Rome.[49]

Pippin's campaigns were followed by a rapprochement with Radbod. We hear from the late-eighth-century *Life of Liudger* of a leading Christian Frisian exile who returned home in about 713, and there may have been others.[50] More spectacular, however, was a marriage between Radbod's daughter Theudesinda and Pippin's son Grimoald, which took place sometime after 711. It might seem that at this point the Frisians had become firm allies of the Pippinids. But when in 714 a crisis in the Pippinid family gave them an opportunity to take back the area to the south of Utrecht, they seized it with a vengeance, and joined with the Neustrians in an attack on the Pippinid heartlands.

The Saxons had been tributaries to the Franks, sending them 500 cows yearly until 631 when Dagobert stopped the tribute in return for Saxon defence against the Wends. Like the Frisians, the Saxons were pagan, which means that we know very little about them. It is clear that they dominated a massive area of northern Germany, and that they were capable of mobilising large numbers of troops who could withstand even the bigger Frankish armies, but unlike the Frisians we do not hear of named Saxon leaders in

---

46 Fritze, 'Franken und Friesen', 110–20.
47 *Bede's Ecclesiastical History of the English People*, ed. and trans. B. Colgrave and R. Mynors (Oxford 1969), V, ch. 11, pp. 484–8.
48 In a letter written in 753 the English missionary Boniface complained to Pope Stephen II that Cologne was continuing to claim authority over Utrecht: *Sancti Bonifatii et Lulli Epistolae*, ed. M. Tangl, *MGH Epistolae Selectae* I (Berlin 1955), no. 109, pp. 234–6, trans. E. Emerton, *The Letters of St Boniface* (New York 1940), pp. 181–3.
49 Below, ch. 5.
50 Fritze, 'Franken und Friesen', 130–2.

this period, and we shall return to the intriguing question of their social structure in Chapter 4. At the end of the seventh century the Saxons were pushing southwards until they were pressing hard against Frankish territory along a line which ran from the River Saale in the east to the Rhine in the west. In this latter area they were uncomfortably close to Pippinid lands in the region of Cologne. According to Bede, two English brothers, the Hewalds, who went to preach to the Saxons in 692 were murdered and their bodies thrown into the Rhine.[51] They were followed by Swidbert, who was one of the English missionaries in Frisia. He went to preach among the Boructuarii, a Frankish people living near the Rhine in northern Austrasia, but then, said Bede, the Saxons conquered the area and Swidbert was forced to flee to Pippin. Thus at the end of the seventh century the Saxons were continuing to expand, and would continue to press against Frankish territory until Charlemagne put in hand a systematic Frankish conquest of Saxony. In the Pippinid period they were far from ready for conversion, and equally distant from that development of political institutions and social structure which would allow a measure of acculturation to Frankish ways.

The author of *LHF* wrote in positive terms about the period 687–714. Things were going well for the Franks, especially in comparison with the infighting of the previous generation, and certainly in terms of Pippin's campaigns against the Frisians and Alemans. But the author heaps most praise on another leader, King Childebert III (694–711). Childebert was an adult king who reigned long enough to make a firm impression on the political scene. In the words of the *LHF* he was 'the famous and just lord, King Childebert of good memory'.[52] The toning down of this high reputation in the *Continuations of Fredegar*, and the insinuation in the *Earlier Annals of Metz* that Childebert ruled only on sufferance from Pippin, show perfectly how the Carolingians rewrote history to their advantage. It was, however, under Childebert's presidency that the royal court made three judgements against the Pippinids, and it is under Childebert that, for the last time in the Merovingian period, we see magnates from the far south attending the court. Childebert was also the last Merovingian whose name appears on coins minted in Marseilles. With Childebert on the throne, Pippin leader in Austrasia, and his son, the 'just' and 'religious' Grimoald, mayor of the palace in Neustria, the Merovingian regime seems to have been working as well as it had ever done. There was peace in Francia, and victory beyond its borders.

---

51 *Bede's Ecclesiastical History*, V, ch. 10, pp. 480–4.
52 *LHF*, ch. 50, p. 94.

The young Charles Martel

It was in the reign of Childebert that Charles Martel, born in 688, reached adulthood. In the *LHF* he is described as a *vir elegans*, which might just mean that he was well educated,[53] rather than 'handsome', though if he were educated, how, where, and by whom is unknown. To his mother, Alpaida, there is just one reference which many historians refuse to accept as genuine on the grounds that it is a later and imaginative interpretation of events. In about 705 Lambert bishop of Tongres-Maastricht was killed in a dispute with the family of one Dodo, a follower of Pippin, who was *domesticus*, presumably in the Liège area. Though according to the mid-eighth-century *Vita Landiberti Vetustissima*, Dodo killed Lambert to avenge two relatives slain by the bishop's men,[54] a late-tenth- or early-eleventh-century tradition had it that Dodo was Alpaida's brother, and that he killed Lambert because the bishop had upbraided Pippin for taking his sister as a concubine.[55] This reinterpretation of events, which followed a well-established convention in which brave churchmen criticised the sexual morality of leaders, we need not believe. There is nevertheless reason to think that Dodo was indeed Alpaida's brother, for in a ninth-century manuscript of the *LHF* a copyist not only named Alpaida as Charles Martel's mother, but also over the name were added the words 'Dodo's sister'.[56] Another of Lambert's killers, Godobald, would later under Charles Martel be made abbot of St Denis, which could indicate that Charles was at least allied with Dodo's circle.

It is interesting to note that no contemporary source made this connection between Dodo and Alpaida, and it is striking that we know so little about Charles's immediate family. Did he have uterine siblings? When did Alpaida die? Did she have family lands in the Liège area? These are all unanswerable questions. The silence might suggest that Charles had a rather undistinguished background, on his mother's side, even if one family member was a *domesticus*. There is no record of the activities of Charles in his homeland before the year 714, but we can see that Plectrude was active there. Her close relative Hubert followed Lambert as bishop, and in 714 Plectrude was the prime mover in endowing a monastery at Süsteren to the

---

53 See note 19, above.
54 *Vita Landiberti Vetustissima*, ed. B. Krusch, *MGH SRM* VI (Hanover and Leipzig 1913), pp. 353–84, chs 11–17, pp. 364–70.
55 *Vita Landiberti auctore Sigeberto*, ed. B. Krusch, *MGH SRM* VI, pp. 393–406, ch. 16, pp. 397–8.
56 Gerberding, *Rise*, pp. 118–19.

north of Liège. With her were the sons of Adela of Pfalzel, who, as we have seen, was probably her sister. Süsteren was given to Willibrord and to Echternach. Charles and Alpaida were obviously in a much weaker position than Plectrude, even in their homeland.

Pippin's eldest son Drogo died in 707, when Charles would have been about 19 years old, but Pippin did not call upon him to take Drogo's place in any way. Then in 714 when Pippin's second son Grimoald was killed, Pippin and Plectrude preferred to make Grimoald's infant son Theudoald, rather than Charles, mayor of the palace. The appointment of a child to this high position was unprecedented and it would turn out to be disastrous. That Charles was passed over in this way must mean that he was seen at best as a peripheral member of Pippin's family.[57] Charles by this stage was aged about 26 and married, to a lady named Chrotrude, about whom we know virtually nothing, despite the fact that she was the mother of Pippin III, who would become the first Carolingian king. Pippin was in fact Charles and Chrotrude's second son. The first-born was named Karloman.[58] We do not know when Karloman was born, but we can see that Pippin's birth came in 714 or 715, for when he died in 768, Pippin was said to have been aged 54. The fact that Charles was well into manhood, married and certainly had one son, and possibly two, makes it all the more striking that he apparently occupied no important position in 714. Although he would later make grants of land which he said had been inherited from Pippin, this does not necessarily mean that Pippin actually meant to include him amongst his heirs. Had Charles not emerged as leader after 714, it seems certain that we would have remained quite ignorant of the fact that Pippin had taken a second wife and had had a third son. Let us now turn to the events which pushed that son into the limelight.

---

57 W. Joch, 'Karl Martell – ein minderberechtiger Erbe Pippins?', in Jarnut, Nonn and Richter (eds), *Karl Martell in Seiner Zeit*, pp. 149–69.

58 *Fred. Contin.*, ch. 23, p. 97, Karloman is referred to as *primogenitus*.

CHAPTER THREE

Crisis, Survival and Victory, 715–724

In 715 the Pippinid family was faced with annihilation. Pippin's success had been at the cost of making enemies throughout Francia and beyond, and crisis within the family gave those enemies a chance to make up for ground lost in the previous generation. In this chapter we shall look at how Charles Martel came from behind to beat all his opponents within, as well as outside, the family. It is for this early part of his career that we can build up the most detailed narrative, because for events up to 721 we can draw on the *LHF* as well as *Continuations of Fredegar* and the *Earlier Annals of Metz*. In addition there are far more charters surviving from the period before 724 than from the later part of Charles Martel's career. What the detail allows us to demonstrate is the weakness of Charles's position in his early years, and how it was some time before he could even establish himself in Austrasia. But it also shows us that once he had beaten the Neustrians, Charles Martel took a far firmer grip on Neustria, and on its premier institutions and families, than his father had ever done. In this sense Charles Martel's victory marked the end of an era, as the mayor established an unprecedented degree of control over the royal palace, for we now enter the time of the real 'do-nothing kings'. The victory also marks a watershed in that all our narrative sources now become pro-Carolingian. It is therefore especially important to examine in detail the early part of Charles Martel's career as it unfolded in Austrasia and Neustria, for this is our last chance to see who in these regions opposed him, and how difficult it was for him to overcome that opposition.

Crisis

As we saw in the last chapter, Pippin's eldest son Drogo died in 707, and his young son Arnulf may at this point have succeeded him as duke in Austrasia. In early 714 Pippin himself fell ill, and when his son Grimoald came to visit him in April of that year, he was assassinated while praying at the shrine of St Lambert at Liège. His slayer was one Rantgar, sometimes said to have been a Frisian because the *LHF* called him *gentilis*, a pagan. But the name Rantgar is also Frankish, and the term *gentilis* could be an insult rather than a description. If Lambert's own death a decade earlier really had been the result of his denigration of Alpaida, Charles Martel's mother, one might read Grimoald's visit to the saint's shrine as a further slight upon her, to which Rantgar, possibly a supporter of her family, reacted with violence. But there is no hard information with which to support speculation about the motive for Grimoald's murder, and there was surely any number of people who might have wished him dead. Here, as in every reference to the Liège area in the period 688–715, Charles Martel and his mother are conspicuous by their absence. Pippin lay ill at nearby Jupille. The clear impression is that it was Plectrude, not Alpaida, who was at his bedside.[1] After the event, as we know, Pippin ordered Grimoald's young son Theudoald to succeed him as mayor of the palace in Neustria, and we have already noted that the appointment of this *parvulus* would turn out to be disastrous.

In December 714 Pippin finally died, and, in the words of the *LHF*, 'Plectrude along with her grandchildren and the king [Dagobert III] directed all the affairs of state under a separate government'.[2] According to the *Earlier Annals of Metz*, things now started to go wrong because Plectrude, 'with feminine cunning', ruled with too much cruelty.[3] This looks like typical medieval misogyny, and it has parallels in what was said about Charlemagne's queen, Fastrada,[4] but by portraying Plectrude as unfit to rule, the author was also able to present Charles Martel as 'the only surviving heir worthy of great power'. That he did not inherit such power at once was, said our author, because Plectrude plotted to keep him down in favour of

---

1   *MGH DD*, ed. G. Pertz (Hanover 1872), *Diplomata Maiorum Domus*, no. 6, pp. 95–6. Pippin stated that he was unable to sign the charter on account of his illness, and that he had asked his wife Plectrude to affirm it in his place.

2   *LHF*, ch. 51, trans. P. Fouracre and R. Gerberding, *Late Merovingian France. History and Hagiography 640–720* (Manchester 1996), p. 94.

3   *AMP*, trans. Fouracre and Gerberding, *Late Merovingian France*, p. 365.

4   Einhard, *The Life of Charlemagne*, ch. 20, ed. and trans. P. Dutton, *Charlemagne's Courtier. The Complete Einhard* (Ontario 1998), pp. 29–30. Fastrada's cruelty was said to have caused Charlemagne's son Pippin to revolt.

her grandson Theudoald, a mere child. The result was a disaster from which only the heroic Charles could rescue the family. Apart from building Charles up as the family's (and the Franks') saviour, it was further necessary to deal with events in this way in order to explain how Pippinid fortunes could so quickly be reversed, for the lengthy first section of the *Earlier Annals of Metz* had been devoted to a celebration of Pippin's divinely sanctioned triumph. Yet the author faced another problem in writing the family's history: he or she seems to have had no information about Charles's life before 715. This is the first reference to him in the work, and when we first meet him he is (in contrast to Theudoald) already fully grown. Since he is portrayed in the *Annals* as a hero whose achievements outstripped those of Pippin his father, the silence about Charles's origins and early life cannot have been simply inadvertent. That the author of the *Annals* started his or her account with Pippin's career allowed the Carolingian dynasty effectively to backdate its supremacy into the later seventh century. It also, however, had the effect of enabling the author to name some of Charles's paternal ancestors, including, importantly, female ancestors in Begga and Gertrude, his grandmother and his great-aunt. It may likewise have been ignorance, or reservations, about Charles Martel's origins on the maternal side which made Einhard so taciturn about Charlemagne's ancestry.[5]

Plectrude's regime held together for the first six months of 715. In June of that year Theudoald was referred to as mayor in a charter granting land to St Wandrille.[6] In the same month Drogo's sons Hugo and Arnulf, and Pippin and Godefrid (two more of his sons to whom there is no other reference), are seen granting land to the church of St Arnulf in Metz in order to honour their father's grave there. In this charter, Arnulf used the title *dux* and Hugo was termed *sacerdos*, which means that by this stage he was in holy orders.[7] Charles Martel, by contrast, was at this time in prison, probably in Cologne.[8] He had been put there by Plectrude. Charles, remember, already had one son, Karloman. His second son was born some-time between September 714 and September 715. He named this child

---

5   Einhard famously began his *Life of Charlemagne* with a passage on the last Merovingian kings rather than with an account of his hero's ancestry.

6   The reference comes in the *Gesta Sanctorum Patrum Fontanellensis Coenobii*, ed. F. Lohier and J. Laporte (Rouen 1936), III, ch. 4, p. 29. This work refers to many charters which are now lost.

7   *MGH DD, Diplomata Spuria*, no. 7, pp. 214–15. This document is preserved only in a later Metz collection, but is regarded as essentially genuine: see I. Heidrich, 'Titular und Urkunden der arnulfingischen Hausmeier', *Archiv für Diplomatik*, 11/12 (1965–66), 17–279, at 251–2.

8   The chronology here is vague. We must rely on the phrase *his diebus* ('in these days'), *LHF*, ch. 51, p. 94.

Pippin after his grandfather, despite the fact that, as we have just seen, one of Drogo's sons already bore the name. The name Pippin may have been chosen to announce Charles's claim to his father's inheritance, but however it was announced, his incarceration was surely Plectrude's reaction to that claim. We next hear from the *LHF* that the Neustrians rose up against Theudoald, and, added the *Continuations of Fredegar*, against the followers of Pippin and Grimoald.[9] Near Compiègne, on the River Oise close to the frontier between Neustria and Austrasia, in a battle which took place on 26 September 715, Theudoald was defeated and driven out.[10] According to the *Earlier Annals of Metz*, he died soon after, but a Theudoald, said to be Charles Martel's nephew, witnessed a charter of January 723 in which Charles gave land to the church of Utrecht,[11] and three of the early Carolingian annals stated that a Theudoald was killed in the same year that Charles Martel himself died. We may therefore suspect that the author of the *Earlier Annals of Metz* killed Theudoald off prematurely in order further to justify Charles Martel's seizure of the mayoralty in 717.[12]

After Compiègne the Neustrians chose their own mayor, Ragamfred, and formed an alliance with Radbod, leader of the Frisians. They then attacked the Austrasians, advancing to the River Meuse, thus into the Pippinid heartland. At some point in 715, the early Carolingian annals report, the Saxons also attacked and laid waste the 'land of the Hettuarii', which probably means that they advanced from east of the Rhine, also towards the Meuse.[13] At the end of the year, or early in 716, the Merovingian king, Dagobert III, died and the Neustrians crowned a monk called Daniel, said in original charters to be a son of Childeric II (d. 675). In 716 this ex-monk would have been in his early forties.[14] He took the name Chilperic, thus Chilperic II. The author of the *LHF* seems to have had doubts about his legitimacy, or was at least uncomfortable in the knowledge that Dagobert had a son,

9 *LHF*, ch. 51, p. 94, *Fred. Contin.*, ed. and trans. J.M. Wallace-Hadrill (London 1960), ch. 8, p. 87.

10 For an excellent discussion of the narrative and chronology of events 714–23, see J. Semmler, 'Zur pippinidisch-karolingische Zuksessionskrise 714–723', *Deutsches Archiv für Erforschung des Mittelalters*, 33 (1977), 1–36. On the date of Compiègne, 7.

11 *Diplomata Belgica ante Annum Millesimum Centesimum Scripta* I, ed. M. Gysseling and A. Koch (Brussels 1950), no. 173, pp. 305–6.

12 R. Collins, 'Deception and Misrepresentation in Early Eighth-Century Frankish Historiography: Two Case Studies', in J. Jarnut, U. Nonn and M. Richter (eds), *Karl Martell in Seiner Zeit*, Beihefte der Francia, 37 (Sigmaringen 1994), pp. 229–35.

13 E. Ewig, 'Die Civitas Ubiorum, die Francia Rinensis und das Land Ribuarien', *Spätantikes und Fränkisches Gallien. Gesammelten Schriften (1952–1973)* I (Zurich and Munich 1976), pp. 472–502, at pp. 488–90.

14 E. Ewig, 'Studien zur merowingische Dynastie', *Frühmittelalterliche Studien*, 8 (1974), 15–59, at 50, n. 192.

Theuderic, who should have followed his father. But Theuderic was an infant, and as Theudoald's demise had just demonstrated, rule by regency cannot have been feasible at this time of severe crisis. Shortly before Dagobert's death, Charles escaped from Plectrude's custody and was on hand in the Liège area when a second attack came. This time, while the Neustrians moved in from the west, Radbod and the Frisians advanced from the north. Charles Martel tried to stop Radbod, but was soundly beaten in battle. He lost many men and was forced to flee. This is the first battle Charles is recorded as having fought, and it is the only one he is ever said to have lost. Chilperic and Ragamfred now moved through the Ardennes forest and met up with Radbod on the other side. Together they marched on Cologne and Plectrude. Plectrude gave them 'much treasure' and they withdrew, but on their way back Charles ambushed them at Amblève, near Malmedy in the heart of Pippinid territory, and inflicted heavy losses upon them.[15]

The battle of Amblève took place in April 716, and is generally regarded by historians as the turning point in Charles's fortunes, although to contemporaries, of course, the outcome of the struggle between Charles and Ragamfred would not become clear for some time to come.[16] After Amblève, Charles went on the offensive, and for the next twenty-five years, right up to his death, he continued on the attack year in year out. The secret of his success in turning the tide in 716 remains elusive. It has been argued that initially he drew upon the resources and supporters of his mother's family in the Liège area, but as we have seen, we cannot identify Alpaida's lands, her family, or her allies. It has nevertheless been assumed that those who stood by Charles at this time would have been supporters of Alpaida rather than Plectrude. With one exception, however, the few people we know anything about turn out to be former supporters of Pippin and Plectrude who had come over to Charles. This is true, for instance, of Plectrude's relative, Hubert bishop of Maastricht. In May 716 Hubert presided over the translation of St Lambert's relics from Maastricht to the basilica dedicated to the saint in Liège. According to the *Vita Landiberti*, the translation was at the behest of the leaders of the area, and Charles Martel was certainly one of the latter.[17] We may, therefore, place Hubert in Charles's camp. Another family member who may have switched sides at this time was Plectrude's nephew Alberic. Alberic was mentioned in the Süsteren charter of 714 as one who had sold land to Plectrude. His sons would nevertheless become firm supporters of Charles Martel, according to the 'Life' of one of them,

---

15 *LHF*, ch. 52, p. 95.
16 R. Gerberding, '716: A Crucial Year for Charles Martel', in Jarnut, Nonn and Richter (eds), *Karl Martell in Seiner Zeit*, pp. 203–16.
17 Gerberding, 'A Crucial Year', pp. 213–14.

Gregory of Utrecht. We learn from his biographer that Gregory reached manhood in the early 720s, and that he had been educated at court.[18] Conventionally, such an education began at age 7 and ended at age 15. This means that Gregory must have been educated in the years following Pippin's death, and since it is unlikely that he was brought up at the Neustrian court under Ragamfred, we must assume that he was educated in the palace at a time when Charles Martel was mayor, which makes it highly probable that his father was on good terms with Charles. Gregory certainly was, for he served Charles faithfully thereafter.

Likewise Willibrord, the Anglo-Saxon missionary whose monastery of Echternach had been so closely associated with Pippin and Plectrude, was on close terms with Charles before Plectrude's defeat in 717. In the *Vita Willibrordi* we are told that Willibrord baptised Charles's son Pippin, and this probably took place at Easter 716.[19] It has been suggested that Willibrord might actually have performed this baptism as a way of reconciling the two branches of the Pippinid family.[20] If Willibrord was on the side of Charles Martel in 716, so too might have been Heden duke of Thuringia, another Echternach patron, who gave land to Willibrord in 717.[21] The land was at Hammelburg deep into Thuringia, and it was given to found a monastery as a base for missionary work. Willibrord, it seems, turned his attention to Thuringia after being forced out of Frisia by Radbod. This is in fact the last we hear of Heden. It has been reasoned that he may have been killed fighting for Charles at some point after the issue of the Hammelburg charter (April 717), but for this there is no evidence. We shall come back to Heden and the situation in Thuringia in the next chapter.

We may also reckon Liutwin and his son Milo as Plectrude supporters who switched sides: Liutwin, who was the bishop of Trier, witnessed three early Echternach documents, and Milo attested the Metz grant of Drogo's sons in 715. Milo followed his father as bishop of Trier sometime in 717–22, and in either 717 or 718 was given charge of the bishopric of Rheims as well.[22] We shall return to Milo later, for his career as Charles Martel's right-hand man would be taken by the Anglo-Saxon missionary Boniface to

---

18 Liudger, *Vita Gregorii Abbatis Traiectensis*, ed. A. Holder-Egger, *MGH SS* XVI (Hanover 1887), pp. 66–79, ch. 2, p. 67.
19 Alcuin, *Vita Willibrordi Archiepiscopi Traiectensis*, ed. W. Levison, *MGH SRM* VII (Hanover and Leipzig 1920), pp. 113–41, ch. 23, pp. 133–4.
20 I. Wood, *The Merovingian Kingdoms* (London 1994), p. 271.
21 J. Pardessus (ed.), *Diplomata, Chartae, Epistolae, Leges, Aliaque Instrumenta ad Res Gallo-Francicas Spectantia* (2 vols, Paris 1843, 1849, reprinted Aalen 1969), no. 500, p. 308.
22 E. Ewig, 'Milo et eiusmodi similes', in *Sankt Bonifatius Gedenkgabe zum zwölfhundertsten Todestag* (Fulda 1954), pp. 412–20, reprinted in *Spätantikes und Fränkisches Gallien* II (Zurich and Munich 1979), pp. 189–219, here, pp. 192–6.

symbolise all that was wrong with the Frankish church.[23] Milo, Liutwin and others may nevertheless have become supporters only after Charles defeated Plectrude. People who appear later as Charles Martel's closest allies and who came from areas in or near to his homeland, such as Count Wido (a relative), Godobald (later abbot of St Denis), and Rotbert, or Chrodobert (who is mentioned alongside Martel in various charters), might have been with him in 715–16, or they could have joined him later. They could, therefore, have been on either side of the Charles/Plectrude dispute. Although Wido might conceivably have been a maternal relative, he too in 715 witnessed the charter of Drogo's sons. In the unlikely case that Wido was a relative of Alpaida, then apart from Dodo, he would be the only one we know of.

The one person we should be able to identify as a supporter of Charles Martel in 715 is Ermino, abbot of Lobbes. According to his *Vita*, Ermino backed Charles as Pippin's heir from the outset. He foretold his victory, and upon hearing of the birth of Pippin, Charles's second son, he predicted that he would have great power and become a king.[24] But since the *Vita Erminonis* was composed in the reign of that same Pippin (751–68), we must suspect strongly that Ermino's 'predictions' were the product not of foresight, but of hindsight, and that the author's claim that Ermino had always supported Charles was likewise an expedient geared to the politics of a later age. Nevertheless, fond memories of Charles at Lobbes might well have related to a long history of support and reward. It is also interesting to see a positive image of Charles in a later-eighth-century saint's Life. We shall return to this point in a later chapter when we examine the question of how the church viewed Charles Martel.

Although we can only guess at the nature and extent of the support for Charles in the months leading up to Amblève, we can see very clearly that the situation in the Meuse–Rhine region was desperate. The people there were under pressure from the Neustrians to the west, from the Frisians to the north and from the Saxons to the east. To the south of Trier, from Rheims in the west to Worms in the east, the Austrasians were, to say the least, unhelpful towards their beleaguered compatriots, although there is no evidence that they actually joined in the attacks upon them. In these circumstances it is not surprising that the eldest of Pippin's male descendants, Charles Martel, was readily accepted as leader in preference to Plectrude and her young grandsons. Now aged 27, Charles presumably had already

---

23 Below, ch. 5, p. 133.
24 *Vita Erminonis Episcopi et Abbatis Lobbiensis*, ed. W. Levison, *MGH SRM* VI (Hanover and Leipzig 1913), pp. 461–70, ch. 9, p. 469.

had considerable military experience, possibly against the very Frisian and Saxon forces which now threatened the area, and if his later record is any indication of his abilities in his younger days, he could already at this stage have had a reputation as a formidable warrior. After his escape from prison he was on hand to provide military leadership, and it must have been very soon after his arrival back in the Liège area that he took the field against Radbod and the invading Frisians. In particular one can see why Willibrord, who owed much to Plectrude, saw fit to support Charles in 716: Radbod was, in the words of a recent historian, 'Willibrord's old nemesis', who in 715 had set about destroying the fruits of a quarter of a century's missionary work in Frisia.[25] Charles Martel provided the only hope of stopping him. If Pippin's erstwhile supporters wished to rally round Charles in defence of their own lands, they would have had to recognise him as Pippin's heir and as the family's leader. Charles could then have made immediate use of the family's wealth around Liège. Even if his claim to inherit the lion's share of this wealth had been weak before 715, the events of that year would have made it irresistible.

After the campaigns of spring 716, no more Neustrian or Frisian attacks followed. Perhaps the treasure Plectrude had been forced to give up had bought peace. A further price paid for the withdrawal of Neustrian and Frisian forces from the Cologne region might have been the recognition of Chilperic's authority in Austrasia. A document in which Arnulf gave to Echternach land he had inherited in the villa of Bollendorf was dated 'in the first year of the king, our lord Chilperic'.[26] If Arnulf here was giving land to Willibrord's monastery of Echternach after Willibrord had baptised Pippin, then perhaps the baptism really had worked as an act of reconciliation, albeit a temporary one. Two years later Charles Martel too would give land in Bollendorf to Echternach, perhaps symbolically to underline the fact that he had replaced Plectrude's grandchildren (including Arnulf) as Echternach's patron.[27]

Survival

Success at Amblève allowed Charles Martel to consolidate his support in Austrasia and to build up his army. By March 717 he was ready to take the initiative, and moved into Neustria. Chilperic and Ragamfred met him at

---

25 Gerberding, 'A Crucial Year', pp. 211–12.
26 *MGH DD, Diplomata Maiorum Domus*, no. 7, p. 96. See Heidrich, 'Titular', 239–40.
27 *MGH DD, Diplomata Maiorum Domus*, no. 9, p. 97. See Heidrich, 'Titular', 240.

Vinchy near Cambrai on 21 March, and they were soundly beaten, although according to the *LHF* it had been their decision to fight rather than negotiate.[28] The same source tells us that Charles laid waste the area around Vinchy, took plunder and captives, and then withdrew. The *Continuations of Fredegar* and the *Earlier Annals of Metz* added that Charles marched on to Paris, but the *LHF* version is to be preferred as it is the source closest to events, and because charter evidence supports the view that Paris was untouched by Charles at this time. All three narrative sources agree that Charles then went back to Austrasia and proceeded directly to Cologne where he settled the issue with Plectrude. Finally defeated, she was forced to give up the rest of Pippin's treasure. What happened to her thereafter, we do not know. Charles Martel now had the resources to set up a king for himself. That he did so suggests that despite his victory at Vinchy, he did not have immediate hope of replacing Ragamfred as mayor of the palace to Chilperic. A king was necessary if his authority were to be more widely recognised in Austrasia, and a king was found in the person of one Clothar, about whom we know nothing, except that he had a good Merovingian name and reigned as Clothar IV.

Even after he had been beaten at Vinchy, Chilperic's authority was widely recognised, and this was why Charles Martel needed a king of his own, for, as we have just noted, among those who recognised Chilperic were some Austrasians. For the years 716–17 we find evidence of Chilperic's authority throughout Neustria. Chilperic was predictably generous to the monasteries of St Denis, Corbie, and St Wandrille. The latter's pro-Pippinid abbot, Benignus, was expelled on Ragamfred's orders. St Wandrille tradition had it that Benignus fought alongside Charles at Vinchy, whereas Wando, his replacement as abbot, was on the other side. After the battle, Wando was said to have lent his horse to Ragamfred as the latter fled from Charles. When Charles found out, he imprisoned Wando in Maastricht and restored Benignus.[29]

Chilperic's charters in favour of the monasteries of St Denis and Corbie suggest, however, that his authority was also recognised much further afield in Provence. One of these charters is a confirmation of annual payment from Marseilles to St Denis, and of exemptions for the monastery from tolls throughout the kingdom. The other charter is the confirmation of a *tractoria*, that is, an order to feed and provision the agents of the monastery of Corbie when they were travelling on business. Both documents were concerned

---

28 *LHF*, ch. 53, p. 95.
29 *Gesta Fontanellensis*, III, ch. 1, pp. 23–4, but note that *Gesta* confuse the events following the battle of Vichy (717) with those which followed the battle of Soissons (718).

with the monasteries' agents going to and from Marseilles, almost certainly to buy olive oil.[30] On the face of it they show Chilperic giving orders to underlings all the way from Neustria through Burgundy, down the Rhône valley to the Mediterranean coast. By the same token they would indicate that there was significant trading activity between north and south. On the other hand, since both documents are confirmations of earlier privileges, first granted over a generation ago, they might relate to political and economic conditions of the later seventh century which no longer obtained in the time of Chilperic. But as we saw in the last chapter, magnates from the south had attended Childebert III's court, and when the Aleman dukes and others ceased to come to the court, it was the Pippinids, not the Merovingians, they were avoiding. In a charter from the monastery of St Victor in Marseilles from the year 779, the monastery pleaded with Charlemagne to restore its lands, and said that Antenor, onetime ruler of Provence, had rebelled against the king's great-grandfather, thus against Charles Martel's father, Pippin II.[31] Since Antenor can be shown to have been a member of a judgement tribunal at Childebert's court, it is reasonable to suppose that he revolted only after Childebert's death in 711, and he would surely have kept up his resistance after 714.[32] Charles Martel certainly regarded Antenor as a rebel, for he later confiscated his lands. In Antenor, Chilperic would therefore have had an ally in the far south, and if the ruler of Provence recognised the authority of the northern king, there would have been very practical reasons for St Denis and Corbie to have their privileges there confirmed.

It is possible to demonstrate a few other outlying areas in which Chilperic's authority was recognised. A St Gallen document was dated by Chilperic's reign, and there is a reference to a privilege given by Chilperic to St Maurice d'Agaune.[33] The monasteries of St Gallen and St Maurice d'Agaune are both in modern Switzerland. But most striking of all are the grants Chilperic

---

30 P. Fouracre, 'Eternal Light and Earthly Needs: Practical Aspects of the Development of Frankish Immunities', in W. Davies and P. Fouracre (eds), *Property and Power in the Early Middle Ages* (Cambridge 1995), pp. 53–81, at p. 71. The charter for St Denis confirming its rights of toll is *Chartae Latinae Antiquiores*, ed. A. Bruckner and M. Marichal, vol. 14, ed. H. Atsma and J. Vezin (Zurich 1982), no. 589. The *tractoria* is in L. Levillain, *Examen Critique des Chartes Mérovingiennes et Carolingiennes de l'Abbaye de Corbie, École des Chartes, Mémoires et Documents*, 5 (Paris 1902), no. 15, pp. 236–7.

31 The charter is discussed by P. Geary, 'Die Provenz zur Zeit Karl Martells', in Jarnut, Nonn and Richter (eds), *Karl Martell in Seiner Zeit*, pp. 381–92. See also below, ch. 5.

32 P. Fouracre, 'Observations on the Outgrowth of Pippinid Influence in the "Regnum Francorum" After the Battle of Tertry (687–715)', *Medieval Prosopography*, 5 (1984), 1–31, at 8–9.

33 Semmler, 'Suksessionskrise', 22–3, and n. 148.

made in Austrasia, to the church of St Arnulf in Metz and to the church of Worms. The grant to St Arnulf's came after the battle of Vinchy. Worms had a history of opposition to the Pippinids, its bishop Rupert having been exiled to Bavaria. According to Bavarian tradition, Rupert, who was of Agilolfing stock, eventually returned to his homeland, probably after Pippin's death.[34] As we noted in the last chapter, the Gundoinings, Faronids and Agilolfings in southern Austrasia had in the past allied with the Neustrian kings against the Pippinids, and it seems very likely that that alliance was in operation again in these years.

Others, in more vulnerable positions, were forced to hedge their bets about whom to support. Best known is the case of Bishop Rigobert of Rheims. When Charles Martel was marching towards Vinchy in 717, he asked Rigobert to let him into Rheims to pray, but Rigobert refused as God had not yet decided the outcome of the struggle between Charles and Ragamfred. Charles replied that if he beat his opponent he would return and punish the bishop, and this is of course what happened. Rigobert was exiled, and Rheims given to Milo. Rheims's lands were then despoiled. There is a very similar tradition from the monastery of St Peter's at Ghent in Belgium, which, like Rheims, was in an area contested by the two rivals. As the long struggle between Charles and Ragamfred swung back and forth, Celestinus, abbot of St Peter's, tried, like Rigobert, to remain neutral. But Celestinus's enemies told Charles that he had written letters to Ragamfred and wished to harm Charles's 'kingdom'. As a result, the abbot and some of his monks were driven out, and Charles divided some of the monastery's lands among his own followers. These accounts come from two later sources, the *Vita Rigoberti*, composed at the end of the ninth century, and the even later *Liber Traditionum* of St Peter's,[35] and it is clear that Charles Martel's reputation as a despoiler of church lands has shaped these stories of how impossible choices, made in difficult circumstances, led to unjust punishment. In each case the purpose of the narrative was to prepare a way for the lost lands to be claimed back. We should also note that the theme of defenceless institutions caught between the opposing sides in a civil war would have been all too familiar to tenth- and eleventh-century audiences. We must therefore be wary of taking the detail of these stories too literally, but it does seem likely that the churches of Rheims and St Peter's Ghent were punished by Charles Martel for failing to support him in 717.

---

34 On Rupert's career, H. Wolfram, 'Der heilige Rupert und die antikarolingische Adelsopposition', *Mitteilungen des Instituts für österreichische Geschichtsforschung*, 80 (1972), 4–34.
35 *Vita Rigoberti*, ed. W. Levison, *MGH SRM* VII, ch. 10, pp. 67–8. *Liber Traditionum* of St Peter's, Ghent, ed. Gyselling and Koch, *Diplomata Belgica*, no. 49, p. 125.

No fewer than ten charters, most of them surviving originals, were issued by King Chilperic in the brief period 716–18. By contrast, we have only six charters of Charles Martel over the much longer period 718–41, and of these, the first five were issued in the years 718–23. In addition there are five charters issued by Theuderic IV, Charles's puppet king. All of the latter are confirmations of earlier charters rather than new grants. No originals have survived. One must not read too much into this contrast, for it may well be explained by differential rates of survival. It could be that we have nearly every charter Chilperic ever issued, but only a fraction of those drawn up for Charles and Theuderic. A high proportion of Chilperic's charters survive as originals because they were preserved in the archive of the monastery of St Denis, and this was an archive which survived the looting and burning of monasteries in the French Revolutionary period. Charles Martel's charters exist only in later copies, and from the later ninth century onwards after he had acquired his reputation as one who took from, rather than gave to, the church, there may have been little incentive to keep, copy or forge his charters.

It has been argued that the charter evidence shows Charles breaking with the traditional forms of palace government: officers such as the 'referend-ary' and the 'seneschal' disappear from royal charters after Chilperic's reign, and we have no more *placita* with tribunal lists which show a mass gather-ing of magnates at court.[36] But again there is no real basis of comparison, for the tribunal lists (three of them) are exceptional and a feature only of charters surviving as originals. The identification of offices and officers is also by and large a feature of originals. Copies tended to lose these details, and always left out the so-called 'Tironian notes' which give additional information about how the charter was drawn up. It is, moreover, the three tribunal lists which contain the bulk of our information about offices and officers. We cannot therefore compare originals and copies and conclude that there had been a change in court procedure, or that magnate assem-blies no longer took place. What can be said, however, is that five of the people who appeared in Chilperic's documents as officers of the court had also appeared in the documents of Childebert III's reign. This includes Ragamfred himself. It is against this background of continuity in royal government and court personnel that we should understand Charles Martel's need for a king of his own.

In the civil wars of the later Merovingian period, when Francia was united under one king, battles were not in themselves decisive unless they enabled the victors to take control of the royal palace. Thus the battle of

---

36   Heidrich, 'Titular', 195–99.

Vinchy did not win the war for Charles Martel because despite his victory he remained excluded from the palace. As we saw in Chapter 1, in any struggle to control the palace much more was at stake than simple access to the machinery of royal government, for those who gained control were able to issue commands which were binding because they were made in the name of the king. Power which was not sanctioned by royal authority was 'tyranny', that is to say, it was power without justice. In the eyes of his enemies Charles Martel would at this stage have been a *tyrannus*, and those who had sworn fidelity to the Merovingians had not only the right, but also the duty, to resist him.[37] Kings, as we have also seen, were necessary for the raising of larger armies. On both counts, that is, in terms of the legitimation of power and the building up of military forces, the elevation of Clothar IV, a Merovingian king, at least in name, seems to have had some effect.

Two charters recording grants to the monastery of Wissembourg, issued between the end of March 717 and 13 February 718, were dated by the reign of Clothar.[38] The next Wissembourg charter, from 18 May 718, was dated according to Chilperic's reign years.[39] It thus seems likely that donors to Wissembourg, who included the Gundoinings and who should generally be counted among Charles's opponents, recognised Clothar as king, and that through Clothar, Charles Martel may have been able to exercise some influence in an area previously closed off to him. The content of one of these charters, in conjunction with two others, may suggest a reaction to that influence.[40] The charters record grants in which Chrodoin, who was closely associated with the Gundoining family, donated the bulk of his land to Wissembourg. Chrodoin's generosity could be interpreted as the transfer of his assets to a safe haven in the face of Charles Martel's rising power. That in May 718 the Wissembourg charters switched back to dating by the reign of Chilperic probably means that Clothar was by then dead (there is no evidence of him beyond this date), not that the monastery had decided to turn its back on the new regime. Charles himself issued a charter in February of Clothar's first year, thus in February 718. It is the charter in which

---

37   In the *Vita Rigoberti*, ch. 12, p. 69, Charles is called a tyrant (*non rex, sed tyrannus*), but this is a late-ninth-century source. In the late-seventh-century *Passio Leudegarii*, ed. B. Krusch, *MGH SRM* V (Hanover 1910) ch. 6, p. 223, the mayor of the palace Ebroin was said to be a tyrant. If the term was used in this way in the seventh and ninth centuries, it is reasonable to suppose that it would have been similarly used in the early eighth century too.

38   *Traditiones Wizenburgenses*, ed. L. Glöckner and A. Doll (Darmstadt 1979) nos 227/194, 261, pp. 447–54, 502–3.

39   *Traditiones Wizenburgenses*, no. 195, p. 453.

40   *Traditiones Wizenburgenses*, no. 227/194, pp. 447–54, in conjunction with nos 195 and 196, pp. 447–57, 401–2.

he gave land in Bollendorf to Echternach.[41] The land was said to have been 'inherited from my father Pippin', and he had received it *'contra allodiones mei'*, which means 'against my co-heirs' or 'against my co-proprietors'. It looks as if Charles had entered into an inheritance formerly denied to him, and he may have been reissuing in his own name a grant previously made by Arnulf. The raising of Clothar IV to the throne of Austrasia and the making of this grant to Echternach both demonstrated that Charles was Pippin's heir and leader of the Austrasians. It was, finally, under Clothar's nominal leadership that Charles raised an army which would crush the Neustrians for once and all, and then raid deep into Saxony.

If we can follow the author of the *Continuations of Fredegar* in reading cause and effect into the narrative sequence of the *LHF*, Chilperic and Ragamfred reacted to Clothar's elevation by forming an alliance with Eudo, duke of Aquitaine.[42] The involvement of Eudo in an anti-Martel alliance confirms the impression that Charles's stature and authority in Austrasia had greatly increased since Vinchy. The *Continuations of Fredegar* added that Eudo's help was bought with gifts and a *regnum*, a kingdom, or rule over a territory, which might mean he was offered Aquitaine's independence, but this assertion seems to have been designed to denigrate all three of Charles Martel's opponents. We shall see later how this source built Eudo up as a dangerous villain, who made a similarly self-serving deal with the Arabs.

In the event, Eudo brought an army northwards and joined up with Chilperic and Ragamfred. Again adding to the *LHF* text, the Continuator said that Eudo's army was composed of *Wascones*, Basques. This may well be a further denigration of the alliance, for the Basques were seen as non-Christian enemies of the Franks. In the spring of 718 Chilperic, Ragamfred and Eudo fought with Charles at Soissons on the eastern border of Neustria.[43] Charles won, and this time he did pursue his enemies to Paris. In fact he chased them across the Seine, then on to Orléans, where they took refuge beyond the River Loire. Along with Chilperic went the royal treasure. Now, says the *LHF*, King Clothar died.[44] His death was very timely, perhaps suspiciously so, for it opened the way for Charles to negotiate the return of Chilperic, without Ragamfred, but with his treasure. Also in 718, we learn from the early Carolingian annals, Charles invaded Saxony and penetrated

---

41 *MGH DD, Diplomata Maiorum Domus*, no. 9, p. 97. See Heidrich, 'Titular', 240.
42 *Fred. Contin.*, ch. 11, p. 89.
43 The early Carolingian annals give the year of the battle of Soissons as 719, but the date 718 is more reliably derived from the Wissembourg charters which show that Clothar IV died in 718.
44 *LHF*, ch. 53, p. 96.

as far as the River Weser, thus marching about 200 kilometres eastwards from the River Rhine, through a land without Roman roads, into the very centre of the country. The feat is all the more impressive when we remember that before this he had taken an army to Orléans and back, thus moving at least 1,300 kilometres over the course of the year. Energy and military skill must rank high among the reasons for Charles Martel's growing ascendancy at this time.

Following his victory at Soissons, Charles can be shown to have taken control of the Paris region. He now appears as the champion of the monastery of St Denis, and by 719 Benignus had been restored to St Wandrille. Rich gifts from Hugo, Drogo's son, followed the restoration. In the west, Hugo in fact became Charles's principal agent. A memorable passage in the *Gesta* of the monastery of St Wandrille describes how Hugo held an astonishing number of posts in the church. He succeeded Benignus as abbot of St Wandrille sometime between 723 and 725.[45] During his abbacy there he was also abbot of nearby Jumièges, bishop of Paris, bishop of Rouen, and bishop of Bayeux. In addition to the posts listed in the *Gesta*, Hugo was quite possibly also bishop of Lisieux and of Avranches as well, for his name appears in the lists of bishops from these two sees.[46] Interestingly, the St Wandrille *Gesta* were hardly critical of this spectacular pluralism, and the reason is that Hugo was very generous to the monastery, even before he became abbot. It is also clear from the *Gesta* that Hugo's maternal ancestry was celebrated at St Wandrille. Through his mother Anstrude, Hugo was connected with the family of Waratto, and thus with the pre-Pippinid mayors of the palace in Neustria. We may detect here a lingering anti-Carolingian sentiment, or at least nostalgia for the days of Neustrian independence.[47] It can be argued that this sentiment was a genuine feature of earlier eighth-century politics, rather than a product of the familiar anti-Martel rhetoric of the mid-ninth century (when the *Gesta* were compiled), because after the death of Charles Martel, the aged Wando returned from his exile and once again became abbot. Wando, remember, had been a staunch supporter of Ragamfred.

It was no doubt because this south-western corner of Neustria remained recalcitrant even after 718 that it was necessary for Charles Martel's

---

45 *Gesta Fontanellensis*, IV, ch. 1, pp. 37–43. There is a discrepancy in the dating because the *Gesta* give the date 723 for Hugo's succession to the abbacy, but 724 for the date of the death of his predecessor Benignus: p. 38, n. 95.

46 L. Duchesne, *Fastes Episcopaux de l'Ancienne Gaule* II (Paris 1910), pp. 222, 235.

47 F. Lifshitz, *The Norman Conquest of Pious Neustria: Historiographic Discourse and Saintly Relics 684–1090* (Toronto 1995), pp. 37–99 develops the argument that the *Gesta Fontanellensis* and other texts from western Neustria were written in opposition to the Carolingians.

supporters to take a firm grip on the bishoprics of the region. After the débâcle of Soissons, it seems likely that Ragamfred had taken refuge in his stronghold at Angers, so it was especially necessary for Martel to surround this area with trusted men. Here, more than anywhere else, we do see what appears to be a secularisation of the church, as four sees passed into the hands of laymen who seem to have added at least part of the revenues of the church to their income as leaders of the *pagus* or county. According to the *Vita Ermenlandi*, which was composed in the first half of the ninth century, at this time a Count Agatheus held the bishoprics of Nantes and Rennes.[48] Since the year 710 at the latest, the *ducatus*, or duchy, of Le Mans had been under the control of a certain Rotgarius and his son Charivius.[49] When Bishop Herlemund of Le Mans died in 721, the see remained vacant. The *Actus Pontificum Cenomannis*, the ninth-century history of the bishops of Le Mans, tells us that Rotgarius's family then proceeded to rob the bishopric. Eventually, Rotgarius's second son Gauziolenus, 'an unlettered and ignorant cleric', was made bishop. He was ordained bishop by Hugo of Rouen, rather than by the bishop of Tours, which, the *Actus* pointed out, would have been more normal for a bishop of Le Mans.[50] We may therefore judge that Rotgarius and family were supporters of Charles Martel, although we do not know where they came from originally.[51]

Finally, we hear of another count, one Rotbertus, who took over the see of Sées. According to the *Vita Opportunae*, which was written by Adalelm of Sées at the end of the ninth century, Opportuna's brother, Bishop Crodegang, went on pilgrimage to Rome, leaving Sées in the care of his friend Crodobert.[52] Crodobert then plundered Sées, made himself bishop, and when Crodegang returned after seven years, he had him assassinated. In the *Vita Opportunae* there is not even a scrap of information which would allow us to date these events. Adalelm made no reference to Charles Martel's oppression of the church, even though such a reference would have given him more to say about Crodobert's wickedness and the injustice suffered by Crodegang. This omission encourages one to believe that the *Vita* is based

---

48 *Vita Ermenlandi*, ed. W. Levison, *MGH SRM* V, pp. 682–710, ch. 13, p. 699.
49 *Actus Pontificum Cenomannis in Urbe Degentium*, ed. G. Busson and L. Ledru (Le Mans 1901). That it had been under the control of the same family since 710 depends on the likely identification of 'duke Crodegarius' of *Actus*, 15, p. 226 with the Rotgarius of *Actus*, 16, p. 245. J. Semmler, 'Pippin und die Fränkische Klöster', *Francia*, 3 (1975), 87–146, at 122–4, argues that the domination of Rotgarius and Charivius went back to about the year 700, but for this there is no firm evidence.
50 *Actus Cenomannis*, 16, p. 245.
51 Semmler, 'Suksessionskrise', 32–3, argues on ground of fairly weak circumstantial evidence that the family originated from the Zülpich area near Cologne.
52 Adalelm, *Vita Opportunae, Acta Sanctorum*, Aprilis III (Antwerp 1675), pp. 62–5, ch. 8, p. 64.

on an independent Sées tradition, and that there is a core of truth to its narrative. We know that there was a Count Rotbertus in the Sées area in 723 and that Charles Martel had a follower called Rotbertus who along with Count Wido witnessed Charles's grant of lands to the church of Utrecht. This grant was made on 1 January 723.[53] A decade later, it was also a Rotbert, leader in the Hesbaye region of Belgium, to whom the exiled Bishop Eucherius of Orléans was entrusted. 'Crodobertus' or 'Rotbertus/ Rodobertus' is a fairly common name among the Frankish arisocracy, so we cannot be sure that the Sées Crodobert was the same man as the Rotbert who appears in an Austrasian context, but it does seem very likely that the Rotbert count of Sées was the same man as the Rotbert of the Utrecht charter, given that the names appear in the same year and both in the presence of Charles Martel. If Rotbert had originated in the Hesbaye, then we may see him as an outsider imposed on the Sées area in the wake of Charles Martel's victory over Chilperic, Ragamfred and Eudo in 718. If we can read Crodegang's seven years' sabbatical as exile, then the *Vita Opportunae* tells a story which is similar to that told of Eucherius of Orléans, who was also exiled after Martel's followers had taken over his territory.

In August 723, the St Wandrille *Gesta* report, Abbot Benignus was involved in the settlement of a land dispute which was heard before Charles Martel at Zülpich, near Cologne.[54] It is in the list of those present that we meet Count Rotbertus, who is described as Benignus's 'advocate', thus a layman. The disputed land lay in the Sées area. The other people listed in this case present a snapshot of Charles Martel's supporters in southern Neustria and in the Champagne. In addition to Benignus and Rotbertus, present too at Zülpich were Rotgarius of Le Mans, Ebbo, bishop of Sens, Hardoinus, bishop of Troyes, and Milo, bishop of Rheims and Trier. Together the areas these people controlled lay along the edge of a massive semicircle which stretched from the Rouen area, down to Maine, then round to the south of Paris, and up through the Champagne, across the Moselle, into the Eifel region. This was the southern rim of Charles Martel's power in the year 723.

As we saw earlier, the evidence of the Wissembourg charters suggests that by 718 Charles also had a measure of influence in southern Austrasia and this impression is confirmed by the *Gesta* of the Bishops of Verdun, which speak of Bishop Peppo's support for Charles in the conflict with Ragamfred.[55] After Charles's victory Peppo and the church of Verdun were

---

53 *Diplomata Belgica*, no. 173, pp. 305–6.
54 *Gesta Fontanellensis*, III, ch. 5, p. 33.
55 *Gesta Episcopum Virdunensium*, ed. G. Waitz, *MGH SS* IV (Hanover 1841), pp. 39–51, ch. 11, p. 43.

rewarded. In 719, according to the early Carolingian annals, Radbod leader of the Frisians died, and we know that Utrecht was back in Frankish hands by 1 January 723, when Charles Martel issued his charter granting extensive lands to the church of Utrecht. How, or when, this reconquest of Frisian occupied territory took place, we do not know. We do hear, however, of another campaign against the Saxons in 720. We also learn from the *LHF* and the *Continuations of Fredegar* that Charles made a treaty with Eudo which resulted in the return of King Chilperic to Neustria, along with gifts, which presumably included part or all of the treasure taken south in 718. Chilperic was said to have died not long after he arrived home. Since he died in 721, we should place his return perhaps in 720 or in 721. He was succeeded as king by Dagobert III's son, Theuderic IV, who would reign from 721 to 737. It is at this point that the narrative of the *LHF* breaks off, with the final statement that 'Theuderic is in the sixth year of his reign'.

With the king, the palace, the royal treasure, and the major churches and monasteries in his hands, Charles Martel, now sole mayor of the palace, really had won the war. He was, in fact, in a stronger position than his father Pippin had ever been, for having broken the power of the old Neustrian families, he was not fettered by their privileges. The monastery of St Denis would never contest the actions of the Carolingians as it had those of the Pippinids. Soon the bishopric of Paris would be in the hands of Hugo, and the abbot of St Denis would be a man from the Liège area. As we have just seen, Charles's followers were able to take control of at least eight bishoprics which stretched from Rouen to Rennes, and there may well have been other cases we do not know about. This was potentially hostile territory, adjacent to the region of Angers, the last area held by Charles's old adversary Ragamfred. In 724 Ragamfred would make one final attempt to regain his influence, but Charles soon had him penned up again in Angers. According to the *Earlier Annals of Metz*, he took Ragamfred's son as a hostage, but allowed him to keep the county of Angers.[56] This is the last we hear of the old Neustrian 'mayor' until the early Carolingian annals report his death in 731.

For the year 723, the early Carolingian annals tell us two things which might well have been causally connected. The first is that two sons of Drogo were 'bound', that is, imprisoned or possibly put in chains. One of them died. In the *Annales Nazariani* version we read that 'two sons of Drogo were bound, Arnold and another who died'. It is usually assumed that this 'Arnold' was in fact Arnulf, last seen as granting land to Echternach in the Bollendorf charter of 716. We know that Hugo certainly did not die in 723 and we

---

56   *AMP*, trans. Fouracre and Gerberding, *Late Merovingian France*, p. 370.

have just noted how close an ally of Charles Martel he was, so Hugo cannot have been the other son of Drogo referred to. This leaves either Pippin or Godefrid as the one who died as a result of his imprisonment. Our second piece of information is that in 723 Charles Martel was ill, and for this to be mentioned as a major event in the annals, he must have been seriously incapacitated.[57]

It may be significant that no military campaign is mentioned in this year and it may have been news of Charles's sickness that prompted Ragamfred to attempt his comeback. We have just discussed how Charles's leading supporters Benignus, Rotbert, Rotgarius, Hardoinus, Ebbo and Milo had come to him near Cologne in August 723. Perhaps the occasion for this dispute hearing was some kind of crisis meeting, or a meeting which followed the resolution of a crisis. It does otherwise look a little strange that the abbot of St Wandrille should travel to Cologne to settle a dispute which was about land in the diocese of Sées. If in August 723 Charles Martel lay sick near Cologne, there may, therefore, have been the prospect of a family crisis. If Charles had died in 723, the situation would have been a kind of mirror image of that faced in 714–15. This time it would have been Charles's adherents who were in control of Cologne and Plectrude's descendants who were older but excluded, with Charles's young sons Karloman and Pippin needing protection from them. Again Ragamfred and the Neustrians would have been in the wings ready to take advantage of any family infighting. In the event, of course, Charles recovered, and the steps taken to end the threat from Drogo's sons, and, in the next year, to destroy Ragamfred as a serious contender for power, meant that by the end of 724 his position was stronger than ever.

Victory

In nine momentous years Charles Martel had battled his way from imprisonment and exclusion to become the most powerful leader in Francia. It is possible to follow the narrative of his rise and triumph as we have done in this chapter, but our sources are either too terse or too partisan to give us any clear explanation of why he was able to come from behind and to win against the odds. The *LHF* makes three comments about Charles's leadership

---

57 Later tradition had it that he was desperately ill and cured only by a miracle after praying to St Maximin of Trier. It is likely that this story was based on little more than an elaboration of the simple entry *Karolus infirmatus* or *Karolus infirmatur* in the *Annales Laureshamenses, Alamannici, Nazariani* and *Petaviani*.

in the light of these events: he was 'a warrior who was uncommonly well educated and effective in battle';[58] when he escaped from prison he did this with difficulty and 'with the help of the Lord'; and when Chilperic, Ragamfred and Eudo were advancing towards him in 718, he was 'steadfastly unafraid'. The *Continuations of Fredegar* did not add to this, but, predictably, the *Earlier Annals of Metz* waxed lyrical in praise of Charles, stressing God's support for his victories. For this author the battle of Vinchy was, like that of Tertry in 687, the 'judgement of divine justice', and, again as at Tertry, bright sunlight bathed the battlefield in a sign of God's approval.[59] This ninth-century view we need not take too seriously, but we should note that the author of the *LHF* was writing no later than 727, and could not, therefore, have been influenced by praise heaped upon Charles Martel after his victory over the Arabs. We may thus conclude that at least one contemporary was struck by Charles's skill and bravery as a warrior.

In the years 715–24 he fought on at least eight occasions and lost only once, on the first. His reputation must have grown with every success, and as it grew, people would have become more and more reluctant to take him on, but readier to join him. There were, as we have seen, people like Rigobert of Rheims and Celestinus of Ghent who maintained a degree of neutrality, waiting to see who would win. As the number of Charles's victories increased, so a growing number of the waverers would have thrown in their lot with him. He also began to build up stocks of treasure, starting with his seizure of booty at Amblève in 716. Once he had control of Plectrude's treasure, and his own king, Clothar IV, he would have been able to offer followers substantial rewards, and after he had driven Chilperic and Ragamfred out of Neustria, these rewards could have included counties and bishoprics, as we saw in south-west Neustria. Hugo, Benignus and Rotgarius were supporters of Pippin in Neustria who made a comeback after Ragamfred's demise. There may have been others in Neustria who had earlier been supporters of Pippin and who now viewed Charles as a liberator. Nor were loyalties cast in stone, for as we noted when discussing the background to Charles's career, lords needed the wealth and opportunity which power and office could bring in order to satisfy their own clients. It is quite sensible to imagine that a figure such as Rotgarius of Le Mans would have in turn supported Pippin, Ragamfred and Charles Martel. One can therefore conjecture that support for Charles at some stage reached a critical mass, at which point neutrals joined his cause, support for his enemies drained away,

---

58 See above, ch. 2, n. 19.
59 *AMP*, trans. Fouracre and Gerberding, *Late Merovingian France*, on Tertry, pp. 356–9, on Vinchy, pp. 368–9.

and victory became more certain in each subsequent confrontation. It would be reasonable to think that this stage was reached after the battle of Vinchy and the defeat of Plectrude, which brought an increasing number of Austrasians into his camp. This allowed him to proclaim his own king and to position himself as mayor of the palace and leader of Austrasia. But all of this depended upon one thing: his ability to win battles.

Charles Martel's triumph in the years 717–24 marked the end of an era in several respects. It was the end of an era for the Pippinid family as power came to focus on Charles Martel to the exclusion of Plectrude's descendants. Historians have traditionally registered the change by referring to the family henceforth as the descendants of Charles: the Carolingians. The period similarly marked a great loss of influence for the Gundoining family and its allies, who for so long had been rivals to the Pippinids. Chrodoin, as we saw earlier, transferred much of his wealth to Wissembourg after Charles had extended his influence over southern Austrasia in 717–18. In 721, Weroald, who was the son of Hodo and the grandson of Gundoin, and a monk at Wissembourg since about 700, made a final donation of his family's land to the monastery.[60] This has been seen as the family's response to their ultimate defeat at the hands of Charles.[61]

The rise of Charles Martel involved an even bigger shift in the balance of power from Neustria to Austrasia. That this decline in Neustria's fortunes marked the end of an era is the palpable sentiment of the *LHF*. Indeed, the wish to remember an old order which was being transformed by the arrival of new leaders from the east has been identified as a primary motivation behind the composition of this chronicle.[62] It was argued in an earlier chapter that what made the Merovingian kings indispensable was their role as umpires between different factions of magnates. We also saw that the kings were necessary for the raising of large armies and for the issuing of legal commands. When one faction of magnates became predominant, the first of these royal functions became redundant. The kings' other functions, the raising of armies and the issuing of commands, still remained important, but unlike umpiring, they could be performed in name rather than person. The fears of an earlier generation that a powerful mayor might 'keep the king in the background and just use his name' had now been realised.[63] With Charles Martel's defeat of Neustria and the eclipse of rival

---

60 *Traditiones Wizenburgenses*, no. 243, pp. 480–1.
61 G. Halsall, *Settlement and Social Organization. The Merovingian Region of Metz* (Cambridge 1995), p. 14.
62 R. Gerberding, *The Rise of the Carolingians and the Liber Historiae Francorum* (Oxford 1987), pp. 166–72.
63 *Passio Leudegarii*, ch. 5, p. 222.

families and factions in both Neustria and Austrasia, we enter the true era of 'do-nothing' kings' – kings, that is, in name only.

What the author of the *LHF* seems to have lamented in particular was the end of a time in which Neustrian *Franci* gathered at the royal palace and together with the king discussed the wellbeing of the kingdom. The turning point here was the rising against Theudoald in 715 when, 'at the instigation of the devil, *Franci* again attacked *Franci*'. We saw too how the author effectively ended his account with the death of Chilperic in 721, an event which marks another significant change, this time in the nature of our source material. It is striking that after this point the fiercely pro-Carolingian *Earlier Annals of Metz* ended its imaginative and argumentative recasting of history. After the final defeat of Ragamfred, the work more or less copied the text of the *Continuations of Fredegar* until it reached the events which followed the death of Charles Martel. Gone are the wonderful descriptions of battles and the long rhetorical speeches which argued the justice of the Pippinid cause. The reason for this loss of originality is surely that the section of the *Annals* up to the 720s had been written as an account which contested the *LHF*'s legitimist and pro-Neustrian view of events. When the Neustrian chronicle came to an end, the *Continuations of Fredegar* took up the narrative and this now became unstinting in its praise for Charles Martel. To the *Continuations'* glowing account of Charles Martel's triumph there was little that the *Earlier Annals of Metz* could add.

With the eclipse of the old Neustrian families, the centre of gravity of the Frankish kingdom shifted towards Austrasia. Neustrian resources massively boosted Charles Martel's power, and with the combined resources of Neustria and Austrasia behind him, he was more than a match for any other group or area. He needed to be, because with the defeat of Chilperic and Ragamfred it seems that those outlying regions which had recognised Chilperic's authority now turned their backs on Charles. In every case the authority of the mayor of the palace would be accepted only after a period of conflict. Like Clovis before him, Charles Martel's great advantage here was that he could use the forces of a recently united north against a south in which political authority had fragmented. And fortunately for Charles, Eudo's duchy of Aquitaine, the one area which might otherwise have had the resources and organisation to lead resistance against him, was at this time distracted and weakened by Arab raids. In the next chapter we shall examine how Charles Martel defeated these regions one by one.

CHAPTER FOUR

Charles Martel and the Periphery: Relations with Aquitaine, Burgundy, Provence, and the Regions East of the Rhine

The massive area subject to Frankish rule and influence was in principle bound together by ties of obedience to the king. This point we have already touched upon several times. We looked in general terms at the king as a figure of mediation between centre and province, and saw that it was through submission to royal authority (however weak) that local rulers and local customs and laws were brought within the Frankish polity. By the same token, because it was built out of a mosaic of local arrangements, this polity was politically brittle. It was noted, however, that although the kingdom might disintegrate politically when consensus failed, there was nevertheless an underlying pull towards cultural integration which meant that the separate regions did not then develop into fully independent units.

In the previous chapter we looked in particular at the way in which Charles Martel made use of the king to reinforce and to extend his power. As soon as he had beaten Plectrude in 717 and had raised Clothar IV to the throne, he became mayor of the palace, and actions done on Charles's behalf, but in the name of the king, now had the stamp of royal authority. Charles was then able to bring all of Austrasia and Neustria within this regime, but his position as mayor did not make his relations with the other regions any easier. For, like Charles himself, the rulers of Aquitaine, Burgundy, Provence, Alemannia, Bavaria and Thuringia all in theory derived their authority from their positions as officers of the Merovingian kings. It was the right of each one to rule his region on behalf of the king, an idea that is strongly expressed in both Alemannic and Bavarian law. The independent stance of these early-eighth-century leaders was thus born not out of separatism, but out of resistance to Charles himself, just as Gottfried duke of the Alemans had earlier refused to deal with Pippin but had remained loyal to the Merovingians. Charles Martel would, as we shall see shortly, force each duke into line, but their submission lasted only as long as the mayor lived. None of them felt bound to obey his sons, with the result that on Charles's death in 741 there was another crisis, and in 743 the raising of another Merovingian king. Ultimately the threat of hostility from dukes who saw their resistance to the Carolingians as perfectly legitimate would be removed only by destroying these ancient dukedoms and by subsuming their authority into that of the Carolingian kings themselves. We shall look at the way in which the Carolingians became kings in the last chapter of this study. For the present, however, we will examine Charles Martel's stormy relations with the dukes. We shall begin by looking at the situation in each region and then draw the threads together to comment on the last fifteen years of Charles's career, the period in which he fought his way to the pinnacle of power.

At this time, after Ragamfred's final defeat, and before his own health failed, Charles mounted campaigns in the outlying regions in most years, and in some years he fought in more than one region. In 724 he campaigned in Saxony. In 725 he fought in both Saxony and Bavaria, and again in 728 he fought in both these regions. He was in Alemannia in 730. In 731 he mounted two raids into Aquitaine, and it was in this region in either 732 or 733 that he won his famous victory over Arab raiders at the battle of Poitiers. After Poitiers he moved into northern Burgundy. In 734 he was in Frisia on a naval campaign, and in 735 he moved down through Burgundy into Provence. In 736 he fought yet again in Aquitaine. Two campaigns were mounted into Provence and Septimania (the former Visigothic enclave between Provence and Spain) in 736–37. In 738 he fought once more against the Saxons, and, finally, he was back in Provence in 739. The breathtaking pace of Charles's military activity slowed only when his health began to decline in 739. We shall look at these events region by region, but presenting them here in stark chronological order serves to emphasise the way in which Charles Martel had to fight in different regions throughout his career. He was apparently unable to concentrate his efforts on any one region for long, for as soon as he had dealt with one area, resistance broke out somewhere else. The great distance between the outlying regions (between Saxony and Aquitaine, for instance) was no doubt a factor here, as it would be in the time of his sons and grandson. That is to say, his opponents were fully aware of where he was and what he was doing, and as soon as they knew that he was far away and fighting elsewhere, they would take the opportunity to throw off his rule. The territory Charles Martel was attempting to bring under his control was huge. Until a measure of consensus gathered around Carolingian rule, and until the Carolingians had established a stable military hegemony, any ruler who wished to hold down the territory by force had to be constantly on the move. For the early Carolingians such movement became a normal way of life.

Aquitaine

Aquitaine, the large area which stretched from the Pyrenees in the south to the River Loire in the north, and from the Atlantic in the west to the Rhône valley in the east, provides a good illustration of how a region with strong ties to the rest of Francia might nevertheless take up an independent stance in the early eighth century. In the late Antique period, Aquitaine, with its fields of waving corn, fortunate climate and rich coastline, was regarded as a particularly prosperous region, and this reputation it retained throughout the Middle Ages. In addition to cereals, it produced increasing amounts of wine. There were lead mines in the Poitiers area which also yielded silver. The extensive pine forests produced pitch, and concentrations of oyster shells along the coastline have been associated with the manufacture of *garum*, a pungent and salty fish sauce which was in high demand in the early Middle Ages, as it had been in Antiquity.[1] The population of Aquitaine was largely of Gallo-Roman stock, and in the age of Charles Martel the authors of the *Continuations of Fredegar* still referred to the people living beyond the Loire as 'Romans'.[2] Poitiers seems to have been one of the last places in Francia to maintain its *gesta municipalia*, that is, a civic archive in which documents were routinely registered, a practice which dated back to the later Roman Empire.[3] Nevertheless, the riches of Aquitaine, and the needs of defence against the Visigoths across the Pyrenees, had always drawn Franks to the south.

For a brief time (629–631/32) there had been a Frankish kingdom based on Toulouse, with which Pippin I had had links. At other times the various *civitates* or counties of Aquitaine were attached to either Austrasia or Neustria. We saw in an earlier chapter how in the year 640 the count of Saintes and his men had marched all the way from the Charente area to the Unstrut in Thuringia in order to join in the attack on Duke Radulf. Saintes was attached to Austrasia.[4] It is clear that in the mid-seventh century Aquitanian

---

1   The major work on Aquitaine in this period is M. Rouche, *L'Aquitaine des Wisigoths aux Arabes 418–781. Naissance d'une Region* (Paris 1979). Though flawed by an over-commitment to a notion of Aquitanian difference and separatism, it is very good on the economy and ecology of Aquitaine, see, for instance, pp. 190–209.

2   For example, *Fred. Contin.*, ed. and trans. J.M. Wallace-Hadrill (London 1960), ch. 25, p. 98.

3   There are extensive references to the *gesta municipalia* in Poitiers at the close of the seventh century in a charter in which Ansoald, bishop of Poitiers, gave land to the monastery of Noirmoutier. See J. Tardif, 'Les Chartes Mérovingiens de Noirmoutier', *Nouvelle Revue Historique de Droit Francais et Étranger*, 22 (1899), 763–90.

4   H. Ebling, *Prosopographie der Amtsträger des Merrowingerreiches*, Beihefte der Francia, 2 (Munich 1974), p. 243, and 'Die inneraustrasische Opposition', in J. Jarnut, U. Nonn and

leaders, of whatever ethnic origin, remained part of that supra-regional elite which was involved in high politics. Dido, bishop of Poitiers, for instance, had been one of the prime movers in the so-called 'Grimoald coup'.[5] Throughout the seventh century, kings and other leaders gave Aquitanian lands to northern churches and monasteries, so that by the year 700 virtually every major church or monastery in Neustria and Austrasia had land in Aquitaine, and the church which seems to have had the most was that of Rheims.[6] When Bishop Rigobert was driven out of Rheims by Charles Martel in 717 or 718, it was in Aquitaine that he took refuge. According to Flodoard's *Historia ecclesiae Remensis*, a tenth-century work, but one which drew upon earlier charters, Dagobert III (711–15) confirmed Rheims in the ownership of all its Aquitanian lands.[7] We therefore have an indication that Aquitaine was seen as part of the Frankish kingdom almost up to the time at which Charles Martel seized power. That Eudo duke of Aquitaine should have joined forces with Chilperic and Ragamfred suggests that he too was prepared to recognise the authority of the Merovingian king as long as the latter was not in the hands of Charles Martel.

There is an alternative view, expressed at some length by the French historian Michel Rouche, that Aquitaine was essentially different from the other parts of the kingdom of the Franks, and that the Aquitanians had long sought to dissociate themselves from the rest of Francia.[8] In this view, power struggles in Neustria-Burgundy in the 670s gave Aquitaine the chance to break away. Led by one Duke Lupus, whose military force was made up

---

M. Richter (eds), *Karl Martell in Seiner Zeit*, Beihefte der Francia, 37 (Sigmaringen 1994), pp. 295–304, at p. 300, argues that a charter of 708 (J. Pardessus (ed.), *Diplomata, Chartae, Epistolae, Leges, Aliaque Instrumenta ad Res Gallo-Francicas Spectantia* (2 vols, Paris 1843, 1849, reprinted Aalen 1969), no. 471, p. 278) shows Wulfoald, count of Verdun, exchanging land near Saintes with the church of Metz, thus demonstrating the continuing links between Saintes and Austrasia. But the land in question cannot be identified as lying in the Saintes region. Its location was in fact *super fluvium Mosellae*.

5 See above, ch. 2, pp. 37–8.

6 Rouche, *L'Aquitaine*, pp. 239–45, and map, pp. 232–3. See also E. Ewig, 'L'Aquitaine et les Pays Rhénans au Haut Moyen Age', *Cahiers de Civilization Médiévale*, 1 (1958), 37–54, reprinted in *Spätantikes und Fränkisches Gallien. Gesammelten Schriften (1952–1973)* I (Zurich and Munich 1976), pp. 553–72.

7 Flodoard, *Historia Remensis Ecclesiae*, ed. I. Heller and G. Waitz, *MGH SS* XIII (Hanover 1881), pp. 405–599, ch. 11, pp. 458–60. A more certain (because contemporary) indication of contact between Aquitaine and the north, and Provence, comes from an original charter in which King Childebert III (695–711) donated to the monastery of St Denis land at Nassigny in the Bourges region. In return the monastery gave up to the king some of its revenues in Marseilles and elsewhere. Nassigny had a few years earlier been held by the church of Lyons, and then exchanged with King Clovis III for land nearer Lyons. *Chartae Latinae Antiquiores*, ed. A. Bruckner and M. Marichal, vol. 14, ed. H. Atsma and J. Vezin (Zurich 1982), no. 577.

8 Rouche, *L'Aquitaine, passim*, but esp. pp. 103–19.

partly of Basques, Aquitaine turned its back on the north. By the year 700, argued Rouche, the northerners were being seen by the Aquitanians as *barbari* (barbarians), and in the minds of the northern Franks *Aquitania* was becoming *Wasconia*, as it became more foreign to them partly because the Basque element in its identity was becoming more pronounced.[9] We have already noted that when Eudo formed his alliance with Chilperic and Ragamfred, the *Continuations of Fredegar* said that Eudo gave his help in return for 'a kingdom and gifts' (*regnum et munera*).[10] Michel Rouche took this to mean that Aquitaine had finally, and formally, won its independence, and that now it was a separate kingdom.[11] For this regnal status there is simply no evidence and the Latin term *regnum* does not necessarily mean 'kingdom' in a formal sense. As Roger Collins has argued, the *Continuations of Fredegar* are at their most distorted when dealing with Aquitaine, and what they say about Eudo cannot be trusted.[12] Nor is there any evidence that Aquitanians had desired independence a generation earlier, in the time of Lupus. The Neustrian court may have been a place too dangerous for Lupus to visit, and no Aquitanians can be identified among those listed in the judgement tribunals of Clovis III and Childebert III, but the northern churches do not seem to have lost their lands in Aquitaine at this time, and one Aquitanian magnate, at least, can be seen owning land outside the duchy.[13] The report of a change in attitudes towards northerners (and vice versa) around the year 700 is misleading as it comes from a ninth-century source, the *Miracula Austregisili*, which confused Pippin II (d. 714) with his grandson Pippin III (d. 768), who waged all-out war against Aquitaine in the years 762–68.[14] There is simply not enough here to allow one to argue that Aquitaine wished to become independent and achieved independence. All in all, as Rouche is ready to admit, we can find out very little about

---

9   For instance the area between Bordeaux and the River Garonne, which Charles Martel attacked in 735, is treated as part of Aquitaine in *Fred. Contin.*, ch. 15, p. 91, but is termed *Wasconia* in the early Carolingian annals when they refer to the same event.

10 *Fred. Contin.*, ch. 10, p. 89. Wallace-Hadrill translates the term *regnum* as 'the kingdom', implying that what was meant was all of Francia.

11 Rouche, *L'Aquitaine*, p. 108.

12 R. Collins, 'Deception and Misrepresentation in Early Eighth-Century Frankish Historiography: Two Case Studies', in Jarnut, Nonn and Richter (eds), *Karl Martell in Seiner Zeit*, pp. 235–41.

13 Ansoald of Poitiers had family land in Burgundy. See P. Fouracre and R. Gerberding, *Late Merovingian France. History and Hagiography 640–720* (Manchester 1996), p. 197.

14 *Miracula Austregisili*, ed. B. Krusch, *MGH SRM* IV (Hanover and Leipzig 1902), pp. 200–8, ch. 5, p. 202. Krusch believed that the language of this work could hardly be earlier than eleventh century. It is this source which refers to the Franks as 'barbarians', but note that this is in a passage where they set fire to Austregisilus's grave and shrine and is, therefore, more likely to be a perjorative term than a literal reference to their separate ethnic identity.

Aquitaine in the period 675–751. Remarkably few charters have survived, and narrative material from the region is equally scarce.

Not surprisingly, therefore, we know nothing about the family background or early career of Eudo, the duke of Aquitaine in the time of Charles Martel. From the moment that he first appears in the *Continuations of Fredegar*, Eudo is treated as a weak leader. Faced with the prospect of fighting Charles in 718, he was 'terrified' and fled back beyond the Loire. He then made a treaty with Charles, but later broke it. Beaten again by Charles he saw that he had become a laughing-stock and stupidly turned to the 'perfidious' Arabs for help against his enemy.[15] But then Aquitaine had to be rescued from an Arab army which was devastating the region. Charles Martel thus became Aquitaine's saviour when he crushed the Arabs at the famous battle of Poitiers. But as has already been stated, the Continuator's account of events in Aquitaine is severely distorted.

The Arabs had invaded Spain in 711. With the help of Berber troops from North Africa, they had by the year 720 consolidated their rule over the former Visigothic kingdom and began raiding north of the Pyrenees. It was perhaps this pressure upon southern Aquitaine which encouraged Eudo to make a treaty with Charles in which he effectively pulled out of the alliance against him. In 721, according to the early Carolingian annals, 'Eudo threw the Saracens out of Aquitaine'. We learn from a near contemporary Spanish source, the *Chronicle of 754*, that Eudo led his troops to victory in a battle at Toulouse in which the Arab leader As-Sham was killed.[16] It is presumably to this success that the Carolingian annals were referring, although the chronology of *Chronicle of 754* and the *Chronicle of Moissac*, an early set of annals, written in the south, perhaps at Narbonne, suggest that it took place in 720 rather than 721.[17]

The Arabs went on to capture Carcassonne and Nimes in 724, and to sack Autun in 725,[18] but it nevertheless seems correct to say that as a result of their defeat at Toulouse, the Arabs were indeed 'thrown out of Aquitaine'. So, far from being a weak leader, as he is portrayed in the *Continuations of Fredegar*, Eudo was something of a hero. This was certainly the view expressed in the biography of Pope Gregory II (715–31), one of the series of contemporary papal 'Lives' written up in the collection known as *Liber Pontificalis*.[19] This work is the essential source for the relations between the

---

15   *Fred. Contin.*, chs 10, 13, pp. 88–9, 90–1.
16   R. Collins, *The Arab Conquest of Spain* (Oxford 1989), p. 87.
17   *Chronicon Moissiacense*, ed. G. Pertz, *MGH SS* I (Hanover 1826), pp. 282–313, at p. 290.
18   *Chronicon Moissiacense*, p. 291.
19   *Liber Pontificalis*, trans. R. Davis, *The Lives of the Eighth-Century Popes* (Liverpool 1992), Gregory II, ch. 11, p. 8.

papacy and its enemies and allies both inside and outside Italy. It tells us that after the battle of Toulouse Eudo wrote to the pope telling him that he had killed 375,000 Saracens in a single day, at the cost of only 1,500 Frankish dead. Eudo added that liturgical sponges sent by the pope the previous year had provided miraculous protection when eaten in small quantities by his troops. Although the source referred to Eudo once as 'prince of Aquitaine', it also described him as a duke of the Franks, who ruled in Francia, and who had Frankish troops. By 720 at the latest, therefore, Eudo was in contact with Rome, and after the battle of Toulouse he was obviously regarded there as an important Frankish leader, much more important at this stage, presumably, than Charles Martel. One can now see why the authors of the *Continuations of the Chronicle of Fredegar* wished to belittle Eudo and show him not as the saviour of the Franks from the Arabs but as the petulant fool who actually invited the Arabs into the region. It is partly because the *Continuations* did their job so well that history has regarded Charles Martel, not Eudo, as the one who turned the tide against the Arab advance, and has judged that decisive victory was won at Poitiers, not at Toulouse. Another early author who helped to form this impression was the Lombard, Paul the Deacon. In his *Historia Langobardorum* written not long after 785, Paul the Deacon used the *Liber Pontificalis* as one of his sources. He took from it the figures of 375,000 Saracen and 1,500 Frankish dead and noted that they fell in a battle in 721, but he had Charles Martel fight this battle alongside Eudo.[20] Later writers, no doubt influenced by the *Continuations of Fredegar*, attributed the Saracen casualties solely to Charles Martel, and the battle in which they fell became unequivocally that of Poitiers.[21]

A second work which reveals the high esteem in which Eudo was held is the *Vita Pardulfi*, the life of St Pardulf, a holy man from the Limoges area, which was composed around the middle of the eighth century. Pardulf died in 737, two years after Eudo, and the author of the *Vita Pardulfi* imagined that the holy man's last words were that he could hear Eudo's war trumpet summoning him, that is, Eudo was calling him to heaven.[22] This work, despite its highly conventional themes, gives us at least a glimpse into life in Aquitaine in our period. It shows us a world of dukes, counts and their underlings, churchmen and peasants which is not recognisably different

---

20 Paul the Deacon, *Historia Langobardorum*, ed. G. Waitz, *MGH SRG* VI (Hanover 1878), ch. 46, p. 233.

21 U. Nonn, 'Das Bild Karl Martells in Mittelalterliche Quellen', in Jarnut, Nonn and Richter (eds), *Karl Martell in Seiner Zeit*, pp. 9–21, at pp. 11–12.

22 *Vita Pardulfi*, ed. W. Levison, *MGH SRM* VII (Hanover and Leipzig 1920), pp. 24–40, ch. 21, p. 38.

from any other part of Francia, except perhaps for the prominence of the *annona*, a fodder tax which seems to have been especially important in Aquitaine.[23] What little charter evidence we have shows us great estates described in terms of their assets, including people. This is a landscape which would have been immediately familiar to northerners, who used identical terms to describe their lands,[24] and as we have already seen, many northern churches held land in Aquitaine. In short, Aquitaine was in terms of its political, social and economic structures, and its culture, language, law and religious institutions, closely bound to Austrasia and Neustria. It had the resources and the organisation to be a serious rival to Charles Martel's growing power. As events in the 760s would prove, to subjugate Aquitaine would require a massive effort.

Even if a respite from pressures elsewhere had provided an opportunity, Charles Martel did not have the resources to conquer Aquitaine, and up to 731 Ragamfred's power base at Angers remained an obstacle to any kind of campaign across the Loire. It is surely no coincidence that Ragamfred's death and Charles's first expedition to the south occurred in the same year. Perhaps Charles was also able to take advantage of Eudo's preoccupation with fresh Arab raids across the Pyrenees. The *Continuations of Fredegar* say that war broke out because Eudo broke an agreement, presumably the one made back in 720 when Chilperic had been handed over to Charles. But the source also mentions the rich booty that was taken in two raids in 731.[25] Booty may have been the main object of the invasions, or Charles may simply have been taking the first chance he had ever had to try and dent the power of his rival Eudo. As we know, the Continuator of Fredegar went on to argue that the humiliated Eudo called upon the Arabs to help him fight Charles. Here we can use the *Chronicle of 754* to show that Eudo had

---

23 *Vita Pardulfi*, ch. 17, p. 35. The *annona* also figures in Charlemagne's legislation of 769 on Aquitaine, and in the so-called Astronomer's *Life of Louis*. Both sources are partially translated in P. King, *Charlemagne. Translated Sources* (Lambrigg 1986), pp. 202–3 and 165–80. Here, the *Life of Louis*, ch. 7, p. 171. All three references to the *annona* are to contexts of abuse, which suggests that it was levied with some vigour. The *Vita Pardulfi*, ch. 9, pp. 29–30 also has a story about the stealing of wild mushrooms which is timelessly Aquitanian.

24 Rouche, *L'Aquitaine*, pp. 217ff. draws on one charter in particular, an extensive donation made by one Nizezius and his wife Ermintrude to the monastery of Moissac in 680 (Pardessus, *Diplomata, Chartae*, no. 393, pp. 184–5), to emphasise the distinctive nature of Aquitanian landholding. The Nizezius charter in fact shows the opposite, for it is very similar to charters issued elsewhere in Francia, apart from the use of the *Lex Falcidia* which stipulated that donors to the church must keep a certain proportion of their lands to hand on to their heirs. This law was in use throughout southern Gaul. On the Nizezius charter, see also C. Higounet, 'L'Occupation du Sol du Pays entre Tarn et Garonne au Moyen Age', *Annales du Midi*, 65 (1953), 301–30.

25 *Fred. Contin.*, ch. 13, p. 90.

not in fact betrayed Francia in this way. Sometime earlier, Eudo had married his daughter to a Berber leader called Munnuza, taking advantage, one supposes, of the growing tensions between Berbers and Arabs in Spain in order to secure his southern border. Munnuza duly revolted against his Arab masters but was defeated and took his own life. Eudo's daughter, it was said, was sent off to Damascus as a gift to the Caliph. It was probably in retaliation for the aid given to Munnuza, and possibly in revenge for As-Sham's death at Toulouse, that the Arab leader 'Abd ar-Rahman attacked Aquitaine and defeated Eudo at the River Garonne.[26] It was now that Eudo called upon Charles, for the Arabs continued their advance, first sacking Bordeaux and then burning the prestigious church of St Hilary's at Poitiers. Charles Martel responded so quickly to Eudo that it has been reasoned that he must already have been on campaign in northern Aquitaine when he received the call for help.[27] He was thus able to intercept the Arab force on the road from Poitiers to Tours, and what followed was the celebrated battle of Poitiers.

According to a clear statement in the near contemporary *Vita Eucherii*, and to a more confused account of events in the later *Gesta Episcoporum Autissiodorensium* (the 'History of the Bishops of Auxerre'), there was a Burgundian contingent at Poiters too.[28] The question of how Charles Martel won the day we shall leave to the next chapter when we review the question of military innovation in this period. The battle is usually said to have taken place in October 732, according to the date given in the early Carolingian annals. Roger Collins, however, has argued that we should prefer the chronology of the *Chronicle of 754* to the traditional dating because the *Chronicle* is the earlier and better informed source. This would give us a probable date of October 733.[29] This argument is sensible, but not without difficulties in that it does not demonstrate that the early Carolingian annals are generally unreliable in their chronology. There is nevertheless no problem in accepting the revised date for the battle of Poitiers, for the redating does not disturb the narrative sequence reported in the Frankish sources. That is to say, Charles Martel is not reported to have been anywhere else in 733, and all that is said to have happened after Poitiers could have taken place in the

---

26 *Chronicon Moissiacense*, p. 291.

27 Collins, 'Deception', p. 239

28 *Vita Eucherii*, ed. W. Levison, *MGH SRM* VII, pp. 46–53, ch. 8, pp. 49–50; *Gesta Episcoporum Autissiodorensium*, extracts ed. G. Waitz, *MGH SS* XIII, pp. 394–400, ch. 27, p. 394.

29 Collins, *Arab Conquest*, p. 91. See also M. Baudot, 'Localisation et Datation de la Première Victoire Remportée contre les Musulmans', *Memoires et Documents Publiées par la Société de l'Ecole des Chartes*, 12, i (1955), 93–105.

order recorded in the narrative sources whether the battle was fought in 732 or in 733.

'Abd ar-Rahman, the commander of the Arabs at Poitiers, was killed in the battle, but his forces do not seem to have been destroyed to the extent that the *Continuations of Fredegar* imagined. The *Vita Pardulfi* tells of how they burned and looted their way through the Limousin *en route* back to Spain.[30] Their campaign should perhaps be interpreted as a long-distance raid rather than the beginning of a war. Defeat at Poitiers no doubt put the Arabs off raiding into Aquitaine again, but they soon turned their attentions to Provence, nearer, more accessible and just as rich. For Charles Martel, however, victory at Poitiers greatly enhanced his reputation. We have of course just seen that in the next generation the scale of his victory would be exaggerated, first by the Continuator of Fredegar and then by Paul the Deacon. It is nevertheless clear that Charles's success had the immediate effect of enabling him to extend his power into Burgundy. It did not, though, seem to have gained him much more acceptance in Aquitaine itself, despite Eudo's earlier defeat at the hands of the Arabs. Charles did not return to Aquitaine until after Eudo's death in 735, and then, according the *Continuations of Fredegar*, he conducted a raid all the way to the River Garonne in the south.[31] The *Earlier Annals of Metz* added that he 'gave the duchy' to Hunoald, Eudo's son, and the *Vita Pardulfi* stated that Hunoald ruled Aquitaine 'with the permission of Charles'.[32]

In 735 Charles may therefore have forced the Aquitanians to recognise his authority, but in 736, the early Carolingian annals tell us, he was back in Aquitaine fighting against the 'sons of Eudo'. These sons were presumably Hunoald and Remistanius. When Charles Martel died in 741, Hunoald was in the forefront of resistance to his sons Pippin and Karloman, and Remistanius carried on fighting the Franks until 768, when he was finally caught and hanged by Pippin.[33] That Charles Martel failed to bring Aquitaine under his control may suggest that he never intended to do more than raid this rich country. To subdue Aquitaine as he had subdued Neustria would have required yearly campaigns and the reduction of numerous well-defended towns, starting with Bourges. We learn from the *Continuations of Fredegar* that Poitiers, Limoges, Saintes, Périgueux and Angoulême also had

---

30   *Vita Pardulfi*, ch. 15, pp. 33–4.
31   *Fred. Contin.*, ch. 15, p. 91.
32   *Vita Pardulfi*, ch. 21, p. 38; *AMP*, ed. B. von Simson, *MGH SRG* (Hanover and Leipzig 1905), p. 28. The author of the *AMP* is here looking forward to the 740s when Hunoald rebelled, for he could then be presented as perfidious, having earlier sworn to be faithful to Charles and his sons.
33   *Fred. Contin.*, chs 50–1, pp. 117–20.

walls and that there were 'many other cities and forts'.[34] The same source describes the great effort it took Pippin to besiege and take Bourges in 762, despite the fact that the Franks had already taken it, and burned it to the ground, twenty years earlier.[35] After the fall of Bourges it would take seven more years of hard fighting to crush Aquitanian resistance. Charles Martel was not in a position to invest this kind of effort in the region.

Burgundy and Provence

Burgundy and Provence were regions which, as we saw in the last chapter, appear to have recognised the authority of King Chilperic II. Northern Burgundy, which included the town of Orléans, was hardly a peripheral region, but lay at the centre of the Frankish kingdom. Southern Burgundy and Provence were more remote, and their rulers, the *patricii* and *rectores*, may have held titles which were different from those held by the leaders elsewhere (the *duces* and *comites*), but there were nevertheless strong family ties between the nobles of the south and those of the north. Again, as we have just seen in the case of Aquitaine, resistance to Charles Martel in these southern regions seems to have been put up by leaders who had in the past accepted the authority of the Merovingian kings, but who were not now prepared to accept Charles Martel as overlord.

It was at one time argued that in the seventh century there was a separatist movement in Burgundy. The Burgundians had in the fifth century occupied the lands between Lyons and Grenoble. They had been conquered by the Franks in the 530s, but, it was reasoned, a degree of Burgundian identity had been preserved in the Merovingian kingdom that was called Burgundy, but which stretched from the original Burgundian lands northwards into the Paris region. One reading of political history imagined that after this kingdom had been united with Neustria in the early seventh century there remained a political faction which sought to re-establish Burgundian independence.[36] Most historians now reject this picture as anachronistic in that ethnic separatism, or regional consciousness, simply did not figure on the political map of early medieval Francia. The two key narratives which had been thought to show the forces of Burgundian separatism at work are now

---

34 *Fred. Contin.*, ch. 46, pp. 114–15.
35 *Vita Pardulfi*, ch. 20, pp. 37–8.
36 This argument was developed at length by M. Chaume, *Les Origines du Duché de Bourgogone* (Dijon 1926).

interpreted as episodes of high politics which, though played out in Burgundy, were determined by supra-regional considerations.[37] An alternative to the separatist view, first articulated by the great scholar of Merovingian history Eugen Ewig, is that in the course of the later seventh century power in Burgundy fell into the hands of the region's bishops, who established a series of what Ewig termed 'episcopal republics', such as Orléans, Auxerre, Autun and Lyons.[38] There were, simply, no secular leaders who could match the strength of these prince-bishops until Charles Martel rooted them out by force. The term 'republic' is in a Merovingian context no less anachronistic than the idea of a separatist movement, and we cannot say that all power fell into the hands of the bishops without noting that our main narrative sources from the region are focused on bishops. We just do not know enough about secular leaders in Burgundy at this time to judge their powers in relation to those of the bishops. Ewig's model does, however, capture the sense that when Ragamfred and Charles Martel were locked in conflict and Burgundy was in effect left to its own devices, what followed was political fragmentation, not a drive to establish any kind of independent regional unit.

According to the ninth-century *Gesta Episcoporum Autissiodorensium*, Savaric, the bishop of Auxerre, took immediate advantage of the fighting in the north.[39] A Bishop Savaric was yet another of those whose attendance at the Neustrian court in the late seventh century is recorded in the lists of judgement tribunal members, but he may not be the same person who was later bishop of Auxerre.[40] The Auxerre *Gesta* tell us that their Savaric became increasingly involved in secular affairs 'more than befits a bishop', until in the aftermath of the battle of Compiègne (715) he 'invaded with military force' the bishoprics of Orléans, Nevers, Tonnerre, Avallon and Troyes. He was on the way to do the same to Lyons when he died of a stroke, probably in 721. Savaric's successor as bishop of Auxerre was Hainmar, 'called bishop', a term of reference which no doubt means that he was a layman who had taken over the bishopric.

Meanwhile in Orléans, Savaric's nephew Eucherius became bishop, having sought the endorsement of Charles Martel for his promotion. This we know from Eucherius's 'Life', the *Vita Eucherii*, which was composed soon

---

37 Fouracre and Gerberding, *Late Merovingian France*, pp. 174–6, 197–8.
38 E. Ewig, 'Milo et eiusmodi similes', in *Sankt Bonifatius Gedenkengabe zum zwölfhundertsten Todestag* (Fulda 1954), pp. 412–20, reprinted in *Spätantikes und Fränkisches Gallien* II (Zurich and Munich 1979), pp. 189–219, here, pp. 207–14.
39 *Gesta Episcoporum Autissiodorensium*, ch. 26, p. 394.
40 An *episcopus* Savaric appears in *Chartae Latinae Antiquiores* nos 576 and 581, two *placita* held in 692/93 and 697 respectively, but Savaric bishop of Auxerre held office 715–21. In 692 Savaric might have been bishop of Orléans, that is, prior to becoming bishop of Auxerre. Alternatively he could have been a relative of the later bishop of Auxerre.

after the bishop's death in 738 or 739. We shall have much more to say about this source, for it played a key role in the development of Charles Martel's reputation as a despoiler of church lands. One other source of information on the situation in northern Burgundy at this time is the eleventh-century cartulary of the monastery of Flavigny, situated between Avallon and Dijon. The Flavigny cartulary preserves versions of a charter in which Abbot Widerad endowed the monastery, and versions of his will. There is some confusion over the order in which, and the dates upon which, the charter and will were drawn up, but it seems most likely that the charter was issued in 719–20, and the will in 721–22.[41] The significance of these documents is that they suggest that Widerad recognised the authority of kings who were under the control of Charles Martel. One version of the will even had Theuderic present as it was drawn up. In addition, they allow us to see that patterns of landholding in this area of Burgundy were identical to those we see in charters from Neustria and Austrasia. Drawing together the indications from these three sources, it can be said that there was a degree of political and military conflict in Burgundy in the years after Compiègne, but that this does not seem to have been of an order to threaten social stability. The bishops of the region seem to have gained a measure of independence and to have built up military forces, but were not at this stage in conflict with Charles Martel. Indeed, as we have seen, the Auxerre *Gesta* and the *Vita Eucherii* indicate that troops from this area joined Martel on the Poitiers campaign, which suggests that their leaders must have been in some sort of alliance with him. All this, however, was to change with Charles's victory at Poitiers.

The *Vita Eucherii* tells us that relations between Eucherius and Charles Martel were good until people who were envious of the bishop suggested to Charles that he exile Eucherius and his family and give their lands and positions (*honores*) to his own followers.[42] In hagiography, envy is often a catch-all explanation for why a holy and successful religious leader might have enemies who wished to do him or her harm. The context which gives a more direct meaning to the term is one of rivalry and competition for

---

41 *The Cartulary of Flavigny*, ed. C. Bouchard (Cambridge Mass. 1991), nos 1, 2, 57, 58, pp. 19–26, 28–32, 135–40, 140–4. Bouchard, pp. 14–16, argues that the will came first: although it is dated according to the regnal years of Theuderic IV, it can be put back into the reign of Chilperic, because he was not recognised as king in Burgundy. Bouchard also argues that the charter must come after the will because it refers to the Rule of St Benedict which came to Burgundy only later. But there is evidence both that the rule was known there as early as the reign of Chilperic, and that Chilperic was recognised as king in Burgundy. There is therefore good reason to accept the dating clauses of the two documents at face value.

42 *Vita Eucherii*, ch. 9, pp. 50–1.

positions of authority and wealth. If we add to this the fact that Orléans lay on the south-eastern boundary of Neustria with Burgundy and was a strategically important crossing point on the River Loire which led into Aquitaine, it is not hard to see why Charles should have coveted the *honores* of his erstwhile ally. In the event, Charles stopped at Orléans on his way back from Poitiers, summoned Eucherius and then exiled him and his family to Cologne. Eucherius was then handed over for safer keeping to Chrodbert, the duke of Hesbaye, and confined in the monastery of St Trond.[43] After six years of exile he died, in either 738 or 739, depending on whether one dates the battle of Poitiers to 732 or to 733. The Auxerre *Gesta* tell a similar, if more confused story: Hainmar, bishop of Auxerre, actually fought against the Saracens and killed their king. He was then ordered to fight against Eudo, duke of Aquitaine, but people eaten up with envy suggested to Pippin (here confused with Charles Martel) that he had allowed Eudo to escape. Hainmar was summoned to Pippin and put in custody at Bastogne in the Ardennes. After a few days he escaped but was hunted down and killed at Lifold in the diocese of Tulle.[44] These accounts can be matched with the *Continuations of Fredegar* to suggest that the exile of Eucherius and Hainmar was the first step in the occupation of Burgundy as a whole. In the year following Poitiers, reported the Continuator, Charles Martel moved through the whole region and established his most trusted and able men everywhere in order to crush the rebellious and disloyal.[45] When the area around Lyons had been pacified he gave it over to his followers, and 'legal agreements having been made', he returned home 'acting confidently', which probably means that he had secured binding agreements from the inhabitants to accept the jurisdiction of his followers and thus felt that the area was secure.[46]

The late-ninth-century *Chronicle of Ado* referred to the destruction of churches around Vienne and Lyons at this time.[47] According to Ado, Willicarius the bishop of Vienne could not bear to watch his church being brought low

---

43   On Chrodbert, see above, ch. 3, pp. 72–3.

44   *Gesta Episcoporum Autissiodorensium*, ch. 27, p. 394.

45   *Fred. Contin.*, ch. 14, p. 91. In this passage Wallace-Hadrill translated the phrase, *ad resistendas gentes rebelles et infideles* as 'to curb disaffection as well as pagan penetration', but there is no reason to suppose that the *infideles* were 'pagan'.

46   *Fred. Contin.*, ch. 14, p. 91. Wallace-Hadrill's translation is again very loose and adds to the original. He translated the sentence, *Firmata foedera iudicaria reversus est victor, fiducialiter agens*, as 'having regularised his grants by charter, he came home, his victories consolidated by the honesty of such administrative dealings'. On these events in Burgundy, see A. Stadt-Lauer, 'Carlus Princeps Regionem Burgundie Sagaciter Penetravit. Zur Schlacht von Tours und Poitiers und die Eingreifen Karl Martells in Burgund', in Jarnut, Nonn and Richter (eds), *Karl Martell in Seiner Zeit*, pp. 79–100.

47   *Chronicon Adonis*, ed. G. Pertz, *MGH SS* II (Hanover 1892), p. 319.

when the Franks seized its property for their own use, and so he retreated to the monastery of Agaune. The provinces of Vienne and Lyons were devastated and plundered, and both churches remained without a bishop while laymen sacrilegiously and barbarously helped themselves to ecclesiastical property. Although Ado's tale of woe may have been informed by the conventional view that this was generally a time of secularisation of church property, there can be no doubt that Charles Martel's occupation of the Lyonnais was remembered in terms of violent expropriation.

We must therefore assume that more local families were driven out in the manner of Eucherius, Hainmar and Willicarius, but of this we have no further evidence. We might, however, be able to detect one family which moved in: it was none other than that of Charles's old rival Plectrude. According to the late-eighth-century *Vita Gregorii Abbatis Traiectensis*, the Life of Gregory of Utrecht, who was a grandson of Plectrude's sister, Adela of Pfalzel, Gregory's older brothers were sent by Charles to 'a distant part of Gaul'. They were followed by younger half-brothers.[48] This has been taken to mean that they were among the followers to whom Charles entrusted the region of Lyons.[49] If this assumption is correct, we learn, or rather confirm, two things: first, that Charles Martel relied upon nobles from his Meuse–Moselle homeland to control the newly conquered region, and second, that descendants of this powerful Austrasian family who had once fiercely opposed him were now trusted supporters. This is certainly true of Gregory himself, whose career unfolded in service to Charles. In 735 Charles Martel returned to the Lyons area and, says the *Continuations of Fredegar*, brought the 'chief men' and the ruler (the *praefectus*) under his control.[50] It may be that southern Burgundy had thrown off his rule in the intervening period, or that the Continuator had exaggerated the success of the first campaign into Burgundy. This time, however, Charles went even further south and installed his men in the whole area between Lyons and the Mediterranean, placing them in the cities of Arles and Marseilles. That is to say, he occupied Provence. It is to this area that we now turn.

As we saw in the last chapter, Antenor, the *patricius* of Provence in the early eighth century, had been in revolt against Pippin II. He seems to have recognised the authority of Chilperic II, who confirmed the privileges which the monasteries of St Denis and Corbie held in Provence. From these confirmations we inferred not only that Antenor had backed Chilperic and

---

48   Liudger, *Vita Gregorii Abbatis Traiectensis*, ed. A. Holder-Egger, *MGH SS* XVI (Hanover 1887), pp. 66–79, ch. 9, p. 74.

49   M. Werner, *Adelsfamilien im Umkreis der Frühen Karolinger. Die Verwandtschaft Irminas von Oeren und Adelas von Pfalzel*, Vorträge und Forschungen, 28 (Sigmaringen 1982), pp. 268ff.

50   *Fred. Contin.*, ch. 18, p. 93.

Ragamfred against Charles Martel, but also that trade links between Neustria and Provence were evidently being maintained in this period.[51] Control of Provence had always provided Francia with access to Mediterranean trade and to Mediterranean wealth, and the port of Marseilles was so important that in the sixth and seventh centuries its revenues had often been shared between the kings of Austrasia and Neustria. If the St Denis charter is to be believed, revenue from Marseilles in 716 was still sufficient to assign the monks 100 *solidi* per year to spend when they visited the port. At the neighbouring port of Fos was the entrance into the River Rhône, and the beginning of a trade route which ran up the Rhône–Saone river valleys up into the heart of Francia. The route was punctuated by lucrative toll stations, starting with Fos itself which was a depot for goods collected for the king. The Corbie charter of 716 granted the monks 10,000 pounds of olive oil per year from the depot.

Various kings may have granted exemptions from tolls along this trade route, but no ruler ever surrendered the right to collect the tolls, for the southern trade was too important a source of cash and of expensive commodities to allow others to control it. By the time of the first Carolingian king (751) the situation had altered dramatically. Provence seems to have become much poorer and the flow of trade from south to north had reduced to a trickle. By 779, when Charlemagne confirmed a toll privilege for the Parisian monastery of St Germain-des-Prés, Marseilles was no longer mentioned as a place the monks might go to buy provision for lighting.[52] Previously it had been envisaged that monks would visit the port for this purpose, for olive oil (which came from the south, being either produced in Provence or imported into Marseilles) was the preferred fuel for the lamps which churches burned night and day.[53] Now, apparently, there was little oil to be had. Churches were increasingly turning to the use of wax candles, and Marseilles was no longer a favoured destination. The impoverishment of the south must be considered a part of a wider economic picture in which long-distance Mediterranean trade slowly declined over the period 400–800. Archaeologists and numismatists have indeed traced Marseilles's decline back into the seventh century, an early sign being the disappearance of a copper coinage from the city.[54] It nevertheless appears that Provence's

---

51 Above, ch. 3, n. 30.
52 *MGH Diplomata Karolinorum* I, ed. E. Mühlbacher (Hanover 1906), no. 122, pp. 170–2.
53 P. Fouracre, 'Eternal Light and Earthly Needs: Practical Aspects of the Development of Frankish Immunities', in W. Davies and P. Fouracre (eds), *Property and Power in the Early Middle Ages* (Cambridge 1995), pp. 68–72.
54 On the changing fortunes of Marseilles in the fifth and sixth centuries, see S. Loseby, 'Marseille: A Late Antique Success Story', *Journal of Roman Studies*, 82 (1992), 165–85.

trade, perhaps ailing but definitely still going in 716, was more or less killed off in the age of Charles Martel, and the reason was the political instability and military conflict brought about by the region's resistance to Charles and by the Saracen attacks which occurred at the same time.

It was reasoned in the last chapter that Antenor continued his revolt into the time of Charles Martel. In the late eighth century, Antenor's tenure of the patriciate of Provence was certainly remembered as a time of great upheaval. Our evidence for this consists of two charters concerned with the monastery of St Victor at Marseilles.[55] One of them is a fragment of a unique report from one of Charlemagne's agents, or *missus*, sent to Provence to inquire into the history of three properties which Maurontus, the bishop of Marseilles, claimed belonged to St Victor. The other charter is a version of a court hearing in Provence which similarly inquired into the ownership of one of these properties and judged the issue in St Victor's favour. Both documents date from about the year 780. They both say that during his revolt Antenor helped himself to St Victor's property and treated it as his own. In the court case he is even said to have asked to see all St Victor's charters and then to have ordered them to be burnt. The set of charters dealing with the property in question (Chaudol, near Digne) had been spirited away and saved, and Maurontus was able to produce a further document which showed that Charles Martel had ordered the property to be restored to St Victor. But then in 'the strife and struggles which there were in Provence', St Victor again lost the land, and then by mistake it was treated by Charlemagne as if it had been part of Antenor's own land which had been confiscated. Chaudol had, claimed Maurontus, belonged to St Victor, but first the *patricius* Metranus and then the *patricius* Abbo had leased it out (or 'given it in benefice'). This is a very brief synopsis of the first part of a highly complex case, and as Patrick Geary has argued, there is reason to think that Bishop Maurontus may have presented a distorted version of Chaudol's history in order to protect his own family's part in the 'strife and struggles', for he bears the same name as one of the chief protagonists in Provence a generation earlier.[56]

The other document is much simpler, though this may just be because less of it survives. The *missus* reported that according to the testimony of local freemen, when Antenor rebelled against Pippin, Charlemagne's great-grandfather, the *patricius* seized St Victor's property by force and then kept it as his own for as long as he lived as a rebel. But Charles Martel ordered

55 P. Geary, 'Die Provenz zur Zeit Karl Martells', in Jarnut, Nonn and Richter (eds), *Karl Martell in Seiner Zeit*, appendix, pp. 390–2.
56 Geary, 'Provenz', pp. 387–8.

the *patricius* Abbo to return the three properties to St Victor, and it was after Abbo's death that they were again lost when they were taken by one Arding, an Aleman, who gave them in benefice to his followers. There can be no doubt, therefore, that Antenor did seize church property during his patriciate, and that Provence continued in a state of disorder, despite Charles Martel's attempt to restore property to the church. We also learn that Charles's chief agent in the area was the *patricius* Abbo, who was well rewarded for his efforts, but that the process of giving church land to followers was actually more marked in the generation after Charles Martel. We are thus afforded a rare glimpse of Charles as restorer, rather than despoiler, of church land.

Abbo's will survives in a later copy, and this document tells us more about who he was and how he was rewarded for supporting Charles Martel.[57] As we have just seen, Charles Martel invaded Provence in 735. No doubt he received help from Abbo. There was, however, another leader in Provence, Maurontus, who continued to resist. Maurontus was a *dux* (duke), not a *patricius* or *rector*, and it has been reasoned that he came from outside the region, possibly being a Burgundian leader who had retreated to the far south in the face of Charles's advance.[58] According to the *Continuations of Fredegar*, Maurontus, like Eudo in 732, invited the Arabs to help him against, Charles. This time it seems likely that the Continuator was not making up this detail in order to vilify a rival leader, for the more neutral *Chronicle of Moissac* confirms that the Arab leader Jusuf ibn 'Abd ar-Rahman moved from Arab-held Septimania into Provence and peacefully entered the city of Avignon.[59] Charles Martel's reaction was to send an army south under his half-brother, Duke Childebrand, in 736. This is the first time we hear of this brother, and we know remarkably little about him, except that it was Childebrand who commissioned the first *Continuation of Fredegar*.[60]

Not surprisingly, the source devotes more space to this campaign in Provence than to any other single episode in the age of Charles Martel. From it we learn that Maurontus had allies other than the Arabs. Childebrand was accompanied by fellow dukes and counts. He prepared for a siege of Avignon and held the field until Charles Martel himself arrived and led a storming of the city. It is in the Continuator's description of the fall of Avignon that Charles Martel was compared to the Old Testament hero Joshua.[61]

---

57 Abbo's will is edited, translated and discussed in detail in P. Geary, *Aristocracy in Provence: The Rhône Basin at the Dawn of the Carolingian Age* (Stuttgart 1985).

58 Geary, *Aristocracy*, pp. 127–8.

59 *Chronicon Moissiacense*, p. 292.

60 *Fred. Contin.*, ch. 20, p. 94: Charles sent '*germanum suum virum inlustrium Childebrando ducem*' to Avignon. For Childebrand and the writing of the *Continuations*, ch. 34, pp. 102–3.

61 See above, Introduction, p. 2.

After taking Avignon the army crossed the Rhône, moved into Septimania and besieged Narbonne, thereby outflanking 'Abd ar-Rahman. When the Arabs sent a relieving army up from Spain, the Franks fought them at the mouth of the River Berre (in the Département of Aude) and won a resounding victory, pursuing the fleeing Arabs into the nearby sea-lagoons, taking much booty and many prisoners. They then ravaged the area, razing the cities of Nîmes, Agde and Béziers, before returning to the land of the Franks. In the early Carolingian annals all this is reduced to a single sentence: 'Charles fought against the Saracens in Gothia (Septimania), on the lord's day'. One must wonder whether other campaigns, for which similarly laconic references in the annals are our only source, were equally extensive. Despite these successes of Childebrand and Charles, a second expedition was needed that year to regain control of Provence, for the Arabs had returned. This time Maurontus was driven to seek refuge 'in impenetrable places, highly defended by rocks and fortified by the sea'.[62] From Paul the Deacon we learn that Lombard help was sought and given, and that when the Arabs perceived this, they fled.[63] Provence had finally been beaten into submission, but as the charters we discussed earlier indicate, things were still unsettled there in the next generation, and if the Bishop Maurontus of the charters was a descendant of the rebel Maurontus last seen clinging on in a coastal fastness, this suggests that there was finally some sort of political settlement with the rebel families in Provence.

Abbo's will was drawn up in the year 739 and casts further light on the situation in the 730s. Abbo was the son of a couple named Felix and Rustica, and in 726 he founded the monastery of Novalesa in the Susa valley. In Novalesa's foundation charter Abbo was termed *rector* of Susa and Maurienne. It is very likely that he was the same person as the Abbo *patricius*, to whom the charters of 780 referred, and he may have been identical with an Abbo who appears as a follower of Charles Martel in the charter of 723 in which land was granted to the church of Utrecht. It seems eminently reasonable to suppose that he was *rector* in 726 and was, as it were, promoted to *patricius* following the help he gave Charles Martel in the conquest of Provence.[64] As leader of the Susa–Maurienne region, Abbo controlled a vital trans-Alpine route into Italy. His will shows that he had inherited and by other means acquired a massive chain of estates which stretched from southern Burgundy down the Rhône valley to Marseilles,

---

62 *Fred. Contin.*, ch. 21, p. 96. Wallace-Hadrill assumed that the Continuator here meant that Maurontus had taken refuge on an island, but the Latin does not actually say this. The source does not mention the Arabs in this campaign.

63 Paul the Deacon, *Historia Langobardorum*, VI, ch. 54, p. 237.

64 Geary, *Aristocracy*, pp. 34–55.

and across to the Susa and Aosta valleys on the border with Lombardy. His family connections were wide, and on his mother's side the names of his more distant relatives suggest ties with Austrasia, possibly even with Dodo, who was said to have been Alpaida's brother.[65] It is therefore conceivable that Abbo was a distant relative of Charles Martel himself. His father's family, on the other hand, seems to have been native to the Alpine region of Burgundy. Abbo's lands were a typical patchwork of small units, and his will shows the familiar process of exchanging, buying and acquiring units in a way that attempted to rationalise the whole pattern. One striking difference with other wills and charters, however, is a preponderance of properties in the hands of freedmen who were pastoral farmers, a feature which reflects the nature of the agrarian economy of the Provençal and Alpine regions where there was relatively little arable land. We get a similar picture from an early-ninth-century inventory of the estates of St Victor, Marseilles,[66] and it reminds us that once Provence had lost its lucrative Mediterranean trade, it was thrown back on a rather poor agrarian hinterland.

Abbo's will tells us of several properties he acquired via confiscation from rebels. Among these rebels was a *clericus* called Maurengus. His name suggests he might have been related to Maurontus, and if he is the same person as Abbot Maorongos who attested Novalesa's foundation charter in 726, we might conclude that he had lost his position as well as land for his part in the revolt. The other rebels were Riculf, Rodbald and Rodurf, who were members of the same family. In the case of Riculf's lands in the *pagus* (counties) of Die, Gap and Grenoble, the will says that they were confiscated by the order of King Theuderic and Charles Martel because Riculf 'associated himself with the people of the Saracens in infidelity against the kingdom of the Franks, and did many evil things with this pagan people'.[67] From this we can see that it was not just Maurontus who allied with the Arabs. It is also the case that Charles Martel must have confiscated these lands very soon after he had put down the first revolt, for Theuderic died in 737.

In an extensive study of Abbo's will, Patrick Geary has argued that the confiscations show that the revolt cannot be interpreted as 'Roman' resistance to Frankish expansion, for the rebels seem to have been no less Frankish than the invaders. In Geary's view, Provence was the theatre for a last stand of the Neustro-Burgundian aristocracy against Charles Martel. Maurontus, he argues (albeit on sometimes tenuous circumstantial evidence), was actually related to the old Neustrian mayoral family of Waratto. At the same time

---

65 Geary, *Aristocracy*, p. 116.
66 *Descriptio Mancipiorum Ecclesie Massiliensis*, ed. B. Guérard, *Cartulaire de l'Abbaye de Saint-Victor de Marseille*, II (Paris 1857), pp. 633–54.
67 Geary, *Aristocracy*, trans. p. 77.

there was a settling of scores between different families resident in the area and this exacerbated the disorder. That disorder was sufficiently widespread to threaten social stability is suggested by another passage in Abbo's will. It reads: 'since these provinces were desolated and destroyed by the people of the Saracens both our freedpersons and our male and female servants were dispersed by necessity through many neighbouring places'.[68] The will gave the agents of the monastery of Novalesa the permission to round up these people and to bring them back to servitude. Abbo's will is, therefore, an important document because it shows that even in a distant region such as Provence, family connections with the rest of Francia, and the local dynamic of competition for power, meant that Charles Martel could find allies and could recruit local leaders to his cause, although as the will also shows, these allies would expect substantial rewards. Let us now turn to southern Germany, where, as Geary argues, the situation was not dissimilar.

Southern Germany

Southern Germany, that is, Bavaria, Alemannia and Alsace, was ruled by leaders who were in theory officers of the Merovingian king. As in Provence, families of Frankish origin had intermarried with descendants of the late Roman leaders, and the population was similarly of mixed descent. One family in particular struck Geary as being very like that of Abbo of Provence. This was the so-called 'Victoriden' family who dominated the area of Chur in Rhaetia (south-east Switzerland).[69] Like Abbo's family, the Victoriden were important as controllers of an Alpine border region. That they continued to be prominent under the early Carolingians suggests that they became supporters of Charles Martel. Southern Germany, though, was in other respects very different from Provence. Though it had a substantial Romance-speaking population, even in areas such as Salzburg, this cultural element seems to have been on the retreat, at least in the eastern part of the region. Unlike Provence, southern Germany had no major urban centres. It had no mints and coinage was scarce. There were very few monasteries there before the eighth century, and even fewer bishops. Unlike the rest of Francia, Bavaria and Alemannia were not divided up into counties, or *pagus*, and there were few counts in the region.[70]

---

68 Geary, *Aristocracy*, trans. p. 77.
69 Geary, *Aristocracy*, pp. 120–2.
70 M. Borgolte, *Geschichte der Grafschaften Alemanniens in fränkishe Zeit*, Vorträge und Forschungen, 31 (Sigmaringen 1984), pp. 27–32.

In these peripheral areas the dukes seem to have exercised quasi-regal powers, but, in principle, if not in practice, they looked to the Merovingian kings to guarantee their privileges. According to the seventh-century law of the Bavarians, Bavaria can could be ruled only by members of the Agilolfing family, who had been made dukes by the Merovingians.[71] Bavarian law also named five other leading families who were subordinate to the dukes but set above all other Bavarians. Two of these families appear later as local leaders. Of the other three we know nothing.

The general impression is that in terms of economic development, political institutions, ecclesiastical organisation, and the structure of the nobility, Bavaria and Alemannia lagged behind the other regions of Francia, including Alsace. But an equally strong impression is that they were catching up fast. It is, of course, quite possible that these impressions are false, because we have so little evidence from seventh-century southern Germany that what appears to be new or changing in the eighth century could have been features of an earlier period about which we are simply ignorant. A case in point here is the apparent spread of charters in eighth-century Alemannia, which is associated with the development of monastic landholding, the forms of which were quickly adopted by laymen too. In Duke Lantfrid's recension of the law of the Alemans, drawn up probably in the 720s, laymen who held land from the church were required to have a charter to show the nature of their holding.[72] But the charters themselves, including large numbers of originals from the monastery of St Gallen, suggest that there was nothing new in making a written record of landholding and of land transactions. The form of the charters owes so much to the later Roman bureaucratic traditions of Rhaetia that we must consider it a possibility that these kinds of document had been in continuous use since Roman times.[73] And if they had been, it might follow that Aleman society in the seventh century was both more literate and more bureaucratically organised than we would otherwise have supposed. On the other hand, if large numbers of charters were produced in this earlier period, it is hard to explain why there is no trace of them.

One explanation could be that late Roman bureaucratic traditions had indeed been conserved in Rhaetia, but that they were adopted in other regions only when monasteries there began to build up their lands and

---

71 *Leges Baiwariorum*, ed. E. de Schwind, *MGH Legum*, sectio I, 5 (Hanover 1888), iii, 1, pp. 312–13.

72 *Leges Alamannorum*, ed. K. Lehman, *MGH Legum*, sectio I, 5, i–ii, pp. 63–7, xvi–xviii, pp. 79–81, xlii, p. 103.

73 This is the argument of R. McKitterick, *The Carolingians and the Written Word* (Cambridge 1989), pp. 81–3. See also Borgolte, *Grafschaften*, p. 32.

influence in the eighth century. We can see this process more clearly in the region of Hesse in central Germany, where we can be more certain that there was no charter tradition prior to the foundation of the monastery of Fulda in the year 744. Within a decade of its foundation, Fulda and the local nobility were recording their property ownership and property trans-actions in charters, and their charters are essentially identical to those pro-duced in areas which did have a much older tradition of written records. In other words, the use of charter forms which had their origins in late Roman bureaucratic tradition does not necessarily indicate the survival of that tradi-tion in the particular areas in which the charters were produced. The point is that the use of charters spread rapidly in areas when and where monasteries were newly founded and where the nobility soon emulated, and imitated, the church by securing its own property by charter. If we accept the view that in eighth-century southern Germany the use of charters was indeed spreading in this way (as opposed to the view that the charters were in widespread use in an earlier period, but have not survived), then this is one important reason for thinking that the church and the nobility in the region were in the process of coming to resemble their counterparts elsewhere.

Place-name evidence from across the region, which is available from the later seventh century onwards, shows a significant number of personal place-names. In a few cases people who gave their name to a settlement appear in charters: an example is Poapintal, modern Pfaffhofen in the Tyrol. It was called after Poapo, who founded the monastery of Scharnitz in the Tyrol, and whom we know from the charters of this monastery.[74] Poapo was in fact a Huosi, a member of one of the five superior families mentioned in the law of the Bavarians, and one of the few Huosi we can trace into the Carolingian period. The spread of place-names with a personal element has been taken to indicate the growing landed power of the nobility, and it tallies with archaeological evidence which shows the development of settle-ments grouped around a church, with a few graves set apart from the rest of the community.[75] These separate graves, it is reasoned, are those of the

74 F. Prinz, 'Frühes Mönchtum in Südwestdeutschland und die Anfänge der Reichenau', in A. Borst (ed.), *Mönchtum Episkopat und Adel zur Gründungszeit des Klosters Reichenau*, Vorträge und Forschungen, 20 (Sigmaringen 1974), pp. 37–76, at p. 42 and n. 21.
75 Prinz, 'Frühes Mönchtum in Südwestdeutschland', pp. 40–6; J. Jahn, *Ducatus Baiwariorum. Das Bairische Herzogtum des Agilolfinger*, Monographien zur Geschichte des Mittelalters, 35 (Stuttgart 1991), pp. 35–40; H. Steuer, 'Archäologie und die Erforschung des germanischen Sozialgeschichte', in D. Simon (ed.), *Akten des 26 Deutschen Rechtshistorikertages*, Studien zur Europäischen Rechtsgeschichtes, 30 (Frankfurt 1987), pp. 443–53, at pp. 446–50; F. Damminger, 'Dwellings, Settlements and Settlement Patterns in Merovingian Southwest Germany and Adjacent Areas', in I. Wood (ed.), *Franks and Alemanni in the Merovingian Period. An Ethnographic Perspective* (Woodbridge 1998), pp. 33–89, esp. pp. 56–71.

local lord's family who may have founded the church and who dominated the settlement, in some cases giving their name to it.

There is, one must repeat, very little evidence from pre-Carolingian southern Germany, and hardly enough to support generalisations about changes in settlement patterns and the development of landlordship, but what little evidence there is, from archaeology, place-names and charters, all seems to point in the same direction: towards noble power based on land, on the control of churches and monasteries, and on service to the dukes. Charters from the mid-eighth century onwards show these nobles consolidating their power by acquiring the right to pass their land on to chosen heirs, rather than dividing it among all the family. We also see the familiar shuffling of holdings, through which families and churches tried to rationalise their dispersed portions of land. Interestingly, in late-eighth-century Bavaria, that is, from the time we first have a decent amount of charter evidence, sales were more common than exchanges as the medium through which land changed hands, although, as we have just seen, there was very little coinage in the region, with land being paid for in kind rather than cash.[76] One explanation for the prevalence of sales might be that some nobles were forced to liquidate their landed assets in order to meet increasing charges and military obligations laid upon them first by the Agilolfings and then by the Carolingians.

From the time of Duke Odilo of Bavaria (736 onwards) we see the political impact of this better-organised and better-resourced nobility. Those serving the duke were given the right to pass fiscal (or 'ducal') land on to their descendants; when Boniface sought to reform the Bavarian church in the later 730s this was with the permission of the leading nobles (*optimates*) as well as that of the duke; nobles (not just the five leading families) seem now to have been recognised as a separate legal group; and finally, in 740 Odilo was driven out of Bavaria in what looks like a revolt against Agilolfing power and Frankish interference. After his return to power in 741, Odilo may have been in a weaker position *vis-à-vis* his nobles. The terms *nobiles*, *iudices* and *comites* appear more frequently after 741, and after the Frankish suppression of the Agilolfing dukedom in 787–88, Bavaria was finally divided up into counties.[77] That is to say, by the time southern Germany was integrated into the Frankish empire, its social structure and ecclesiastical organisation had become very similar to that of the regions west of the Rhine. This cultural assimilation was indeed a precondition for the Frankish

---

76 C. Hammer, 'Land Sales in Eighth- and Ninth-Century Bavaria: Legal, Social and Economic Aspects', *Early Medieval Europe*, 6 (1997), 47–76.

77 Jahn, *Ducatus*, pp. 224–54.

take-over. The late-eighth-century *Royal Frankish Annals* is a work which expresses a strongly pro-Carolingian point of view, but its author may not have been simply indulging in wishful thinking when he or she said that in 787 the Bavarians abandoned their duke, Tassilo, preferring to be ruled by the Carolingian king. Some of the Bavarian nobles might have thought that they would have more prospects of power and reward under a Carolingian rather than an Agilolfing regime. As we have seen, at least one of the old families, the Huosi, apparently continued to prosper under Carolingian rule, so it is reasonable to think that they were among those who switched their allegiance to the Carolingians in 787.

As has already been stated, the growth of the church was an important aspect of southern Germany's development in the early eighth century. King Dagobert I (629–39) was said to have begun the organisation of Alemannia and Bavaria into bishoprics, and there had always been bishops in Chur, but, despite these early beginnings, Bavaria of the mid to late seventh century seems to have been a land without bishops, although it had plenty of smaller churches. It was under Duke Theodo that the church began to be reorganised. In the late seventh century three missionary bishops came to Bavaria. One of them, Rupert of Worms, we have already met as a refugee from the Pippinids.[78] He was of Agilolfing stock and after arriving in the duchy in 696 was given sweeping powers to organise the church in eastern Bavaria. This he did by setting up an ecclesiastical centre at Salzburg.[79] As we know, Rupert returned to Austrasia after the death of Pippin in 714. The other two missionaries were Emmeram, who came from Poitiers and was active in the ducal centre of Regensburg, and Corbinian, said in his 'Life' to be from Melun in Neustria, who organised the church around Freising. This is not the place to go into the fascinating details of these missionary careers, but it is important to note that though each missionary worked independently, and two of them came into conflict with the Agilolfings, their work had the combined effect of reinforcing the dukes' powers. The first Bavarian monasteries were in effect under ducal control, and the importance of the ducal strongholds of Salzburg, Regensburg and Freising was heightened when they became prestigious ecclesiastical centres too. The memory of Rupert, Emmeram and Corbinian would also feed an anti-Carolingian sentiment in Bavaria, in the view that the duchy had created its own church rather than had church organisation imposed upon it by the Carolingians. In the works of Arbeo of Freising, who wrote the 'Lives' of

---

78   Above, ch. 3, p. 67.
79   H. Wolfram, *Die Geburt Mitteleuropas. Geschichte Österreichs vor seiner Entstehung* (Vienna 1987), pp. 122–4.

Emmeram and Corbinian in the later eighth century, we get what is a kind of counter-Carolingian picture of missionary activity, one which ignores the work of Boniface and the other Anglo-Saxon missionaries who were the Carolingians' heroes.[80]

In 715 or 716 Duke Theodo travelled to Rome. He was, according to the *Liber Pontificalis*, the first Bavarian ever to visit the pope. What Theodo wanted was Rome's backing for an independent Bavarian church, and this he effectively got. That he should visit Rome in 715–16 has been taken to mean that he took advantage of the strife in Francia to make his bid for independence. But a more likely reason is that it was the violent death of the missionary Emmeram which prompted his journey.[81] Emmeram had been accused of making Theodo's daughter Ota pregnant. Her enraged brother mutilated Emmeram and left him at a crossroads to die, a customary punishment for adultery.[82] Theodo may thus have wished to gain forgiveness for this act. In 715 he was already old, and since he died soon after his return from Rome, it may also be that Theodo simply wished to make a pilgrimage to Rome before he died.

The Agilolfings had been in close contact with the Lombards since the latter's arrival in Italy. One Lombard king was called Agilulf, and he was married to a Bavarian, Theudelinda. Their daughter Gundeberga would also become a queen, and a kingmaker.[83] At the end of the seventh century these contacts were reinforced as the deposed Lombard king Ansprand and his son Liutprand sought refuge with the Agilolfings in Bavaria. In 712 Ansprand and Liutprand returned to Italy with Bavarian troops and re-gained the throne. When Liutprand followed Ansprand as king, he became one of the most successful rulers the Lombards ever had. His alliance with the Agilolfings was further strengthened when he married the daughter of Theotbert, Theodo's son. Later he would intervene in conflict in Bavaria by supporting Theotbert's son Hugbert.[84] Papal interest in the Bavarian church was no doubt stimulated by the Agilolfings' close ties to Liutprand and the Lombards, whom the popes saw as a great threat. And the same ties must have influenced Charles Martel's desire to build up his own alliance with Liutprand. This would culminate with the adoption of Charles's son Pippin by Liutprand in 737. One can see why affairs in Bavaria were of

80 Arbeo, *Vitae Sanctorum Haimhrammi et Corbiniani*, ed. B. Krusch, *MGH SRG* (Hanover 1920). On Arbeo's view of the Bavarian mission, Jahn, *Ducatus*, pp. 69–73 and I. Wood, *The Merovingian Kingdoms* (London 1994), pp. 307–9.
81 Wolfram, *Die Geburt Mitteleuropas*, p. 121.
82 Arbeo, *Vita Haimhrammi*, chs 15–18, pp. 47–53; Jahn, *Ducatus*, pp. 41–8.
83 *Fredegar*, chs 34, 51, 70–1, pp. 22, 41–3, 59–60.
84 Paul the Deacon, *Historia Langobardorum*, VI, chs 35, 43, pp. 227–8, 232.

such great concern to the Carolingians, for the dukes of Bavaria were becoming increasingly powerful. Not only did they now have influence in Lombardy and Rome, they had also built up their military power in the face of Slav and Avar incursions from the East. And, remember, the Agilolfings had a long history of opposition to the growth of Pippinid power.

The ducal family of Alemannia was related to the Agilolfings, and so too possibly were the Etichonids, the family who ruled Alsace, although this latter relationship is inferred only on the basis of similar family names. As we have already seen, Charles Martel's father Pippin had directed four campaigns against the Alemans (or 'Sueves') in the years 709–12.[85] It seems that on the death of Duke Gottfried in 709 there was conflict between his sons, and that the Franks intervened to support Lantfrid against his brother Willeharius. There were possibly four other brothers too: Liutfrid, Theudebald, Huoching and Odilo, the latter becoming Duke of Bavaria in 736, and in 741 marrying Charles Martel's daughter. Huoching was, according to later tradition, the great-grandfather of Hildegarde, Charlemagne's wife.[86] Relations between Lantfrid and Charles Martel seem initially to have been good, at least up to 725 when Charles passed through Alemannia on his way to campaign in Bavaria.[87]

In 719 the monastery of St Gallen was refounded. Otmar, the new abbot of St Gallen, and Waltram, the monastery's leading patron, travelled to the royal court to seek protection for their institution.[88] This they did with the permission of 'Duke' Nebbi, Huoching's son. Then in 724 when the monastery of Reichenau was founded, its abbot Pirmin received a gift of land from the king, Theuderic IV, and a letter of protection from Charles Martel. The two documents which granted these benefits have long been known as forgeries, but careful analysis has shown that they incorporate parts of genuine originals.[89] The historian Friedrich Prinz refused to believe that King Theuderic and Charles Martel could possibly have had any influence in Alemannia at this time, and on this basis he argued that the two documents

---

85 Above, ch. 2, pp. 51–2.

86 J. Jarnut, 'Untersuchungen zu den fränkisch-alemmanische Beziehungen in der ersten Hälfte des 8 Jahrhunderts', *Schweizerische Zeitschrift für Geschichte*, 30 (1980), 9–24. The Hildegarde tradition comes from Thegan, *Gesta Hludowici Imperatoris*, ed. G. Pertz, *MHG SS* II, pp. 585–605. This work was written in 837.

87 *Fred. Contin.*, ch. 12, p. 90. Wallace-Hadrill's translation suggests that Charles 'punished' the Alemans, but the Latin says simply that 'he traversed them' (*lustrat*) on the way to the Danube.

88 *Vita Galli, auctore Walafrido*, ed. B. Krusch, *MGH SRM* IV, II, ch. 10, p. 319.

89 I. Heidrich, 'Die Gründungsausstatung der elsässischen Klöster St Gallen und Reichenau in der ersten Hälfte des 8 Jahrhunderts', in P. Classen (ed.), *Die Gründungsurkunden der Reichenau*, Vorträge und Forschungen, 24 (Sigmaringen 1977), pp. 31–62.

were simple forgeries which could bear no relationship to the reality of power in the region. In Prinz's view the missionary bishop and abbot, Pirmin, was no doubt an anti-Martel figure, possibly linked with the Agilolfings, who, like Rupert in Bavaria, was as much refugee as missionary.[90]

This way of thinking divides all the Frankish world into two camps: pro- and anti-Charles Martel. Pirmin's career, however, cut across these party lines. He was, it seems, a genuinely neutral figure. And between any pro- and anti-Carolingian factions there still stood the figure of the Merovingian king. Theuderic IV may look to us now as if he were simply Charles Martel's mouthpiece, but he was a legitimate Merovingian and still viewed as a source of wealth and authority. When Duke Lantfrid issued a version of the Aleman laws at roughly this time, he stressed the ultimate authority of the king, as leader of the army and as having the decision over who should be duke. We can likewise see the ducal family of Alsace, the Etichonids, peti- tioning Theuderic for privileges for their monasteries.[91] Again, Pirmin was involved. It has been argued that the Etichonids were seeking to build up their own influence by founding new monasteries, and by having the king, rather than Charles Martel, guarantee their privileges and independence.

Pirmin went to Alsace in 727 having been expelled from Alemannia, 'because of the hatred of Charles'. Prinz took this to mean that he was expelled because Charles hated him,[92] but read in context this phrase, which comes from the much later *Chronicle of Hermann the Lame*, can only mean that it was because of the duke's hatred for Charles that Pirmin was driven out. In other words, the alliance between Lantfrid and Charles was over. It was perhaps now that Lantfrid issued his new version of the Aleman laws. In 730 Charles attacked Lantfrid, who died in the same year. He was succeeded by his brother Theudebald. In 734, according to Hermann the Lame, 'because of hatred for Charles', Theudebald expelled Eto, Pirmin's successor as abbot of Reichenau. In the same year Theudebald was driven out, and Charles reinstated Eto.[93] This, in effect, marked the end of the Aleman ducal line. When Charles Martel divided the Frankish kingdoms

---

90 Prinz, 'Frühes Mönchtum in Südwestdeutschland', pp. 57–60. The mid-ninth-century *Vita Pirmini*, ed. O. Holder-Egger, *MGH SS* XVi, ch. 1, pp. 21–2, says that Pirmin came from Meaux, near Paris.

91 Heidrich, 'St Gallen und Reichenau', pp. 40–1.

92 Prinz, 'Frühes Mönchtum in Südwestdeutschland', p. 70. He admits that his interpretation is the *lectio difficilior*.

93 *Chronicon Herimanni Augiensis*, ed. G. Pertz, *MGH SS* V (Hanover 1844), s.a. 732, p. 98. Eto was driven out *a Theudebaldo ob odium Karoli*. There can be no doubt that it was Theudebald who hated Charles. Since the author a few lines earlier used the same phrase for Pirmin's expulsion, it seems impossible to construe this as a result of Charles's hatred for Pirmin.

between his sons prior to his death in 741, Alemannia was included in the division, along with Neustria, Austrasia, Burgundy and Provence. It was, in other words, his to give away. Theudebald would in fact return to Alemannia as soon as Charles died, but as we shall see in the last chapter, a final Aleman stand against the Carolingians would end in disaster.

Alsace also lost its status as a dukedom in the age of Charles Martel. Nearly all we know about Alsace in this period comes from the charters in which the Etichonid family made donations to the monasteries of Honau, Murbach and Wissembourg. Honau, just north of Strasbourg, had been founded by Duke Adalbert sometime before 722. In a fragment of a charter in which Adalbert donated land to Honau in 722, we learn that the act of donation was drawn up in Strasbourg in the royal palace (*curtis regia*) 'which was in the new suburb of the town which I [Adalbert] built as a new work'. This interesting snippet of information tells us that Strasbourg was expanding in the early eighth century, which is very rare for a town in this period. It seems likely that increasing traffic on the River Rhine was the cause of its expansion, and the placing of a royal palace in the new suburb suggests that the king and his mayor sought to profit from the growing trade.[94] In the documents of this time Adalbert's son Eberhard was termed *domesticus*, that is, the officer responsible for the royal fisc, which indicates that he was active on behalf of the Merovingian regime. By 723 Adalbert was dead, and another son, Liutfrid, appears as duke. Eberhard went on to found the monastery of Murbach in the Vosges. This he did with the help of Pirmin, recently expelled from Alemannia. Then sometime after 735 Eberhard separated from his wife Himiltrude and entered the monastery of Remiremont, with Himiltrude probably joining the convent there. In a charter which injects a note of personal sadness into the usually dry formulae of land grants, Eberhard said that having lost his only son, and having become blind, he wished to retreat from the world. In this donation, Eberhard gave the rest of his worldly goods to Murbach, a monastery which he had already richly endowed.[95] We last see Duke Liutfrid in a document of 739. Thereafter there were no more dukes of Alsace, and the Etichonid family monasteries passed into the hands of the Carolingians.[96] Since no mention is ever made of a son of Liutfrid, it seems that the Etichonid line of dukes simply died out, allowing the Carolingians and their allies to step into their shoes unopposed. Some people bearing Etichonid names do appear among the nobility of Alsace in the late eighth and ninth centuries, but it is clear that like the

---

94 C. Wilsdorf, 'Le Monasterium Scottorum de Honau et la Famille des Ducs d'Alsace à VIIe Siècle. Vestiges d'un Cartulaire Perdu', *Francia*, 3 (1975), 1–87, at 58–9.

95 Pardessus, *Diplomata, Chartae*, no. 544, pp. 355–7.

96 Wilsdorf, 'Honau', 69–72.

old Neustrian families a generation earlier, they had been forced out of the leading positions in their region.

Charles Martel failed to extinguish the dukedom of Bavaria as he had that of Alemannia. As we have just seen, the Agilolfing dukes were, if anything, growing stronger in the age of Charles Martel. Another factor in Agilolfing–Carolingian relations was the fact that two families became entwined with each other, which meant that Bavaria was not just a rival in military and strategic terms, but also a possible magnet for dissaffected members of the Carolingian family itself. When looking at the background to Charles Martel's career we noted that one of Plectrude's sisters, Regentrude, may have married the Bavarian duke Theodo.[97] The evidence for this marriage is late, but according to Arbeo's *Life of Corbinian*, a work of the later eighth century, a certain Frankish lady Regintrude did come to Bavaria along with one Pilitrude who may have been her daughter. The name Pilitrude is quite close to 'Plectrude', and Theodo's sons, Hugbert and Grimoald, bore the names of Plectrude's father and son, so it does seem reasonable to suggest that Regintrude married Theodo. Pilitrude cannot, however, have been his daughter, because after his death she in turn married his sons Theudoald and Grimoald. Arbeo tells us that Corbinian condemned this last marriage, and prophesied Grimoald's downfall. First, says Arbeo, Pilitrude sent a witch to kill Grimoald's son, and then Grimoald was himself murdered.[98] Pilitrude was clearly a very important lady. She had a niece called Swanahild (or 'Sunnichild' in the *Continuations of Fredegar*). Swanahild was also said to be the niece of Hugbert of Bavaria, and of Odilo who later became duke of Bavaria.[99] Given that Odilo was probably a son of Gottfried, duke of the Alemans, Swanahild's ancestry gave her links with the Bavarian and Aleman ducal families, and with the family of Plectrude. From Charles Martel's point of view she might in theory be the linchpin of a nightmarish alliance against him. One way to neutralise this threat, and at the same time to gain more influence in southern Germany, would be for Charles to marry Swanahild.

Strife in Bavaria after the death of Theodo in 717 or 718 gave Charles Martel the opportunity to intervene there, rather as conflict after the death of Gottfried had given Pippin an entry into Alemannia a decade earlier. In Bavaria there was a struggle for power between Theodo's son Grimoald, and Grimoald's nephew Hugbert. After Grimoald's murder in 725, Charles Martel invaded in support of Hugbert, and it was on this campaign that

---

97 Above, ch. 2, p. 44.
98 Arbeo, *Vita Corbiniani*, chs 24–31, pp. 215–24.
99 J. Jarnut, 'Untersuchungen zur Herkunft Swanahilds, der Gattin Karl Martells', *Zeitschrift für bayerische Landesgeschichte*, 40 (1977), 254–9.

Charles passed through Alemannia. Hugbert received support too from the Lombard king, Liutprand. Also in 725 Charles Martel's first wife Chrotrude died, the notice of her death in the early Carolingian annals being the only reference we have to her. According to the *Continuations of Fredegar*, Charles conquered Bavaria, took from it much treasure and then returned home taking with him Pilitrude and her niece Swanahild.[100] Swanahild then became his second wife. Whether Chrotrude was already dead before he set out for Bavaria, or whether the capture of Swanahild was incidental or actually an objective of the campaign, we have no way of knowing, but the result of these events is clear: Charles's forging of family links with the Agilolfings, and at the same time his forcing of the duke into a degree of dependence upon the Franks, meant that Bavaria was neutered as a rival, at least for the time being.

In 728 we have a reference to another campaign in Bavaria, but since it comes from the typically laconic early Carolingian annals, we cannot say what was going on here. The next reference to Bavaria is the *Earlier Annals of Metz*, which tell us that upon Hugbert's death in 735 or 736, Odilo was made duke, with the permission of Charles.[101] This phrase echoes the statement that Hunoald was made duke of Aquitaine with Charles's permission and, as in Hunoald's case, it prepares the way for a later portrayal of Odilo as disloyal and lacking in due gratitude to the Carolingians. How, exactly, Odilo became duke of Bavaria we cannot tell, but it does seem likely that the Bavarian branch of the Agilolfings had died out with Hugbert and that the Bavarian law's requirement that the duke be from this family was satisfied by bringing in an Agilolfing from Alemannia. Odilo nevertheless seems to have needed Charles Martel's support.

In 739 the Anglo-Saxon missionary bishop Boniface came to Bavaria, in which he had long had an interest. Two letters from Pope Gregory III tell of how Boniface was to reorganise the Bavarian church into four dioceses based on Freising, Passau, Regensburg and Salzburg.[102] This he did, consecrating new bishops for all the sees except Passau, where the existing bishop, Vivilo, had already been consecrated by the pope. We shall return in the next chapter to Boniface and his attitude towards the Bavarian church when we consider Boniface's career in the age of Charles Martel. It has been argued that this reorganisation of the Bavarian church, which essentially put into effect those plans for an independent church tied to Rome which Theodo had first discussed in Rome in 715–16, was an anti-Frankish

---

100   *Fred. Contin.*, ch. 12, p. 90.
101   *AMP*, ed. von Simson, *MGH SRG*, p. 33.
102   *Bonifatii Epistolae*, no. 45, trans. E. Emerton, *The Letters of St Boniface* (New York 1940) pp. 72–4.

move.[103] But since it was done with Odilo's approval, and since the next year Odilo took refuge with Charles Martel, this seems unlikely. This is another case in which it seems simplistic to categorise developments in southern Germany as either pro- or anti-Carolingian. The reasons for Odilo's expulsion from Bavaria in 740 are nowhere stated, but it is usually supposed that being an outsider, and having been installed by Charles Martel, resentment may have been building up against him from the outset. Yet again, this is guesswork. We do know, however, that while at the Frankish court, Odilo formed a relationship with Charles Martel's daughter Hiltrude. Around the time of Charles's death (22 October 741) Odilo returned to Bavaria, and shortly after that Swanahild encouraged Hiltrude to run off and join him there. She may already have been pregnant by Odilo when she left Francia. This scandal would send a shiver down the spines of Carolingian writers for generations to come. One reason it was so shocking was that Odilo then fought against Hiltrude's brothers Karlomann and Pippin. Charles Martel's intervention in Bavaria thus had mixed results. Swanahild's capture and marriage had for the moment made Bavaria a much less dangerous place, but it also served to make it more, rather than less, hostile in the next generation, for one reason that Odilo turned against his brothers-in-law was that they had excluded their half-brother Gripho from power. Gripho was the son of Charles and Swanahild. Then in the next generation after this, Tassilo, the son of Odilo and Hiltrude, would become a dangerous rival to Charlemagne, the son of Pippin. Tassilo and Charlemagne were both grandsons of Charles Martel. Genetically, therefore, Tassilo was every bit as Carolingian as Charlemagne himself, but he had the added advantage of being an Agilolfing, the representative of a family which traditionally had derived its ducal status from a recognition of Merovingian authority. When the *Earlier Annals of Metz* said that Odilo had been made duke of Bavaria with Charles Martel's permission, the author was signalling that this tradition of authority had been broken, but the very determined and careful way in which Charlemagne eventually set about removing his cousin Tassilo suggests that it had not.

Central and northern Germany

Central and northern Germany are the areas we know least about in the age of Charles Martel, and again the reason for our ignorance is that there was no organised church in these regions. Central Germany, that is, Hesse

---

103   J. Wallace-Hadrill, *The Frankish Church* (Oxford 1983), pp. 153–4.

and Thuringia, is hardly mentioned at all in the Merovingian period, and with regard to the lands of the Saxons and Frisians in the north, our only references are to warfare with the Franks. We last looked at Thuringia when we discussed the revolt of Duke Radulf in 639–40.[104] Fredegar's narrative of this affair also provides one of the two references to the region of Hesse in the pre-Boniface period, in as much as he says that the forces sent to tackle Radulf marched across 'Buchonia' on their way to Thuringia.[105] The forest of Buchonia covered much of Hesse. The Radulf story shows Frankish power stretching far to the east beyond the forest of Buchonia and towards the River Saale, which formed the border between the Franks and the Slavs in Carolingian times. Radulf, we know, had a stronghold on the River Unstrut, but this is about all we can glean about the situation in the area, apart from the fact that Radulf was a military leader and involved in frequent conflict with the Slavonic Wends. We know too that there were strongholds in Hesse, at least at Würzburg and at the site which later became the monastery of Fulda. The whole region was nominally Christian. There are the remains of a seventh-century church at Fulda, and as we have seen, Duke Heden of Thuringia was a supporter of Willibrord who in 717 donated lands at Hammelburg in the Saale area for the foundation of a monastery. There were, however, no bishops in these regions, nor were there any mints, nor, apparently, counts. Throughout the Merovingian period, writers spoke of the population of the region as the 'peoples' beyond the Rhine. A letter from Pope Gregory II to the Anglo-Saxon missionary Boniface names eight of them.[106] One, the Borthari, we have probably already met, if they are the Boructuarii, whom Bede tells us were conquered by the Saxons in the early eighth century. Five of the others were the inhabitants of the different *Gaue* (districts) of central Germany, to some of which they gave their names. The other two 'peoples' were the Hessians and the Thuringians, who were probably larger groups.

In several ways central Germany resembles Saxony as we see it in the later eighth century. That is, the land seems to have been under the control of different 'peoples' whose leaders are rarely named. There were, apparently, no paramount leaders, and no reference to any leader having an 'office', apart from the dukes of Thuringia. We cannot tell whether the region had always been like this, or whether its apparent decentralisation

---

104 Above, ch. 2, pp. 35–7.
105 *Fredegar*, ch. 87, p. 73. The other reference relates to the reign of Clovis and it comes from Gregory of Tours, *Decem Libri Historiarum*, ed. B. Krusch and W. Levison, *MGH SRM* Ii (Hanover 1951), II, ch. 40, trans. L. Thorpe, *Gregory of Tours. The History of the Franks* (Harmondsworth 1974), p. 155.
106 *Bonifatii Epistolae*, no. 43, trans. Emerton, *Letters of St Boniface*, pp. 69–71.

was a later Merovingian development. There are, however, some hints that the situation was unstable in this period, and a likely cause of destabilisation was the advance of Saxons from the north and of Slavs from the east. As we have seen, one of the region's peoples, the Boructuarii, had fallen under Saxon control at the beginning of the eighth century. Eigil, in his *Life of Sturm*, the first abbot of Fulda, written in the later eighth century, emphasised how the Grabfeld region of northern Hesse was vulnerable to Saxon attack, and Einhard in his biography of Charlemagne spoke of a long history of border conflict in the region which was the precursor to all-out war between the Franks and the Saxons from 772 onwards.[107] At Fulda in the Grabfeld a stone building which had formed part of the Merovingian stronghold had been burned down around the year 700. It is possible that the burning took place in the context of Saxon raids. Eigil also speaks of a great crowd of Slavs in the region, and a charter of Charlemagne from the year 813 refers to mixed Frankish and Saxon settlement in the forest of Buchonia, with one (friendly) Saxon clearing forest land in the area.[108] This had taken place at least one generation earlier and was followed by the assertion of royal control over the land, which suggests that previously it had been under no overall control.

The Thuringians too seem to have been under pressure from the Saxons, although the history of the dukedom of Thuringia in the later seventh and early eighth century is almost impossible to reconstruct. According to the *Passio Kiliani*, an account of the career and murder of the Irish missionary bishop Kilian, which was written shortly before 840, there was a duke of Thuringia called Hruodi.[109] He was followed by his son Heden. His son was Duke Gozbert, and Gozbert's son Heden also became duke, possibly ruling alongside one Theotbald who is mentioned in the late-eighth-century *Life of St Boniface*. The name 'Hruodi' has been seen as a short form of 'Radulf', which would make the Heden family his descendants, although opinion on this is divided.[110] Alternatively, the Heden family have been seen as Austrasian

---

107 Eigil, *Vita Sturmi*, ed. G. Pertz, *MGH SS* II, pp. 366–77, ch. 5, p. 367, trans. C. Talbot, *The Anglo-Saxon Missionaries in Germany* (London 1954), pp. 181–202, at p. 183; Einhard, *The Life of Charlemagne*, ch. 7, ed. and trans. P. Dutton, *Charlemagne's Courtier. The Complete Einhard* (Ontario 1998), pp. 20–1.

108 Eigil, *Vita Sturmi*, ch. 7, p. 367, trans. Talbot, *Anglo-Saxon Missionaries*, p. 186. The charter is *MGH Diplomata Karolinorum*, no. 218, pp. 291–2.

109 *Passio Kiliani*, ed. W. Levison, *MGH SRM* V, pp. 722–8, ch. 3, p. 723.

110 W. Schlesinger, 'Das Frühmittelalter', in H. Patze and W. Schlesinger (eds), *Geschichte Thüringens I. Grundlagen und frühes Mittelalter. Mitteldeutsche Forschungen* 48, I (Cologne and Graz 1968), ch. 5, pp. 317–80. Schlesinger, p. 337, did not believe that the name 'Hruodi' could be a form of 'Radulf'. H. Mordek, 'Die Hedenen als politische Kraft im Austrasischen Frankenreich', in Jarnut, Nonn and Richter (eds), *Karl Martell in Seiner Zeit*, pp. 343–66, at p. 363 and n. 103 believes that it could be a form of 'Radulf'.

Franks sent to guard the Würzburg region from Radulf and his Slav allies further to the east.[111] It is certainly true that by the end of the seventh century Würzburg, rather than Radulf's stronghold on the River Unstrut, had become the ducal residence.

In a story which bears a suspiciously strong resemblance to that told about Corbinian in Bavaria, Kilian is said to have converted Duke Gozbert to Christianity, and then to have demanded that he separate from his wife, the pejoratively (and therefore rather suspiciously) named Geilana ('the sexy one').[112] She was the widow of Gozbert's brother, and this was why Kilian wanted the union to end. Gozbert, though he loved Geilana very much, loved God even more, and did as he was told. Geilana, mad with envy, had Kilian and his companions beheaded. Gozbert was then killed by his own servants, and the inhabitants of the region drove out his son Heden and all his family.[113] According to the chronology of the *Passio Kiliani*, these events took place in the later 680s, although we know that Heden was still duke of Thuringia in 717. It is quite possible that Kilian and his career in Thuringia are a Carolingian invention, but the idea that the demise of the Heden family was accompanied by violence and disorder is also to be found in the *Life of Boniface*, a work which has a much more certain historical content. Willibald, the author of the *Life of Boniface*, says that the leading men of Thuringia were Christian but were oppressed by Heden and Theotbald, who drove them to seek help from the Saxons.[114] Those who remained in Thuringia were subjected to pagan Saxon rule until Heden and Theotbald were finally driven out.[115] The people of Thuringia were also vexed by four false priests who were fornicators and adulterers. The four, who had Anglo-Saxon names, were expelled by Boniface when he preached in the region in 725.[116] Two pieces of contemporary information allow us to make some sense of these colourful stories. First, we have already seen that in 717 Duke Heden granted to Willibrord land at Hammelburg in the east of Thuringia for the foundation of a monastery. This is the last ever reference to Heden or to any other duke of Thuringia. It has been suggested that Heden was a

---

111 Mordek, 'Die Hedenen', pp. 348–56.

112 *Geil* in modern German means 'randy'. The later-ninth-century author Notker the Stammerer said that Geilana was *petulca*, that is 'frisky' or 'wanton', surely a play on her name.

113 *Passio Kiliani*, chs 8–14, pp. 725–7.

114 Willibald, *Vita Bonifatii*, ed. W. Levison, *MGH SRG* (Hanover 1905), ch. 6, pp. 32–3, trans. Talbot, *Anglo-Saxon Missionaries*, pp. 25–6, at p. 46.

115 Mordek, 'Die Hedenen', p. 349 places these events in the time of Heden's grandfather, also called Heden, but his reconstruction of events is highly speculative because there is so little information from Thuringia throughout the Merovingian period.

116 Willibald, *Vita Bonifatii*, ch. 6, pp. 32–3, trans. Talbot, *Anglo-Saxon Missionaries*, p. 46.

close ally of Charles Martel who fought alongside him at the battle of Vinchy in' March 717 and may have been killed fighting for Charles in a subsequent campaign. An alternative view is that he had fallen out with Charles and was driven out by him sometime after 717, or one can speculate that he simply died soon after 717. Whatever the case, the duchy of Thuringia ceased to exist after Heden. Second, in a letter of 722 which prepared the way for Boniface's mission in Thuringia, Pope Gregory II addressed five leading men of the region, and congratulated them as Christian leaders who had refused to abjure their faith when put under pressure to do so by pagans.[117] It thus seems likely that there was indeed a degree of political and religious confusion after the exit of Heden, possibly linked to a growing Saxon presence in the region. The four fornicating priests may well have been Anglo-Saxon missionaries left behind at Hammelburg by Willibrord when the latter left Thuringia to return to Frisia after the death of Radbod in 719.[118] If so, the terms in which Willibald described them suggest that they had, one might say, 'gone native' and taken local partners. That Gregory II should have addressed five men as the leaders of Thuringia could indicate that after the disappearance of the ducal family, the duchy had undergone decentralisation, perhaps under Saxon pressure, and that the situation there now resembled that in Saxony itself and in Hesse.

Unlike the Saxons, the 'peoples' of central Germany do not seem to have been prepared to resist Charles Martel. If political authority in these regions had become fragmented, Charles Martel was certainly ready to pick up the pieces, and we have already noted how the charters from Fulda show the rapid acculturation of local leaders to Romano-Frankish bureaucratic traditions. The imposition of an ecclesiastical organisation and the foundation of monasteries are the visible means by which these areas came to resemble the areas to the west of the Rhine. The letters and 'Life' of Boniface of course stress Boniface's leading role in the Christianisation of central Germany, but the evidence of Heden's Hammelburg charter and of Gregory's letter to the Thuringians suggests that local leaders may have taken the initiative in trying to set a fledgling church on a more organised basis. It is interesting to see that the papacy was interested in these moves. Kilian is said to have sought Rome's permission to preach in Thuringia. Kilian may be a character of fiction rather than history, but the notion that the papacy was interested in a Thuringian mission is supported by Gregory's concern for those Thuringian leaders who refused to abjure their faith. His concern may not simply have been prompted by Boniface, but may relate

---

117 *Bonifatii Epistolae*, no. 19, trans. Emerton, *Letters of St Boniface*, pp. 44–5.
118 Schlesinger, 'Das Frühmittelalter', p. 344.

to a much older interest in the region. In this light the Thuringians look similar to the Aquitanians and Bavarians as a people in contact with Rome, and on the threshold of developing an independent church. The fact that Boniface could proceed to organise central Germany into a diocesan structure suggests that it had reached a level of development at which it could be fully absorbed into the Frankish polity. In 741 Charles Martel would bequeath Thuringia to his son Karloman, and in the next generation Hammelburg would be donated to the monastery of Fulda as if it had always been the personal property of the Carolingians. No more do we hear of the 'peoples east of the Rhine'. By the late eighth century they have become simply the 'eastern Franks'.

Developments in northern Germany, that is, Frisia and Saxony, are even more closed to us than those in Hesse and Thuringia. Apart from one charter from Utrecht, to which we have already alluded, all our information comes from narrative sources. We noted in Chapter 3 that following Radbod's death in 719, Frankish control was reasserted over southern Frisia, but that how this happened is unknown. The Utrecht charter can be dated to 723. Two of the early Carolingian annals stated that in 722 there were 'wars against the North'.[119] This could be a reference to a campaign which brought southern Frisia, including Utrecht, back under Frankish control. Our next, and last, reference to Frisia is to a campaign of 734, which is reported in both the early Carolingian annals and the *Continuations of Fredegar*.[120] In the latter's account we are told that Charles Martel assembled a large naval force and attacked the Frisian islands. This was in response to 'rebellion'. Charles set up strongholds on the banks of the River Boorn, and killed the rebel leader, Bubo. He then destroyed the pagan religious centres in the region before returning home with much booty. Sometime between 723 and 734 Charles made gifts of land in the Kennemerland to the monastery of Echternach. Kennemerland lies well to the north of Utrecht, so it may be that after 719 the Franks had been moving deeper into Frisian territory, that is, beyond Utrecht, and that Bubo's 'rebellion' was a reaction to this advance. It has been argued that the successful campaign of 734 established the Franks up to the River Lauwers, in the present-day province of Groningen.[121] The Lauwers would remain the limit of Frankish control until the time of Charlemagne, but although the major part of Frisia had been 'conquered' in 734, the northern region remained largely pagan and occasionally hostile. Finally, we should note the Continuator's reference to

---

119 *Annales Nazariani* and *Annales Petaviani*.
120 *Fred. Contin.* ch. 17, p. 92.
121 W. Fritze, 'Zur Entstehungsgeschichte des Bistums Utrecht. Franken und Friesen 690–734', *Rheinische Vierteljahrsblätter*, 35 (1971), 107–5, at 145–7.

the use of a naval force. It is extremely rare to see the Franks taking to ships, but it clearly did not strike the Continuator as unusual that they did so in this instance.

In the age of Charles Martel the Saxons were, as we have seen, continuing to press down southwards into Thuringia and Hesse and westwards towards the River Rhine. Quite why the Saxons should have been expanding so vigorously in this period is a mystery. What little we know about them, from the *Life of Lebuin* and from later Carolingian sources, presents an intriguing image of a near acephalous and pagan society. The *Life of Lebuin*, which is a mid-ninth-century account of the work of yet another Anglo-Saxon missionary, who flourished in the 770s, describes Saxon warriors meeting at an assembly in which they discussed the affairs of their people. This assembly had no obvious leader, but its authority seems to have been feared by the two local chiefs who tried to protect Lebuin.[122] The Carolingian narratives of Charlemagne's long wars against the Saxons allow a similar picture to be drawn in that they name few Saxon leaders and show the Franks finding that pacts with particular leaders, or even with different groups of Saxons, were not sufficient to secure peace across the region as a whole. And Charlemagne's two capitularies which deal with the Saxons give ample indication of their resolute paganism.[123] Saxony thus presented a strong contrast with Francia in terms of its religion and social organisation, the one pagan and decentralised, the other Christian and with a single leader. In other ways, however, the Franks and Saxons had much in common. There is, for instance, little to distinguish Frank and Saxon in terms of material culture. The Saxons, in fact, have no distinctive archaeology. Eastern Franks and Saxons also spoke closely related languages, and shared many of the same personal names. That the two peoples were similar in appearance is clear from one of the episodes in the long war between them: in 775, according to the Revised version of the *Royal Frankish Annals*, Saxons broke into the Frankish camp by mingling with Frankish foragers as they returned to base. The Saxons appeared to the Franks 'as if they were their fellows'.[124]

Throughout the Merovingian period there are references to Saxons fighting for the Franks, and in 673 Saxon warriors were in Visigothic Septimania,

---

122 *Vita Lebuini*, ed. A. Hofmeister, *MGH SS* XXX, ii (Hanover 1926–34), pp. 789–95, trans. Talbot, *Anglo-Saxon Missionaries*, pp. 229–34, at pp. 230–3.

123 The First and Second Saxon Capitularies, trans. King, *Charlemagne, Translated Sources*, pp. 205–8, 230–2. For the argument that the Saxon mortuary customs banned in the Capitularies were not as unusual or strange as Charlemagne's legislation makes them seem, since there were recent parallels in Francia, B. Effros, '*De Partibus Saxoniae* and the Regulation of Mortuary Custom: A Carolingian Campaign of Christianization or the Suppression of Saxon Identity?', *Revue Belge de Philologie et d'Histoire*, 75 (1997), 267–86.

124 *Revised Annals of the Kingdom of the Franks*, trans. King, *Charlemagne. Translated Sources*, p. 112.

fighting for a rebel leader called Paul. We can therefore see that despite their rather different political organisation and religious culture, the Saxons had a long history of contact with, and involvement in, the Frankish kingdom. That they should have absorbed so little Frankish influence in the course of this history points to the resilience of Saxon culture. It is sensible to ask whether this culture even had a colonising propensity, like Frankish culture itself. As we have just seen, many Thuringians allegedly opted for Saxon rule and paganism when oppressed by the Heden family. And when the Boructuarii were said to have been conquered by the Saxons, it seems that they were thereafter counted as Saxons. One could imagine other peoples of Hesse being absorbed into the Saxons while keeping their own group identity, for like the Franks, the Saxons were a confederate mass, made up of different subgroups. Nor should we forget the extraordinary success of Anglo-Saxon language, culture and religion in displacing their Romano-British counterparts in England. Anglo-Saxon colonisation in England of course took place in very different circumstances from Saxon expansion on the Continent, and in England there was a very important insular input into the development of Anglo-Saxon culture, but both movements demonstrate the same combination of cultural conservatism and military power which meant that it was they who gave their identity to those they conquered, rather than the other way round. It thus seems that of all the enemies of the Franks, the Saxons were the ones most able to resist them, in cultural as well as in military terms.

Charles Martel's campaigns against the Saxons were probably aimed at limiting their expansion rather than at conquering Saxony itself. We saw that the Saxons had joined in attacks against the northern Austrasians in 715, and that in 718, at the height of his struggle with Ragamfred, Charles still found the time and energy to launch a raid deep into Saxony.[125] In 720, according to the early Carolingian annals, he fought against the Saxons again, and the reference to 'wars against the North' in the year 722 could refer to another Saxon campaign, rather than to an attack upon the Frisians. In 724, say the *Continuations of Fredegar*, Charles punished a Saxon rebellion, and he was back in Saxony in 728.[126] In 729 he apparently wanted to campaign there, but was somehow prevented, possibly by growing resistance in Alemannia, to which he attended in the next year. Finally, in 738 Charles attacked the Saxons who lived in the vicinity of the River Lippe, and, according to Fredegar's Continuator, ordered that they pay

---

125 Below, ch. 3, pp. 70–1.
126 *Fred. Contin.* ch. 11, p. 90. The 728 campaign is reported only in the early Carolingian annals.

tribute.[127] This may indicate that the Lippe Saxons were forced to recognise Frankish overlordship, an advance which led Boniface to write optimistically about the prospects for converting Saxony. His optimism was, however, premature. It is significant that this whole sequence began with Saxon attacks across the Rhine in 715 and ended with a Frankish attack up the Lippe which flows into the Rhine just north of present-day Essen. In other words, after twenty years of counter-attack into Saxony, the Franks had made painfully little progress. Nor would they do so until Charlemagne made all-out war on the Saxons from 772 onwards, and even then it took a decade of heavy fighting before the area around the River Lippe was properly subdued. If Charles Martel had made the Lippe Saxons pay tribute in 738, one imagines that they stopped paying it as soon as Charles was dead and his sons had started to fight for their own survival. It is surely right to conclude that the Franks had had more influence over the Saxons in the age of Gregory of Tours than they would ever have in the age of Charles Martel. Let us now consider how Charles Martel's dealings with the different regions reflect his rise to the height of power in Francia.

Conclusions

In each of the regions we have discussed in this chapter we have seen that at almost every turn we lack the kind of detailed information which would tell us exactly how and why Charles Martel was successful in his operations. When we take all of the campaigns together, though, what is immediately striking is the frequency and range of Charles's military activities. Few years were without a campaign, and if we start with the conflict that arose with the death of Pippin in 714, we can see that there was nearly a generation of almost yearly campaigning, with some years seeing more than one expedition. With the probable exception of central Germany, fighting ranged across all the outlying regions, and distance seems to have been no object to Charles Martel's forces. In 734, for instance, we see them on separate campaigns in Alemannia, Frisia and Burgundy. This pattern of widespread and frequent military activity directed by the ruler would remain an essential feature of Carolingian government for the next three generations. In an earlier chapter it was pointed out that the ability to campaign across

---

127   *Fred. Contin.* ch. 19, p. 93. Wallace-Hadrill's translation of *gentem illam saevissimam ex parte tributaria esse praecepit* as 'he taught the men of that region of savages the lesson of paying their taxes', is loose. A more accurate translation is: 'he ordered the savage people of the region to be tribute payers'.

massive distances can be identified in Merovingian Francia too, and that without that ability a huge territory subject to a single ruler was inconceivable. But it remains true that we have to go back a century into Merovingian history to find a ruler who campaigned on the scale of Charles Martel. That ruler was King Dagobert I (629–39), but whereas his activity was basically crammed into a single decade, Charles Martel was active for more than a quarter of a century. Some of Charles's campaigns were no doubt little more that plundering raids, into Aquitaine, for instance, and one region, Burgundy, was too divided to put up much resistance against him. Nor, apparently, were the campaigns into Aquitaine, Alemannia, Bavaria and Saxony aimed at conquest. Charles Martel did, nevertheless, sometimes meet stiff resistance, especially in Provence and in Saxony.

The obvious answer to the question of why Charles Martel was so successful in his campaigns against the outlying regions is that he had a large, enthusiastic, and increasingly self-confident military following. But we cannot go much beyond this statement of the obvious, for we know very little about the make-up or size of that following. Whether his troops fought in the tens of thousands, thousands, or even hundreds is unknowable, although it would be sensible to assume that Charles Martel's armies were at least equal in size to those they fought against. The speed and range of their movement also suggest that a significant proportion of his men were mounted warriors, and this is a subject to which we will return in the next chapter. Some, perhaps most, of his followers were Austrasians from the Pippinid heartland, like Adela's grandson Gregory and his brothers. Others, like Abbo of Provence, were recruited in the outlying regions, and in each region we must suppose that Charles could find willing allies who sought to profit by joining his cause. It must, indeed, have been highly profitable to be on Charles's side after about 724. The sources invariably state that much booty was taken on campaign, and we have seen that in Burgundy and Provence, at least, supporters were rewarded with land and office as they had been in Neustria in the previous five years. No land or office seems to have been available for the provision of rewards in Alemannia, Aquitaine or Bavaria, so that we must presume that booty was the main incentive for the soldiers fighting there.

Give or take some violent factional fighting, the mid and later seventh century was relatively peaceful compared with the age of Charles Martel. The contrast may suggest that the fighting between Neustria and Austrasia at the end of the seventh and at the beginning of the eighth centuries had occasioned a remilitarisation of society.[128] Charles Martel seems to have

---

128   See below, ch. 5.

benefited from this phenomenon. One can certainly imagine that the military following built up by Ragamfred would have been keen to find new sources of employment and wealth after Neustria's defeat, and what happened, one wonders, to the forces built up by Savaric and Hainmar in northern Burgundy? Such people would surely have provided a reservoir of manpower for campaigns in other regions. Here, we are thrown back on the adage that nothing succeeds like success, that is to say, Charles's successes would have brought fresh recruits to his following, so that his support grew and victory became more certain year by year. It is surely apparent, for instance, that it was his success against the Arabs in 732 or 733 which enabled him to push into Burgundy the next year. Charles thus built up his power piecemeal until it was irresistible. By 737, when King Theuderic IV died, Charles was the unchallenged strongman of the whole area under Frankish influence. He was so strongly supported, in fact, that from 737 until his death in 741 he was able to rule without a king, an interregnum which is unique in Frankish history. At the same time the papacy began to regard Charles as the unquestioned leader of the Franks, and as the individual to whom their concerns about growing Lombard power should be addressed. We can say, therefore, that Charles Martel's power grew throughout his career as he met and defeated his enemies and rivals one by one. We shall see in the final chapter that where the outlying regions were concerned, loyalty to Charles was based on a fear and respect which did not outlive him, and which had to be rebuilt anew by his sons. First, however, we will look more closely at the effect Charles Martel's rule had upon Francia, and here we must return to the difficult question of whether or not he orchestrated military and social change, or whether he was in fact the beneficiary of changes already taking place.

CHAPTER FIVE

Francia under the Hammer

In the Introduction to this survey we looked briefly at the Brunner thesis, which gave the firm impression that Charles Martel was the harbinger of widespread social, political and economic change to Francia. It is now time to look more carefully at the issues raised by this idea. 'Harbinger' (one who announces the approach of something) is a rather appropriate term to use in this context, for it is derived from two ancient German elements *heri* and *berg* which together referred to someone sent to find lodgings for an army. It was the need to find resources for his army which, according to the Brunner thesis, lay behind the changes that Charles Martel introduced in Francia. Brunner, remember, postulated that Charles systematically made use of church lands to reward his followers, hence his later reputation as a despoiler of the church. In the short term, it was argued, the appropriation of ecclesiastical land provided Charles with the mounted warriors he needed to defeat his many enemies, including the Arabs. In the longer term new social relations arose as it became usual for land to be held in return for military services, and as the landholders developed into a class of nobles who held local power in each region, and who took firm hold of the local peasantry which supplied them with the wherewithal to perform those military services. This so-called 'feudal system', whereby land was held in return for service, and in which each person in society owed loyalty and service to those above them, used to be a cornerstone of textbook descriptions of medieval society, and indeed the model, represented as a pyramid of loyalties and services, is still to be found in some textbooks used in the early years of secondary schooling. In this modern account of the early Middle Ages, those who held the land from superior lords are termed their 'vassals'; the lands they held are known as 'fiefs', and the loyalty they expressed to superiors in return for 'fief-holding' is called 'homage'. And all of this is ultimately traced back to Charles Martel's need to raise armies composed of mounted warriors. Today this model is generally seen as much too simplistic, and many would argue that it in effect invented its own terminology by drawing selected terms from different times and different places and using them as if they could be applied everywhere, at all times, even when they do not appear in the sources.[1] One historian, for instance, recently termed the missionary Willibrord a 'vassal' of the Carolingians, although this term was never used of him in any contemporary source.

In order to examine the Brunner thesis and its implications more closely, we must first ask how Charles Martel did in fact treat the church. A discussion of what happened to the church will also require us to think about the role and context of missionary activity, for this has a direct bearing upon the issue of social, as well as religious and cultural, change. The two missionaries with whom Charles Martel was most closely involved were Willibrord and Boniface, so we must give their careers particular consideration. In addition some of Boniface's letters have been used as evidence in the argument that Charles did secularise church property. This material we must discuss in some detail. Having looked at the question of whether or not Charles Martel deserves his reputation as an enemy of the church, we can return to the wider issue of how the need to furnish troops might have affected property relations and could have led to social change. This discussion will first of all focus on precarial tenure, that is, the form of landholding most closely associated with the giving out of land, especially church land, in return for military service. We shall then consider the nature of the Frankish armies of the period in order to see what evidence there is that they were becoming the predominantly cavalry force which the Brunner school imagined them to be. And finally, we shall consider the third element in the thesis, the apparent rise in social importance of the 'vassals'. In all three areas it will be necessary to point out great holes in the traditional arguments. Far from being a simply negative exercise which cuts straw men to pieces just for the sake of it, this approach is designed to construct a much more realistic assessment of the changes taking place in the age of Charles Martel.

Charles Martel and the Church

We have of course seen that Charles Martel's rise to power was, to put it mildly, a bruising affair which left numerous casualties in its wake. With the

---

1 This is the fundamental argument of S. Reynolds in her major work, *Fiefs and Vassals. The Medieval Evidence Reinterpreted* (Oxford 1994).

exception of our two central narratives, the *Continuations of Fredegar* and the *Earlier Annals of Metz*, the bulk of our source material comes directly from the church in the form of saints' Lives, episcopal histories such as the *Gesta* of the Auxerre bishops, and charters which recorded flow of property to various ecclesiastical institutions. It is the case, therefore, that our impressions about how Charles Martel treated those he defeated are based on what happened to churchmen, and at first sight the church appears to have fared badly. Wando, abbot of St Wandrille, Celestinus, abbot of St Peter's at Ghent, and bishops Rigobert of Rheims, Crodegang of Sées, Eucherius of Orléans, Hainmar of Auxerre and Willicarius of Vienne were all driven out by Charles, and we hear that the lands of their churches were then distributed to his followers. Thus far, the picture of Charles as one who despoiled the church to provide rewards for his men seems to hold good. We must, however, be careful to divide off the rare contemporary reports of despoliation from the bulk of accounts which are informed by Martel's later reputation. The case of Rigobert of Rheims provides a clear example of how a later source was influenced in this way. What the late-ninth-century *Vita Rigoberti* had to say about Martel's seizure of lands was demonstrably modelled on the account of what happened to the church of Orléans when Eucherius was banished. It is in fact the *Vita Eucherii*, composed shortly after Eucherius's death in about 738, which is the key to the construction of Charles Martel's reputation as a plunderer of church property. What the *Vita Eucherii* actually said was that, 'people full of envy suggested to the prince, Charles, that he condemn the holy man [Eucherius] to exile along with all his kindred, and some of their lands and positions [*honores*] he should take for his own uses, and some he should heap upon his followers [*satellites*]'.[2] It is, of course, possible that the *honores* of Eucherius's kinsmen had nothing to do with the church of Orléans, but seeing this as an attack on the bishopric as well as upon the bishop and his family, the crucial question is whether the passage indicates the way in which Charles Martel treated the church in general, or whether the treatment of Eucherius and his church in particular should be regarded as opportunistic and exceptional.

It seems to have been Hincmar, first a monk at St Denis and then highly influential archbishop of Rheims from 845 to 882, who made Eucherius's demise stand for the ill-treatment of the Frankish church as a whole. In 858 Hincmar wrote a letter from the Synod of Quierzy to Louis the German and Charles the Bald, kings respectively of East and West Francia. In this letter Hincmar appealed for the return of church land which had fallen into

---

2   *Vita Eucherii*, ed. W. Levison, *MGH SRM* VII (Hanover and Leipzig 1920), pp. 46–53, ch. 7, p. 49.

the hands of laymen, and he claimed that 'of all the kings and princes [*principes*] of the Franks', Charles Martel 'was the first to take property away from the church and to divide it up'.[3] This statement he underlined with an account of a vision which Eucherius had had when he was in exile. This is the vision of Charles Martel languishing in hell, having been dragged out of his tomb in St Denis by a dragon.[4] It was Boniface and Fulrad, the abbot of St Denis, who discovered the empty tomb. Although later in 878 in his *Vita Remigii* (the 'Life' of Remigius, a fifth-century bishop of Rheims) Hincmar said that Eucherius's vision had first been revealed in the reign of Charles Martel's son Pippin (751–68), one must suspect that it was Hincmar himself who was author of the vision text, especially as visions were a genre in which Hincmar was keenly interested.[5] The story would thereafter become very widespread. It was indeed the single most important text in the construction of Charles Martel's reputation as a seculariser or despoiler of church lands. Why did Hincmar fix on Charles as the prime mover in secularisation?

Hincmar found the general context for secularisation in the *LHF*'s narrative of the wars between Ragamfred and Charles Martel, from which he concluded that this was a period of such severe conflict that Christianity almost died out. In his view, few bishoprics had remained, and others were given to laymen who divided up the church's property. Hincmar, whose aim was to recover property lost by his own see, considered Rheims to have suffered badly in the conflict, and in the figure of Charles's right-hand man, Milo, he found the villain surely responsible for its troubles. Milo, as we have already seen, replaced Rigobert as bishop of Rheims. Though he was actually a cleric, according to Hincmar, Milo behaved like a layman, and in his care Rheims lost much of its property. It seems to have been knowledge of Rheims's losses during Milo's forty years as bishop, an awareness that Boniface had castigated Milo as a typically bad bishop, and the fact that Charles had ordered Rigobert's exile and Milo's appointment, which led Hincmar to claim that Charles was the first to sanction the taking of church land. Charles was, moreover, a figure sufficiently distant from the mid-ninth century to allow Hincmar to criticise him with impunity, especially as he was not a king, which meant that Hincmar was not, strictly speaking, criticising the Carolingian dynasty itself. He was, however, the direct ancestor

---

3 Hincmar, *Epistola Synodali Carisiacensis ad Hludowicem Regem Germaniae Directa*, ed. A. Boretius and V. Krause, *MGH Capitularia* II (Hanover 1897), pp. 427–41, at p. 432.
4 See above, Introduction, p. 2.
5 The vision is related in *Vita Rigoberti*, ed. W. Levison, *MGH SRM* VII, pp. 58–80, ch. 13, p. 70. On Hincmar and vision texts, see P. Dutton, *The Politics of Dreaming in the Carolingian Empire* (Lincoln and London 1994), pp. 169–94.

of the two kings whose granting out of lands in the mid-ninth century was what Hincmar was attacking in 858.

Did Hincmar actually know of any secularisation which took place in this period other than that suffered by Orléans and by Rheims? There is no evidence that he did. Nevertheless it became increasingly common for churches to follow him in assuming that land over which they had lost control at some unspecified time in the past had been taken by Charles Martel. It is for this reason that we must suspect that the accounts of the churches of Rheims, Ghent, Auxerre and Vienne losing land in this way may in part be wrongly placed in the age of Charles Martel. It would, on the other hand, be naïve to think that Charles never helped himself to ecclesiastical resources when these were in the hands of opponents, and the fact remains that when Rigobert, Celestinus, Crodegang, Eucherius, Hainmar, Willicarius and company were driven out, they were replaced by Martel supporters who were sometimes laymen. This we saw most clearly in the bishoprics of south-west Neustria.[6] In this sense, at least some supporters were indeed rewarded with church property. Rotbertus's appointment to Sées provides a good example of a loyal count taking over a bishopric in this way.

The Brunner thesis rested on the assumptions that such expropriation was systematic and that Charles Martel really was the first to employ this system of reward, as Hincmar claimed. Yet complaints against laymen taking over church property in fact go back at least into the later seventh century. There is, for instance, a well-documented case of successive Neustrian mayors of the palace treating a property of St Denis in this way.[7] In the time of Charles Martel himself it is clear that it was not just Charles who appropriated land for his own use. In the previous chapter, for example, we discussed two documents from the monastery of St Victor in Marseilles which complained about Antenor, the *patricius* of Provence, helping himself to St Victor's estates, and similar complaints of unjust expropriation were levelled at Duke Eudo of Aquitaine. So Charles Martel was certainly not the first, nor the only one to take church property for his own use. Nor, as we shall see shortly, can the way he used it be deemed systematic. There was, nevertheless, genuine complaint that under Charles Martel the Frankish church was poorly led and subject to interference by laymen. The complaint came from the Anglo-Saxon missionary Boniface. Let us review the relationship between Charles Martel and the missionaries, and examine the

---

6 Above, ch. 3, pp. 71–3.
7 H. Wolfram, 'Karl Martell und das fränkische Lehenswesen', in J. Jarnut, U. Nonn and M. Richter (eds), *Karl Martell in Seiner Zeit*, Beihefte der Francia, 37 (Sigmaringen 1994), pp. 61–78. On the St Denis case, pp. 68–71.

substance of Boniface's complaint, before making a final assessment of how badly (or otherwise) the church fared in our period.

Missionaries

Missionaries have so far made several appearances in this study, and it is a reflection of their influence and importance that no account of the age of Charles Martel could avoid discussing their work. Francia had, we know, been a Christian kingdom since the time of Clovis, but since the early seventh century it had attracted a stream of missionaries from Ireland. These holy men, who wished to exile themselves from their homeland in order to move closer to God, were concerned not so much with converting the heathen as with improving the quality of religious devotion in an already Christian society. At the same time as the Irish were active on the Continent, Frankish churchmen were busy organising the fledgling church in southern England, and strong spiritual ties developed between Francia and England, especially between Neustria and East Anglia, Kent and Wessex.

At the end of the seventh century we see the tide turn, with Anglo-Saxon missionaries visiting Francia, following the Irish pattern of *peregrinatio*, or self-exile. As we have already observed, Charles Martel's father Pippin welcomed and supported the Anglo-Saxon missionaries. For not only did they help to bring the region of Frisia more firmly into the Frankish orbit, they also helped to raise the spiritual standing of the Pippinid family itself, and provided a counterweight to the old ties between leading Neustrian families and England. To a greater extent than their earlier Irish counter- parts, these Anglo-Saxons headed for the peripheral regions of Francia, being intent upon converting the heathen. It seems, though, that despite a rhetoric of conversion, they were mainly concerned with organising the church among existing Christian communities. Recent thinking in fact now questions the notion of 'conversion' to Christianity as a simple sequence of preaching, persuasion and acceptance. An alternative picture is of Christian- isation as a much lengthier process of cultural transformation, beginning with the adoption of some outward signs of Christianity alongside existing 'pagan' customs, and only slowly developing towards a proper articulation of the beliefs of the new religion.[8]

---

8   This position is neatly summed up by F. Theuws, 'Landed Property and Manorial Organisation in Northern Austrasia: Some Considerations and a Case Study', in N. Roymans and F. Theuws (eds), *Images of the Past. Studies on Ancient Societies in Northwestern Europe* (Amsterdam 1991), pp. 299–407, at p. 334 and n. 157.

In the age of Charles Martel most of the peoples among whom the missionaries were active had already been subject to this gradual process of Christianisation for some time, arguably for generations.[9] In areas where they had not, that is, in Saxony or in Scandinavia where there was a more resilient non-Christian culture, the missionaries failed to make much impact and often suffered violent rejection. The Anglo-Saxons themselves, of course, did not think in terms of cultural transformation. As they saw it, they were off to convert their fellows in the same way that they believed the English had been converted a century earlier, that is, by missionaries who brought truth to an ignorant people and moved them in an instant from darkness to light. The point here is that when the Anglo-Saxons came to the Continent, they brought much of their cultural baggage with them. It is an important point for two reasons: first, it means that they sought papal support for their work, for their model was the mission sent to England by Pope Gregory the Great at the end of the sixth century, and second, they found some Frankish bishops worldly and arrogant, in contrast to most bishops in England who were much less powerful. In England the church was in effect newly established in this period and bishops had not built up power over the local community. Furthermore, there were very few towns in England, whereas in Francia bishops were powerful partly because they controlled towns. This cultural difference underpinned the hostility which Boniface expressed towards the Frankish church.

The Pippinids and early Carolingians were, as just stated, closely involved with two missionary groups in particular: those led by Willibrord and by Boniface. Willibrord was active, largely in Frisia, for nearly half a century, from 690 to 739. Pippin and then Charles Martel were his patrons, and we have already seen how Willibrord and his monastery of Echternach were lavishly endowed not just by these two leaders but by their allies, including Heden, duke of Thuringia. So close were the ties between Willibrord and the Pippinids that he can be described as their dependant. We saw, for instance, how in 706 Pippin and Plectrude took Echternach under their control. Willibrord's was the case referred to earlier in which the use of 'feudal' terminology not found in the sources is, to say the least, unhelpful: Willibrord did not owe military services to his 'lords'![10]

---

9 J. Wallace-Hadrill, *The Frankish Church* (Oxford 1983), pp. 143–61. See also R. Fletcher, *The Conversion of Europe. From Paganism to Christianity 371–1368 A.D.* (London 1997), pp. 203–4.

10 A. Angenendt, 'Willibrord im Dienste der Karolinger', *Annalen des historisches Vereins für den Niederrhein inbesondere das alte Erzbistum Köln*, 175 (1973), 63–113. The author acknowledges the fact that Willibrord was never termed a 'vassal', but argues that his relationship with Pippin was *vassalitisch*, implying that he would have owed military service. For this there is no evidence.

In an important recent study the archaeologist Frans Theuws has examined the early-eighth-century charters in which people in Toxandria, the modern lower Meuse valley, gave land to Willibrord, land which eventually came to Echternach.[11] Theuws compared the terminology of the charters with the situation on the ground as revealed by the archaeological evidence from some of the Toxandrian settlements mentioned in them. His finding was that in the late seventh and early eighth centuries there was a reorganisation of landed property in this region. Changing terminology in the charters shows a shift in emphasis from relatively independent peasant farmsteads (*casatae*) to peasant holdings grouped around a central hall (*sala*). On the ground this change is associated with the break-up of old burial patterns, in which the elite began to be buried separately from the rest of the community, and in which the practice of placing material goods in graves came to an end. The emergence of the *sala* as the focal point of settlement Theuws matched with the clearance of land, and with the regrouping of the population, first to clear the land and then to till it. Very loosely, this reorganisation can be termed 'manorialisation', and it involved lords creating a central reserve of land which was worked by dependent peasants living around it. These units of production, soon generally to be termed *mansi*, were often part of a string of properties which made up the larger estates we see in the charters of major ecclesiastical institutions such as those of Echternach.

What this change amounted to in social terms is a process of differentiation, or elite formation, in which leading families separated themselves off from their communities, and began to exercise increasing rights over them. What provoked the change is unclear. Theuws has suggested that the impulse was external, and that it began in the later seventh century when Charles Martel's father Pippin turned to Toxandria as a source of new clients and resources to offset the losses the family suffered in the wake of the disastrous 'Grimoald coup'.[12] This is a sensible guess, but a guess all the same. Population growth and the increase in the labour available to work the reserve may be other factors. What is clear, however, is that the background to Willibrord's mission was one of social change, and that the mission worked with the grain of this change by building up a series of estates worked by dependent peasants. The growth of Christian organisation further stimulated the break-up of what has been termed the 'Merovingian burial

---

11 Theuws, 'Landed Property'. See also F. Theuws, 'Centre and Periphery in Northern Austrasia (6th–8th centuries). An Archaeological Perspective', in J. Besteman, J. Bos and H. Heidinga (eds), *Medieval Archaeology in the Netherlands. Studies Presented to H.H. van Regteren Altena* (Aasen and Maastricht 1990), pp. 41–69.
12 Theuws, 'Landed Property', pp. 333–4.

community' by encouraging the shift to new burial sites, in turn helping the elite to separate themselves off from the community. Finally, the spread of charters which accompanied the growth of the church served to define and strengthen the rights which lords had over local communities. One can see why missionaries were welcomed by some people into areas such as Toxandria.

In Bavaria and Alemannia it is possible to describe a similar background to missionary activity. In the last chapter we looked at the work of Emmeram, Rupert, Corbinian and Pirmin in these regions and it was then suggested that the organisation of the church there accompanied the development of noble landholding and the growth of ducal power. Again, the archaeological evidence shows that the arrival of the missionaries was preceded by a process of social differentiation and by a degree of Christianisation, both marked by the appearance of separate elite burials in or near newly founded churches, and by the emergence of settlements bearing the name of a single lord. And again we see these social relations reflected in (and in part created by) the growing use of charters. Missionary activity was therefore not the sole preserve of the Anglo-Saxons, but took place throughout the peripheral regions as part of the process of social and religious development through which they were integrated into the mainstream of Frankish culture. Another feature common to the missions in both north and south was the way in which the missionaries sought papal backing for the organisation of the church into new bishoprics. It used to be thought that this was particularly characteristic of the Anglo-Saxons, who brought with them to the Continent their peculiar reverence for the holy see. Willibrord, for instance, visited Rome shortly after arriving in Frisia, and he returned there in 696 to receive ordination as archbishop of the Frisians. This habit of going to Rome to seek ordination and advice was reckoned to have been of great consequence for their patrons the Carolingians, for it put the latter in contact with Rome, and thus prepared the way for papal support for Charles Martel's son to make himself king in 751. But as we have already seen, the Bavarians, the Aquitanians and, if we can believe the *Passio Kiliani*, the Thuringians, were independently in contact with Rome, as the Neustrians had been in the previous generation. The papacy, it seems, revived its interest in the church north of the Alps in the later seventh century. In 668 it sent Theodore of Tarsus to become archbishop of Canterbury with a brief to sort out the diocesan structure in England. There is good reason to think that it was actually Theodore who did most to promote the cult of Pope Gregory the Great in England, in effect teaching the English that history of conversion which informed the behaviour of Willibrord and Boniface. Thus far from awakening the popes' interest in the church north of the Alps, the devotion of the Anglo-Saxon missionaries to Rome was the fruit of that interest.[13] The papacy from the 660s onwards was, in other words, much more proactive in its relations with leaders outside Italy than historians used to think.

The instinct of rulers, Agilolfings and Etichonids as well as Carolingians, was to welcome the missionaries as holy men. They gave them protection and property, and encouraged them in the foundation of monasteries and in the setting up of bishoprics. As we noted in the last chapter, there was also scope for conflict when holy men, like Corbinian, challenged the legitimacy of certain marriages in the ruling family, but the importance of such conflict may have been exaggerated by hagiographers: churchmen worth their salt had to be depicted as capable of standing up to powerful laymen. Patronage of missionaries therefore brought distinct benefits in terms of bringing order to certain areas, but no doubt to the patrons the main hope was that they would provide spiritual benefits, not least in increasing the chances of good fortune and salvation. Charles Martel does not seem to have had any 'missionary policy' other than to offer support. Willibrord and Boniface apparently went where they pleased, even to Bavaria to serve the Agilolfings in the latter's case. What was there to complain about?

Boniface is unique among the figures of this period in that we can see something of his personality. This is because substantial numbers of the letters he wrote and received between the years 710 and 754 have survived. Of these, 38 letters were written by Boniface, 32 were received by him (including 15 sent by Popes Gregory II, Gregory III, Zacharias and Stephen II) and 14 were written to support his mission. The letters not only chart the progress of Boniface's work, they also reveal his thoughts about how things were going. Boniface's original name was Wynfrith. After an early and promising monastic career in southern England, he travelled to Frisia in 716, at the height of Radbod's drive to oust the Franks from the region. Unable to work in these conditions, he returned to England but was back on the Continent in 718, travelling to Rome in 719. There he received the name Boniface from Pope Gregory II (715–31) and received the pope's backing for a mission against the pagans. Boniface then returned north via Lombardy, Bavaria and Thuringia, joining up with Willibrord in Frisia. In 721 he left Frisia and headed for the borders of Hesse and Saxony, staying *en route* with Plectrude's sister Adela of Pfalzel. At this point, according to his 'Life', Adela's grandson Gregory became Boniface's pupil and eventually accompanied him to Thuringia, where, as we have already seen, Boniface

---

13 On the development of the Gregory cult in England, A. Thacker, 'Memorialising Gregory the Great: The Origins and Transmission of a Papal Cult in the Seventh and Early Eighth Centuries', *Early Medieval Europe*, 7 (1998), 59–84.

expelled those survivors of an earlier mission who had taken wives. First, however, Boniface returned to Rome where Pope Gregory ordained him bishop. He then preached in Hesse where at Geismar he famously felled a great oak tree sacred to the pagans. After his work in Thuringia, he returned to Hesse and founded four monasteries there. In 732 the new pope, Gregory III (731–41), made him an archbishop, though without a fixed see. In 738 he returned to Rome via Bavaria and then went to Saxony where Charles Martel's successful military campaign had given him high hopes of opening a new missionary field. Disappointed in the lack of progress here, he returned to Bavaria, where, as we have seen, he organised the duchy into four dioceses. After Charles Martel's death in 741, Boniface's career took a new turn as Charles's sons Karloman and Pippin threw their support behind him in an endeavour to reform the Frankish church. In 742 Karloman also helped him found the monastery of Fulda in Hesse, which would become a leading monastic centre east of the Rhine. At the same time three new dioceses were created in the east at Würzburg, Erfurt and Büraburg. Reform was promoted through four church councils called between 742 and 744. At the last of these Boniface was made archbishop of Cologne, but facing opposition here, in 745 he became archbishop of Mainz instead. Finally, in 753 he returned to Frisia where in the following year he and many of his companions were murdered by robbers near Dokkum in the far north of the region.[14]

The Carolingians regarded Boniface as one of the heroes of their times, and from this brief outline of his career one can see why. Our problem is that his career casts a long shadow over the Frankish church, which appears lacklustre and complacent when set sharply against Boniface's energy and commitment. Boniface was not, however, much concerned with the Frankish church as a whole until the reform councils of the 740s. Prior to that his letters make very little reference to it, and say nothing about its shortcomings, except to complain about Gerold, bishop of Mainz. In a letter of 724,[15] Pope Gregory II referred to Boniface's complaint that Gerold, having done nothing to convert the peoples living beyond the Rhine, now claimed jurisdiction over this area, which Boniface had made his special missionary field. In the same year Charles Martel had a letter of safe conduct drawn up for the missionary, as he did too for Pirmin.[16] Interestingly, this is the one document which Charles issued in royal form, possibly because there was

---

14 This synopsis is taken from I. Wood, 'Boniface', an entry in *The New Dictionary of National Biography* (Oxford forthcoming).

15 *Bonifatii Epistolae*, no. 24, trans. E. Emerton, *The Letters of St Boniface* (New York 1940), pp. 50–2.

16 *Bonifatii Epistolae*, no. 22, trans. Emerton, *Letters of St Boniface*, p. 47.

no alternative model. It shows that he was willing to protect Boniface, but Gregory's letter equally suggests that Charles was not prepared to advance his cause against that of the bishopric of Mainz. Nor, from the evidence of a much later letter, was Charles prepared to champion Boniface against the see of Cologne which claimed jurisdiction over southern Frisia.

At this stage Boniface's overwhelming concern was to set up a new church in regions which he perceived to have been lacking in proper Christian organisation, and as such his agenda had little to do with whatever Charles Martel was doing elsewhere. Boniface's letters in this respect display a kind of tunnel vision in which he repeatedly referred back to the original mission to the Anglo-Saxons. For example he asked the archbishop of Canterbury to send him a copy of the answers Gregory the Great had given to the missionary Augustine on questions of how to treat pagan customs and marriage among the Anglo-Saxons. The rulings on marriage he obtained from contemporary popes did not seem to satisfy him.[17] Similarly, Boniface was not prepared to take 'no' for answer when he asked Pope Zacharias (741–52) if he might choose his own successor as archbishop of Mainz, even though Zacharias told him that this was 'contrary to every rule in the church'.[18] For Augustine, the first archbishop of Canterbury, had chosen and consecrated his successor Laurence, and it seems to have been this model that Boniface was determined to follow. Discussions on the progress of his work were between himself and the popes, or between himself and people back in England. If he ever wrote to any Frankish bishop about his mission, or if any Frankish bishop wrote to him, the letters have not survived.

It was, as we have just seen, Karloman and Pippin who moved Boniface to the centre stage of church affairs, as they attempted to assert their authority over the church in the wake of the political instability which followed Charles Martel's death. The two brothers sought a mandate for reform by stressing shortcomings in the behaviour of bishops and priests. Boniface's stature as a veteran missionary backed by the popes, and his uncompromising views on how the clergy should behave, made him an ideal mouthpiece for a critique of the Frankish clergy. His main blast against the Frankish church came in a letter written to welcome and inspire the new pope, Zacharias, in 742.[19] In it he said that the church over the last sixty or seventy years had been 'trodden underfoot and scattered'. There had been no synod for eighty years, it had no archbishops and paid no attention to the church canons, and 'now for the most part throughout the dioceses the

---

17 *Bonifatii Epistolae*, no. 33, trans. Emerton, *Letters of St Boniface*, pp. 62–3.
18 *Bonifatii Epistolae*, no. 51, trans. Emerton, *Letters of St Boniface*, pp. 83–8.
19 *Bonifatii Epistolae*, no. 50, trans. Emerton, *Letters of St Boniface*, pp. 78–83.

episcopal seats have been handed over to greedy laymen to hold and given over to exploitation by adulterous and fornicating clergy and by lay tax gatherers'. He went on to say that 'Some are found among the bishops who say that they are not fornicators or adulterers, but even so they are negligent and go hunting. They are warriors who fight in the army, and with their own hands spill the blood of men, be these pagans or Christians.'

Boniface was certainly right that there had been no church council in Francia for a long time, although eighty years is generally regarded as an exaggeration. He was right too that the Franks did not have archbishops. In effect they had never had any. His diatribe against fornicators and adulterers may, however, reflect his own monastic vocation more than any recent slippage in standards of behaviour, and his sense of the worldliness of Frankish bishops may stem from an unfavourable comparison with less powerful Anglo-Saxon bishops who, like himself, very often came from monastic backgrounds. What, one wonders, did he think about a figure such as Eucherius of Orléans who was both 'worldy' and an acclaimed champion of the church? In fact only two bishops are named in Boniface's attacks upon the standards of the episcopate. In a letter reporting on a council held in Rome, Pope Zacharias referred to earlier correspondence in which Boniface had complained about 'Milo and men like him who do much harm to the church of God'.[20] As we know, Milo was bishop of both Trier and Rheims and a close ally of Charles Martel. This one reference would be enough for Hincmar to cast him as a villain whose behaviour was supposedly typical of a degenerate church, and it certainly encouraged Hincmar's assumption that what happened to Rheims under Milo's stewardship was repeated throughout the land. The second bad bishop named by Zacharias in the same letter was Gewilib, now reportedly deposed from the see of Mainz. Gewilib, who was the son of Boniface's old adversary Gerold, had been a 'warrior and a fornicator'. Boniface, we know, had been in conflict with the see of Mainz in the time of Gerold, and he himself became archbishop of Mainz after Gewilib was thrown out. Milo may have been part of the circle which resisted Boniface's attempts to stop Mainz from having influence over the growing church across the Rhine in Hesse.[21] It was suggested earlier that Charles Martel may have protected the interest of Mainz – but his sons may not have followed suit. This background gives a particular slant to Boniface's criticism of bishops in the years after Charles's death. His attack, in other words, may have had more to do with his own

---

20 *Bonifatii Epistolae*, no. 87, trans. Emerton, *Letters of St Boniface*, pp. 159–64, at p. 162.
21 E. Ewig, 'Milo et eiusmodi similes', in *Sankt Bonifatius Gedenkengabe zum zwölfhundertsten Todestag* (Fulda 1954), pp. 412–20, reprinted in *Spätantikes und Frankisches Gallien* II (Zurich and Munich 1979), pp. 189–219, at 199–200.

difficulties in the Mainz area than with the state of the Frankish church as a whole.

Boniface was a stern moral judge who found fault wherever he looked, be it in Bavaria, England, Francia, Thuringia, or even Rome. His letter to Zacharias, for instance, also contained a few sharp words about what he regarded as pagan elements in the festival held in Rome each January (it was still being held in the twelfth century!). To the secularisation of the church under Charles Martel he is therefore hardly a satisfactory witness. There is, however, a more direct reference to Charles as an enemy of the church in a version of a letter Boniface wrote to King Aethelbald of Mercia in 746 or 747.[22] Often regarded as a later insertion, this criticism of Charles has recently been defended as evidence of what Boniface really thought about him.[23] The bulk of the letter is concerned with the familiar issues of fornication and adultery, which, said Boniface, blotted Aethelbald's record as an otherwise good king. Incidentally, when the missionary contrasted the sexual purity of the pagan Saxons with Aethelbald's licentious conduct he quoted from what the Roman author Tacitus had written in his *Germania* about the 'Germans' in the first century AD. That an old missionary who had spent most of his life in the field amongst the German peoples should still be guided by what Tacitus had to say about Germanic behaviour gives us an insight into the extraordinary influence of the *Germania*, which itself had, of course, been written not as 'straight' ethnography but as critique of Roman degeneracy. Though the work seems to have been lost after this period, since its rediscovery in the fifteenth century it has continued to influence historians right down to the present.[24] Two other letters touch on the Aethelbald missive. The first was addressed to Archbishop Egbert of York and asked him to correct and improve the text of the letter to Aethelbald.[25] This is a convention of courtesy often used when one church-man sent a work to another, and it demonstrates respect for the recipient's learning and spiritual authority. Boniface asked Egbert to make the text known 'to his people', that is, to the Northumbrians. The other letter was addressed to the priest Herefrid and it asked him to convey Boniface's words of admonition to Aethelbald.[26]

The letter to Aethelbald as we have it in the Boniface correspondence does not contain the criticism of Charles Martel. This only occurs in a

---

22 *Bonifatii Epistolae*, no. 73, trans. Emerton, *Letters of St Boniface*, pp. 134–30.
23 T. Reuter, '"Kirchenreform" und "Kirchenpolitik" im Zeitalter Karl Martells: Begriffe und Wirklichkeit', in Jarnut, Nonn and Richter (eds), *Karl Martell in Seiner Zeit*, pp. 35–59.
24 J. Ridé, *L'Image du German dans la Pensée* (Lille and Paris 1977), pp. 129–40.
25 *Bonifatii Epistolae*, no. 75, trans. Emerton, *Letters of St Boniface*, pp. 132–3.
26 *Bonifatii Epistolae*, no. 74, trans. Emerton, *Letters of St Boniface*, pp. 130–1.

version quoted by the Anglo-Norman historian William of Malmesbury. When he dealt with Aethelbald's reign in his *History of the English Kings* (written *c*. 1120) William quoted the letter in an abridged version of about a quarter of its original length, but he included this additional sentence, which was meant to draw attention to the fate of rulers who wronged the church: 'Charles prince of the Franks, who ruined many monasteries and diverted the riches of the church to his own uses, suffered long agony and died a fearful death'.[27] Either William of Malmesbury, perhaps copying some earlier interpolator, inserted the words himself in line with the conventional view of Charles's treatment of the church as handed down by Hincmar, or the passage was already there in the version of the letter which Aethelbald actually received. It was once argued that Egbert could have added the words, since he was asked to improve the text, but, as we have just seen, this request was conventional, and, anyway, Egbert was not asked to send the text to Aethelbald but to make it known to the Northumbrians. This leaves the priest Herefrid as one who might have altered the text, and if it was Herefrid who changed it, the argument goes, he would have changed it in line with what he knew to be Boniface's sentiments.[28] It seems more likely, however, that the insertion was indeed much later, and despite some early-looking terminology, it was very probably William of Malmesbury's gloss on the original text, a gloss which was inspired by a reading of Hincmar. No other contemporary source speaks of Charles Martel suffering a terrible death, and there is good evidence that the texts in which Hincmar criticised Charles Martel were available in the Worcester archive which William of Malmesbury is known to have used. Writing at much the same time as William was another historian, John of Worcester. In his *Chronicle*, John quoted freely not only from Hincmar's *Vita Remigii*, but also from the letter from the Quierzy synod, including the whole text of the Eucherius vision.[29] If this was the source for John of Worcester's view of Charles Martel, it seems very probable that the same source, from the same archive, encouraged William of Malmesbury to embellish the Aethelbald letter in the way he did.[30] William of Malmesbury was, after all, a historian who took great

---

27 William of Malmesbury, *Gesta Regum Anglorum, The History of the English Kings* I, ed. and trans. R. Mynors, R. Thomson and M. Winterbottom (Oxford 1998), chs 80–1, pp. 115–19.

28 Reuter, ' "Kirchenreform" ', pp. 51–8.

29 John of Worcester, *The Chronicle of John of Worcester*, II, *The Annals from 450–1066*, ed. R. Darlington and P. McGurk, trans. P. Bray and P. McGurk (Oxford 1998), s.a. 474, pp. 17–19 for John's use of the *Vita Remigii*, s.a. 741, pp. 189–91 for the Eucherius vision.

30 On the Worcester archive as a common source for the histories of William of Malmesbury and John of Worcester, M. Brett, 'John of Worcester and His Contemporaries', in R.H.C. Davis and J. Wallace-Hadrill (eds), *The Writing of History in the Middle Ages. Essays Presented to Sir Richard Southern* (Oxford 1981), pp. 101–26.

pride in his ability to draw on a wide range of sources in order to enrich his narrative.[31]

If we take the Aethelbald letter out of the picture, and stand back from the Hincmar tradition, then we are left with Boniface's general complaints about sexual misconduct and the giving of bishoprics to laymen. We cannot take seriously the notion that the age of Charles Martel was one of unrestrained fornication, but what Boniface said about laymen taking over bishoprics does accord with what the narrative sources tell us. This is that in order to secure certain important areas Charles Martel did eject the bishop and his followers and replaced them with his own men. There seems no doubt that this was a time in which many bishops exercised military functions, although warrior bishops can be found from time to time throughout the Frankish period. We can also find earlier, isolated examples of laymen who seized bishoprics, but it is only in our period that the intrusion of laymen becomes relatively common. It was not the case, however, that Charles Martel was invariably responsible when laymen did this: some warriors, like Savaric or Hainmar of Auxerre, took over bishoprics independently. Most bishoprics maintained lists of bishops and it is true that in this period many lists show either breaks, suggesting that there was no bishop around, or they qualify names with the term 'called bishop', which means that the incumbent was a layman.[32] The gaps in the lists do not, however, always indicate that particular churches were without a bishop, for it may often have been the case that whoever compiled the list in a later period simply did not know who had been bishop at certain earlier times. The gaps are by no means confined to the age of Charles Martel. And the picture is not all negative. Monasteries continued to be founded and endowed. Even the Milos of the Frankish world gave to some churches just as they took from others. Charles Martel himself sometimes restored property to a church, as he did to St Victor's at Marseilles, as well as presiding over another church's loss of resources, as in the case of Orléans. He was generous to Echternach and to St Denis, and in one hagiographic source, the late-eighth-century *Passion of St Salvian*, he was portrayed as a pious ruler, most concerned to seek justice for the murdered Salvian and very generous to the monastery which housed his remains. This work tells of how Charles called upon the saint to settle a dispute in which a wicked noble tried to disinherit his sisters.[33]

---

31 On how William of Malmesbury used other Carolingian sources, R. Thomson, 'William of Malmesbury's Carolingian Sources', *Journal of Medieval History*, 7 (1981), 321–38.

32 The lists of bishops are to be found in L. Duchesne, *Fastes Épiscopaux de l'Ancienne Gaule* (3 vols, Paris 1894–1915).

33 *Passio Sancti Salvii*, ed. M. Coens, 'La Passion de Saint Sauve, Martyr à Valenciennes', *Analecta Bollandiana*, 87 (1967), commentary 131–63, text 164–87.

Though much of the Salvian tradition may be the stuff of legend and the product of hagiographical convention, it does indicate that in the institutional memory of some churches Charles Martel may have been thought of as just and pious, that is, before Hincmar got hold of his reputation.

On balance the fortunes of the church under Charles Martel were mixed – so mixed, in fact, that it is difficult to speak of the church as a whole rather than of the experiences of particular persons, sees and monasteries. We know nothing about what happened to the majority of churches. Where we do see the ejection of bishops, the intrusion of laymen and a tradition that resources had been seized, this is largely in the context of military conflict. The sequence in which churches suffered losses follows the course of Charles Martel's campaigns of conquest, beginning in western Austrasia, and then moving through Neustria into Burgundy and Provence. The sequence does not reflect a systematic expropriation but it is a measure of the violence with which Charles Martel's regime was established. We should also remember that his successes had been preceded by the collapse of central authority in Burgundy, which had allowed the bishops there to build up military power, hence the cluster of episcopal casualties in this region. The impression that expropriation was systematic comes from one form of land tenure which historians have associated with the leasing out of church land to warriors. This is the so-called 'precarial tenure', which is mentioned with increasing frequency in the charters of our period. Let us now look at how important the granting of *precaria* actually was in the wider context of the relationship between property and power, for this brings us to the nub of the Brunner thesis, namely, the proposition that the rewarding of warriors with church land in this way led to social change.

Precaria

Precaria (singular, *precarium*) were a form of lease. The term is used in documents to describe the written record of the lease or to refer to land held in this way. Historians sometimes use the term more loosely, often in modern form such as the German *Prekarien*, to refer to land given out in return for service, even when the Latin word does not appear in the document concerned. Here the term *precaria* is used strictly in relation to contemporary documents, rather than to refer more generally to (i.e. to 'reify') a form of landholding. The word itself is derived from the Latin *precari*, 'to request', and the essence of a precarial grant was that it was made as a favour in answer to a request. Being dependent upon a favour, it could in principle be revoked at the whim of the grantor, and so another characteristic of the arrangement was that it was supposed to be temporary. It might be subject to renewal, but such a lease could not be made in perpetuity. The sense that this form of land tenure was for a limited period only, and subject to revocation, is perfectly conveyed by the modern term derived from the same root: precarial tenure was in theory 'precarious'. This was as it should have been, for churches were not supposed to alienate land permanently as bishops and abbots were the guardians of God's property. Precarial grants thus developed as one of the means by which the church could make grants of property and yet retain its rights.

One can easily see why some scholars attached particular significance to this form of lease as a link in the relationship between property and power, for it was seen to provide a way in which those with sufficient means could lease land out to dependants who would remain in their debt. In order to ensure that the favour would continue to be granted, these tenants would be bound to provide certain services. And since the grants were made in answer to a request, they could be made to a third party, that is to say, one could request a landowner to make a precarial grant to someone else. We have here a putative mechanism through which Charles Martel might have secularised church land and created those relations of dependence charac-terised as 'feudal'. It is logical to suppose, therefore, that he could have requested that particular churches grant *precaria* to his followers. These men, his 'vassals', would have received the grants as a favour, a 'benefice' (*beneficium*), in return for which they would provide Charles with essential services, above all, military services. The moment at which it became the norm for 'vassals' to receive 'benefices' was, according to the great Belgian historian F.L. Ganshof in a still influential work first published in 1944, the moment at which 'feudalism' as a type of property holding and political power was effectively born.[34] It has already been pointed out that in reality this moment never came, for as a coherent 'system' 'feudalism' in this sense is essentially the construct of historians. The terms 'feudal' and 'feudalism' are, of course, used in a rather different sense by Marxist historians to refer to the relations of production, and social formation, pertaining to medieval Europe in general. This very general use of the terms in the wider eco-nomic frame has little bearing on our discussion of whether or not Charles Martel granted out land in return for military service. In Marxist terms, whatever he did was within the framework of a 'feudal society'.

In our period few followers and clients were termed 'vassals'. Nor did the term 'vassal' usually denote a military follower dependent upon a grant of land from a lord. The term *beneficium* rarely meant land held in return for

---

34   F. Ganshof, *Feudalism*, trans. P. Grierson (London 1964), pp. 3–19.

military service, for it covered a great variety of different favours, not least spiritual ones. In his Lexicon of early medieval Latin, J.F. Niermeyer listed no less than forty-one ways in which the term was used, and only a handful of these are to do with land held in precarial tenure or associated with military service.[35] Most recorded leases, that is, grants on favourable terms, or grants with restricted rights, had nothing at all to do with military services, and the basis upon which people did perform military service is largely unknown. Two pieces of evidence have often been quoted to show that Charles Martel did use precarial grants on a massive scale to endow his men, whether or not these endowments can be termed 'feudal'. But what this and other evidence for *precaria* actually suggests is that property relations were complex and even confused. It is the very messiness of the situation, rather than any new and neat arrangement, which provides clues about how Charles Martel may have built up his power. Let us look at the evidence.

In March 743 Charles Martel's son Karloman held a council of the church at Estinnes in present-day Belgium. Apart from the familiar condemnation of fornicating clergy, the council tackled the problem of land lost by the church. Karloman had earlier promised to restore all that the church had lost in previous years, but at Estinnes he announced that adverse circumstances meant that some land would have to be retained in order to support the army. This is the key passage: 'Because of the wars which threaten, and on account of the hostility of the rest of the peoples who surround us, we have decided, with the advice of the servants of God and of the Christian people, to keep for a while longer a portion of church property'. This property would, with God's indulgence, be held as *precaria* by men who performed military service in Karloman's army as part of church contingents. The land would be subject to rent (*census*) paid by those in whose name the *precaria* were held. Only churches which could afford it would be subject to this imposition. Any church brought to penury by the measure would have all its land restored. For the others, the rent would be substantial: one *solidus* from each household (*casata*) each year (each estate would contain dozens, if not hundreds, of *casatae*).[36]

---

35   J. Niermeyer, *Mediae Latinae Lexicon Minus* (Leiden 1984), pp. 91–96. *Beneficium* is by far the largest entry in this impressive work. This is not surprising for a term which could be used to denote all kinds of favours, at a time in which social interaction revolved around the giving, receiving and returning of favours.

36   *Concilium Liftinense*, ed. A. Werminghoff, *MGH Concilia* II, i (Hanover and Leipzig 1906), pp. 6–7, here ch. 2, p. 7. For comment on the measures put forward at Estinnes, see E. Lesne, *Histoire de la Propriété Ecclésiastique en France* (6 vols, Lille 1910–38), II, i, pp. 40–7. Lesne's work on church property in this period remains essential reading. Lesne was influenced by the Brunner school, but his careful use of evidence led him to keep an open mind about Charles Martel's treatment of the church.

One might conclude from this passage that Charles Martel had indeed forced the church to give out *precaria* to his warriors, and that Karloman had been under pressure (from Boniface?) to stop the practice, but that he now found that he could not manage without this new-found military resource. We cannot tell, however, when, how or in what circumstances the original grants had been made, or whether, in fact, they had been made as *precaria* in the first place. This council was intended to introduce reform, so that it could be the case that it was to the church's advantage to decree that all the land previously given out to laymen should now be counted as precarial land. The advantage lay in the fact that to say that a grant was precarial was to confirm the grantor's ownership, and this was signified by the payment of *census*, which in this case was extraordinarily high, fifty times higher, in fact, than it would be in Charlemagne's day. If the payment of one *solidus* per *casata* really was made, the church would have received a large proportion of the temporary landlord's profits. But the rate may have been more symbolic than actual. There were no *solidus* coins in circulation at this time, and the term may denote a token payment by which each *casata* was marked as belonging to the church.

The Council of Estinnes went on to state that when the tenant died the land should return to the church, or if the ruler judged that it was still necessary for the land to be used as a military resource, a new precarial grant should be made, and written down again, thus once again publicly stating that the church was the owner of the land. The measures announced at Estinnes may therefore have been designed to clear up a situation in which the ultimate right to, as well as the occupation of, land had been contested.[37] Far from continuing a practice which had become systematic, the council may, in effect, have introduced a new system in which the ruler claimed the right to make precarial grants in order to defend the 'Christian people', but at the same time pledged himself to guarantee the church's ultimate ownership of the land and to make sure that no church would be reduced to poverty. The provisions of Estinnes were further developed in subsequent Carolingian practice and legislation. Soon it became common to refer to *precaria verbo regis*, that is, grants made at the request, and also backed by the authority, of the king. Another step was to formalise the notion that churches should not be left without the means to carry out their duties by creating a protected reserve of land which could not in any circumstance be granted out.[38] Finally in 779 Charlemagne reduced the

---

37 Wolfram, 'Lehenswesen', pp. 71–3.
38 For a clear statement of the principle and practice of the so-called Carolingian *divisio* of church land, W. Goffart, *The Le Mans Forgeries* (Cambridge Mass. 1966), pp. 6–15.

census to a fiftieth of the Estinnes level. These measures helped the Carolingians to strengthen their control over the lands of the bishoprics and
major monasteries, and this they needed to do in order to help support a
growing number of dependants, clients and functionaries. It is ironic that
Charles Martel's sons and grandson should win reputations as reformers of
the church and yet it was they who made more systematic that use of church
land for which the first Charles was blamed, but which he had engaged in
only in a very limited *ad hoc* way.

Our second piece of evidence comes from the *Gesta* of the abbots of
St Wandrille, and although this work was put together in the mid-ninth
century, what it has to say about the eighth century is generally regarded as
reliable because it is based on archive material. It is, as we saw in an earlier
chapter, a faintly anti-Carolingian work. The *Gesta* say that under Abbot
Teutsind (elected 735/36) St Wandrille was reduced to poverty, having lost
a third of its property, which was given to Teutsind's relatives and to the
king's men.[39] The source then detailed one of the losses, a *precarium* given to
one Count Ratharius. It consisted of twenty-eight *villae* (estates), many of
which had originally come to St Wandrille from the royal fisc. In return
Ratharius paid a yearly rent of sixty *solidi* (a fraction of the Estinnes rate)
which was to fund the lights of the abbey church.

One might take the *Gesta* at its word and imagine that it really had been
reduced to poverty in the age of Charles Martel, and if we see both Teutsind
and the 'king's men' as Charles's supporters, then we appear to have a concrete case of depredation through the grant of *precaria* in return for military
services. But as Ian Wood has recently argued, the St Wandrille case is by
no means as straightforward as this.[40] It was, Wood points out, normal for
the richer churches to make precarial arrangements of their own, without
compulsion, in order to manage lands which had grown too massive to
exploit directly.[41] Usually such arrangements could be made with friends
and clients of the church. What seems to have irked St Wandrille in this
case was that Teutsind, although in other ways generous to the abbey, was
an outsider, and Count Ratharius was no doubt an outsider too. In 787 on
the death of Abbot Witlaic, St Wandrille drew up an inventory of its lands,
and this allows us to see that it had clearly not been impoverished as a
result of Teutsind's grants. In 787 it owned 3,964 *mansi* (farmsteads). Of
these the monks held 1,313 for their own use, and 2,395 were let out as

---

39 *Gesta Sanctorum Patrum Fontanellensis Coenobii*, ed. F. Lohier and J. Laporte (Rouen 1936), IV,
    1–2, pp. 46–51.
40 I. Wood, 'Teutsind, Witlaic and the history of Merovingian *precaria*', in W. Davies and
    P. Fouracre (eds), *Property and Power in the Early Middle Ages* (Cambridge 1995), pp. 31–52.
41 Wood, 'Teutsind', p. 47. See also Reynolds, *Fiefs and Vassals*, p. 78.

beneficia. In addition, Witlaic had let others out to the king's men or to other men 'which he should not have done at all', i.e. it was these ones, not the other 2,395 *beneficia,* which were regarded as 'lost'.[42] In other words, the granting out of land on restricted terms was quite normal. The monastic community might complain bitterly about land that had been lost in precarial grants made to king's men and to others picked by the abbots (his friends and kin) without the consent of the monks, but in relation to the whole, the proportion felt to be 'lost' was in fact small. This evidence puts the issue of *precaria* into a rather different perspective.

Although we can identify essential characteristics common to all precarial grants, it is also true that motives for making the grants and the circumstances in which they were made could be very different. We have just seen how a major ecclesiastical institution like St Wandrille had much more property than it could control directly. The justification for the ownership of property by the church was that property provided the means for each church to carry out its liturgical functions and to support the Christian community with alms.[43] The granting of *precaria,* a form of temporary grant, allowed the church to give to others the control of land it could no longer manage itself, without giving up the ownership of the land. Those others would then be closely associated with the monastery as armed clients and supporters. When the *census* was dedicated to a liturgical purpose or reserved for alms, this both underlined and justified the fact that it was the church which retained the ultimate right to the property. This kind of dedication we saw with Ratharius, whose *census* of sixty *solidi* was to pay for the lights to be burned in the St Wandrille church. Another form of precarial arrangement, and the one which is by far the most common to be found throughout the early medieval period, involved a gift of land to the church, some or all of which was then received back on request, *in precaria.* The donor retained the land in usufruct (that is, they could take the income from the land) for the rest of their life, which meant that they could give to the church without personal impoverishment. After they died the church would have full rights over the land. It is in the countless documents detailing grants of this kind, often concerning small amounts of land, and relating to people of modest means, that we see how churches and monasteries built up a very wide circle of clients, friends and dependants. Families which had a close association with a church did not lose control over land they donated to it, for not only were family members likely to be among the clergy of the

---

42 Wood, 'Teutsind', p. 38.
43 D. Ganz, 'The Ideology of Sharing: Apostolic Community and Ecclesiastical Property in the Early Middle Ages', in Davies and Fouracre (eds), *Property and Power*, pp. 17–30.

church or part of the monastic community, they also often managed to pass on their precarial tenancies to the next generation. It has indeed been argued that in some areas, for example in later eighth-century Bavaria, precarial tenancies became a device for passing on land to a single heir rather than dividing it.[44] This happened when the original donor asked in his or her request that when he or she died the precarial lease be renewed for a limited group of people, which usually meant keeping the land in the line of direct male descendants. In this way the spread of *precaria* has been compared to the development of so-called 'bookland' in Anglo-Saxon England at roughly the same time, for both *precaria* and 'bookland' allowed families to preserve selected properties from division between heirs and to strengthen their rights of disposal over them.[45] Finally, we have what was probably always the least common form of *precaria*, the one with which we began, the grant of land at the request of the ruler.

Why was it now, the mid-eighth century, that these three kinds of precarial grant became more common? A church such as St Wandrille had acquired the bulk of its property in the seventh and early eighth centuries, and it was thus in the mid-eighth century that we see it letting out large numbers of *mansi*. Ratharius's *precarium*, for instance, included estates that we know were originally donated in the early 670s. In the seventh century donations to the church tended to be large-scale, and came from kings, queens and magnates. It is from the early eighth century onwards that we see the smaller gifts of lesser people, and this is the context in which the most common form of *precaria* developed. Their increasing use relates to the foundation of new churches and monasteries and also to the spread of charters, the combination of which provided the opportunity and means to use precarial tenure as strategy for passing on land undivided. Finally, as the Council of Estinnes implied, it was the turmoil of the mid-eighth century which led rulers to claim a right to request the church to let out land as a way of securing a military resource. Interestingly, the Agilolfings in Bavaria were making precarial requests at this time too.[46] But it must be stressed that the systematic use of church land in this way by rulers came after, not in, the age of Charles Martel – that is, if it came at all.

---

44 W. Hartung, 'Adel, Erbrecht, Schenkung: Die strukturellen Ursachen der frühmittelalterlichen Besitzübertragungen an die Kirche' and J. Jahn, 'Tradere ad Sanctum: Politische und gesellschaftliche Aspekte der Traditionspraxis im agilolfingischen Bayern', both in F. Seibt (ed.), *Gesellschaftsgeschichte. Festschrift für Karl Bosl zum 80. Geburtstag* (2 vols, Munich 1988), I, pp. 417–38 and pp. 400–16.

45 T. Reuter, 'Property Transactions and Social Relations between Rulers, Bishops and Nobles in Early Eleventh-century Saxony: The Evidence of the *Vita Meinwerci*', in Davies and Fouracre (eds), *Property and Power*, pp. 165–99, at pp. 171–2.

46 Wolfram, 'Lehenswesen', pp. 66–8.

The effect, and perhaps one of the main purposes, of making precarial grants was to record a tenant's right of possession at the same time as his or her landlord's ownership was publicly stated. The spread of precarial arrangements of all kinds in the course of the eighth century suggests that it was becoming common for the lesser nobility, or small-scale landowners, to possess land in this way, and as we have seen, some people who owned their own land were turning their holdings into precarial tenures by giving them to the church and receiving them back again. Land held in tenure which was in principle precarious, but was undivided, may, it seems, have afforded better protection for social status than land owned outright ('allodial' land). Allods had the further characteristic of being subject to division. Families had to adopt variable and flexible strategies in the ways in which they held land to fit changing and competing interests of family members and family groups. We cannot tell how in an earlier period most nobles who were not magnates held their land, for we do not have sufficient charter evidence. We can see, however, that as in the case of St Wandrille, the great blocs of land held by the kings, magnates and major churches were later reorganised into smaller units, and became subject to that process of 'manorialisation' which Theuws describes for Echternach's estates in Toxandria. It was no doubt this kind of economic unit, worked by the labour of dependent peasants, which was in the hands of precarial tenants, and, of course, in the hands of other kinds of tenants too. The fundamental resources of the unit we may see in the *casatae* of the Estinnes legislation, or in the *mansi* of the Witlaic inventory, that is, peasant households, who were in themselves tenants, paying rent in labour services, cash and kind. It was these which supplied what Estinnes simply called 'our army', although others would have supplied it too: it is only the church lands and church tenants we hear about. It has been convincingly argued that the reorganisation of the large estates in this fashion was led by the church.[47] If so, the Brunner thesis put the cart before the horse: the church leased out its land first, then came Charles Martel.

The provision of secure landholdings with a tied workforce (and not just on church lands) may have provided some of the resources to raise an army, but it no doubt was the opportunities to increase wealth and raise social status which the rewards of warfare offered that made that army willing to serve. We can, of course, only speculate about what motivated people to fight, for no source of our period was ever concerned with what drove ordinary soldiers, as opposed to the motives and morals of leaders. There are a few famous instances in the pages of Gregory of Tours which

---

47 J-P. Devroey, 'Réflexions sur l'Économie des Premiers Temps Carolingiens: Grands Domaines et Action Politique entre Seine et Rhin', *Francia*, 13 (1985), 475–88.

suggest that in the sixth century some Frankish warriors fought simply for the prospect of booty.[48] In the *Continuations of Fredegar* and the *LHF* we see loyalty to king and faction as factors in addition to the lure of booty. And we saw from the narrative of Charles Martel's early years that people also fought for survival. It was argued in an earlier chapter that as Charles Martel became increasingly successful more and more people joined his cause, until he built up a force which was effectively unstoppable. Charles no doubt engendered loyalty among his troops, and one could suggest that honour, prestige, social obligation, and real and fictive kinship were among the other factors which would have encouraged military solidarity and helped build an *esprit de corps*. But what emerges from our narrative sources is that it was, as ever, booty which they saw as the main draw.

After the battle of Vinchy (717), Charles's successes were invariably crowned with the taking of booty, usually described in the sources as 'much booty'. The spoils, as we know, included *honores*, that is, lands and offices, so that we should imagine that supporters received rewards appropriate to their social status, ranging from small amounts of movable wealth or cash for the least honourable, to whole counties or bishoprics for the most honourable. It is generally accepted by both historians and archaeologists that there was intense competition for wealth and social status, and that it was the success-ful competitors who formed the social elite. Although in most areas ruled or attacked by Charles Martel the process of elite formation had taken place long ago, that elite remained relatively open, and an element of strong com-petition continued to govern social behaviour. It was therefore not simple greed, but rather social necessity, and accepted rules and obligations, which drove warriors to seek booty under the leadership of Charles Martel. If we accept this proposition, there is no need to postulate that land would have had to be granted out before people would have agreed to perform military service.

Military organisation

As to the actual form of military organisation in this period, we have very few clues.[49] We know that throughout the Frankish period there was a

---

48 See, for instance, Gregory of Tours, *Decem Libri Historiarum*, ed. B. Krusch and W. Levison, *MGH SRM* I: (Hanover 1951), III, ch. 11, pp. 107–8, trans. L. Thorpe, *Gregory of Tours. The History of the Franks* (Harmondsworth 1974), p. 171, a passage which tells of the events of 534, when King Theuderic I's warriors threatened to desert him unless he led them to plunder.

49 The essential guide to this subject remains B. Bachrach, *Merovingian Military Organisation* (Minneapolis 1972). See also B. Bachrach, 'Military Organisation in Aquitaine under the Early Carolingians', *Speculum*, 49 (1974), 1–33.

general military obligation laid on all free men to defend the land. But the impression from later evidence is that rulers mostly demanded that the obligation be discharged in cash rather than service where the mass of people was concerned. A systematic organisation of the kingdom aimed at providing a general levy seems to emerge only when the Carolingian Empire began to be put under pressure in the early ninth century.[50] It is interesting here to remember the concern with military resources expressed at the Council of Estinnes, for at this moment too the pressing need was for defence. When the Carolingian regime was expanding there seems to have been no shortage of willing recruits, and little reference to resources.

It is logical to argue that the prolonged fighting of this period led to a militarisation of society, that is to say, growing numbers of people were involved in fighting. The basis for this argument is simply that more conflict is recorded in the sources from the later seventh century onwards. Not only was there fighting between Austrasians and Neustrians in the years 676–87 and 714–19, there was at the same time also conflict between Franks and Frisians, Saxons and 'Sueves'. The Aquitanians fought with the Arabs, there was turmoil in Burgundy in the time of Savaric, and of course we have Charles Martel's extensive campaigns after the defeat of the Neustrians. It would nevertheless be wrong to think that Frankish society in this period reverted to a type in which power was based upon plunder and the warband was the principal form of political organisation and leading social institution.

As we saw earlier, both in this chapter and in Chapter 1, it was essentially the income from the soil which supported the social elite. The additional income which came from the spoils of war must have played an important part in giving particular nobles an edge over potential rivals, but by securing and improving their status it reinforced, rather than subverted, the landed base of political power. Moreover, land organised into discrete units and worked by a closely supervised labour force, whose produce could be directly collected by a lord living in or nearby the settlement, was in military terms a far more potent and reliable resource than the tribute and plunder rather haphazardly collected by the warband. On this point the Brunner school was quite right: the organisation of the countryside into the collections of *mansi* or *casatae* that we see reflected in precarial grants did indeed provide the resources for larger numbers of cavalrymen. It was not, however, Charles Martel who called this development into being; rather it was the product of that reorganisation of large estates which we described

---

50 This is the argument of T. Reuter, 'Plunder and Tribute in the Carolingian Empire', *Transactions of the Royal Historical Society*, 5th series, 35 (1985), 75–94, and T. Reuter, 'The End of Carolingian Military Expansion', in P. Godman and R. Collins (eds), *Charlemagne's Heir* (Oxford 1990), pp. 391–405.

earlier, in conjunction with a prolonged period of military conflict and the incentive provided by the prospect of gaining much-needed extra wealth. The Franks had always used cavalry. What was necessary for the spread of cavalry was not technological invention or political genius, but simply wealth and organisation, and as more wealth was gathered in the countryside in the course of the later seventh and eighth centuries, an increasing number of people could afford the expensive horses and more sophisticated equipment needed to become mounted warriors or to enable others to do so.[51] For two reasons it is also unhistorical to think that the introduction of the stirrup suddenly changed the way in which these cavalrymen fought. First, the spread of the stirrup was gradual and its use is not well attested in our period. Second, the evolution of cavalry into the shock force of knights so effectively deployed by the Normans and others was a slow and complex process, again owing more to sociological development than to any technological breakthrough. Most historians would place the so-called 'rise of knighthood' well into the post-Carolingian period, that is, into the tenth and eleventh centuries.

That Charles Martel did make extensive use of mounted warriors must be the conclusion to be drawn from the speed and extensive range of his operations. An example of speed is Charles's rapid intervention against the Arab raiders in Aquitaine in 733 (or 732), and in an earlier chapter we emphasised the extraordinary distances his forces could cover in a single year. It is, however, only from the more detailed narratives and legislation from the reign of Charlemagne that we can form a clear impression of how these warriors fought and of what equipment they used. These later-eighth- and early-ninth-century sources suggest that the Frankish armies were spearheaded by an elite force of mounted warriors who fought with lances, swords and bows. Alongside them fought much larger forces of less well equipped infantry. This is to say very little: all early medieval armies on the Continent appear similar in this respect, and there is no reason why the armies of Charles Martel should have been much different from those of his grandson.

According to the *Continuations of Fredegar*, Charles's son Pippin switched the month of the annual assembly from March to May.[52] This has been interpreted as a response to a change in the composition of the army, from a preponderantly infantry force to one which relied much more heavily upon cavalry, the thinking being that a cavalry force would have to wait

---

51 C. Hammer, 'Land Sales in Eighth- and Ninth-Century Bavaria: Legal, Social and Economic Aspects', *Early Medieval Europe*, 6 (1997), 47–76, at 65–6.
52 *Fred. Contin.*, ed. and trans. J.M. Wallace-Hadrill (London 1960), ch. 48, p. 116.

until later in the spring to campaign, because only then would there have been enough grass for the horses.[53] But all armies had large numbers of horses which needed feeding, whether or not men charged into battle upon them. It may be that the change to May reveals simply that the assemblies and the armies had grown larger, and that now they were expected to go on campaign directly after the meeting, for as we have already seen, by the mid-eighth century, years without a campaign were becoming very rare. Another possible factor could be that Pippin, having recently taken the crown from the Merovingians, wished to alter the time of the assembly in order to stamp the new dynasty's identity upon a gathering which had traditionally been a focal point of loyalty to the Merovingians. As to the actual battles in which Charles Martel fought, we have very few details except from the *Continuations of Fredegar*'s reports on Poitiers in 733 (or 732), and on the storming of Avignon and the Septimanian campaign of 737. These reports are highly stylised. The attack on Avignon, we may recall, was compared to Joshua's storming of Jericho in the Old Testament. Nevertheless the fact that it was stormed does tell us that Charles Martel's army was able to take a strongly fortified town, and the military history in general shows that that army was a versatile force, as we saw when Charles mounted a naval expedition to Frisia. What we do not see in the sources is any reference to the logistics of warfare, but given the massive size of the Frankish kingdom from the sixth century onwards, we must assume a well-developed expertise in moving supplies and troops over large distances.

The Continuator's brief account of the battle of Poitiers has sometimes been taken as evidence that Charles Martel's army did indeed use the massed cavalry charge, and that it was this which gave them victory over the Arabs. Let us first look at the key passage in the original and then at how J.M. Wallace-Hadrill translated it.

Contra quos [the Arabs] Carlus princeps audacter aciem instruit, super eosque belligerator inruit. Christo auxiliante tentoria eorum subvertit, ad proelium stragem conterendam accurrit interfecto rege eorum Abdirama prostravit, exercitum proterens, dimicavit et devicit; sicque victor de hostibus triumphavit.[54]

Taking boldness as his counsellor Prince Charles set the battle in array against them [the Arabs] and came upon them like a mighty man of war. With Christ's help he overran their tents, following hard after them in the battle to grind them small in their overthrow, and when 'Abd ar-Rahman

---

53   B. Bachrach, 'Was Marchfield Part of the Frankish Constitution?', *Medieval Studies*, 36 (1974), 178–85.
54   *Fred. Contin.*, ch. 13, pp. 90–1.

perished in the battle he utterly destroyed their armies, scattering them like stubble before the fury of his onslaught; and in the power of Christ he utterly destroyed them. So did he triumph over all his enemies in this his glorious day of victory.

On the face of it, the passage as Wallace-Hadrill translated it could describe a cavalry charge which burst through the Arab camp, and 'followed hard' into the enemy lines, smashing them to pieces, and 'scattering them like stubble'. It thus seems to support a central tenet of the Brunner thesis: that it was in response to Arab attacks that the Franks developed the effective use of shock cavalry. It is clear, however, both that the Continuator was not presenting a literal description of the battle and that the Wallace-Hadrill translation (which has been in standard use among English-speaking students of the period for nearly forty years) is itself far from literal, and indeed in some respects actually misleading. A more accurate, if less elegant, rendering of the passage would be:

Prince Charles boldly drew up his battle line against them [the Arabs] and the warrior rushed in against them. With Christ's help he overturned their tents, and hastened to battle to grind them small in slaughter. The king Abdirama having been killed, he destroyed [them], driving forth the army, he fought and he won. Thus did the victor triumph over his enemies.

Nowhere in the original is there anything about 'following hard' and 'scattering them like stubble before the fury of his onslaught'. Nor, incidentally, is there anything about the 'power of Christ', or the 'glorious day of victory'. Wallace-Hadrill's embellishments had the effect of magnifying the victory and they reinforced the impression that it was due to a cavalry charge. In the original the only possible hint that we are dealing with a charge comes in the word *inruit*, that Charles 'rushed in' and as a result overturned the tents. But here the author has taken his phraseology from the Book of Numbers, chapter 24, where the Spirit of God 'rushed in' to the tents of Israel. The term for warrior, *belligerator*, is also biblical, from the Book of Maccabees, chapters 15 and 16, which describe huge battles. There is, in short, no way that we can read a cavalry charge into the *Continuations of Fredegar*'s few words about the battle of Poitiers. This is not to say that cavalry could not have played its part at Poitiers, nor in any of the other battles fought in the age of Charles Martel. The point is simply that there is not enough evidence to show that there was a decisive change either in the way in which the Franks fought, or in the way in which they organised the resources needed to support their warriors.

Francia under Charles Martel saw more warfare than it had since the days of Clovis. In some areas, such as Provence, prolonged conflict may have threatened to destabilise the very social order, but more generally there is no sign that any kind of social or economic crisis resulted from the fighting. It is, of course, expecting too much of our sources to imagine that they would have reported any matters of humanitarian concern, such as the displacement of people by warfare, or the damage done by armies. We might nevertheless reasonably expect to hear of widespread famine if it occurred, as we do later in the century, and we might just hope to detect traces of any economic collapse (as we can in Provence) or of steep demographic decline. There is no evidence of either in this period, apart from the collapse of Mediterranean trade in the south. On the contrary, there are faint signs of a growth both in population and in economic activity. Silver coinage became more plentiful. Trading centres, which archaeologists term *emporia*, continued to develop on the coasts and along the major rivers. In the last chapter we also saw how a much older centre, Strasbourg, grew at this time. *Emporia*, it is argued, developed in order to service the needs of the elite in society, as centres in which they owned properties and at which they could concentrate and exchange surplus produce from their estates.[55] They could thus acquire the high-value exotic goods which traders brought to the *emporia* and which were necessary for the display of high status and for the distribution of rewards to followers. Their development therefore complements that process of elite formation which archaeologists and historians have detected in the lands on the periphery of Francia. Militarisation (that is, adding the spoils of war to the income available to the noble) and manorialisation (that is, organising peasant labour in order to provide him with a more dependable income) both helped to maintain a newly emerged social elite, and at the same time facilitated the cultural integration of the peripheral areas with the rest of Francia.

Vassals

Ganshof laid great stress on the growing importance of vassalage in our period. He argued that the vassal was originally a lowly figure in service to a

---

55 *Emporia* are thought to have developed under the aegis of rulers who wished to facilitate the import of those luxury goods they needed for display and gift exchange. See, for instance, R. Hodges and B. Hobley (eds), *The Rebirth of Towns in the West, 700–1050* (London 1988). Recently a more nuanced picture has emerged, one which sees the *emporia* develop to meet the needs of the elite in general, and thus to have a greater impact on the hinterland economies. See C. Scull, 'Urban Centres in Pre-Viking England?', in J. Hines (ed.), *The Anglo-Saxons From the Migration Period to the Eighth Century. An Ethnographic Perspective* (Woodbridge 1997), pp. 269–310, esp. pp. 284–92.

noble. The form of tie between the noble and his servant or vassal, so-called 'homage', was based on that of 'commendation' in which an inferior had once pledged complete loyalty to, and total dependence upon, a superior. Originally the act of commendation had been one in which a desperate person might in effect sell himself and his descendants into servitude in return for a guarantee of food and physical safety.[56] In Ganshof's view, these type of agreements became increasingly common as the conditions of near anarchy which characterised the later Merovingian period forced lords to build up their forces and to recruit men in pacts of service and security. The pacts became the mechanism through which a lord secured the services of his warrior followers, the vassals. As the warrior developed into the cavalryman, his standing rose, until it was no dishonour for members of the elite to become vassals of other lords. The classic example often given of a magnate of high standing becoming a vassal in this way was that of Charlemagne's cousin Tassilo. In 757, Tassilo, the duke of Bavaria, who was the son of Odilo and Chiltrude, was said to have been made the vassal of his uncle, Pippin.[57] As we have already seen, it was when these vassals were rewarded with 'benefices' that Ganshof judged that 'feudalism' had begun. In his view, 'feudalism' was the base upon which Carolingian power was constructed: its development was held to have marked a structural change in the nature of the Frankish kingdom, which was now rebuilt upon foundations of firmer reciprocal obligations between the rulers and their magnates than the Merovingians had ever been able to engineer.[58]

It must be pointed out, yet again, that there is no evidence with which to back up this sweeping hypothesis, and in particular, the impression that later Merovingian Francia was anarchic now seems groundless. Tassilo's vassalage, moreover, is now thought to indicate the opposite of what Ganshof's school believed, that is to say, vassalage was imposed on Tassilo as a way of humiliating him by forcing him to accept a form of service associated with inferiority.[59] Making him a vassal was a way of stating that he was Pippin's servant, not his equal in blood and authority. It could nevertheless be the case that in this period oaths of mutual support and loyalty sworn between

---

56   This form of commendation is late-Roman in origin. No records of cases survive, and what is usually quoted as evidence for commendation is a 'formula' (charter model) from Tours: *Formulae Turonenses*, ed. K. Zeumer, *MGH Formulae Merovingici et Karoli Aevi* (Hanover 1886), no. 43, p. 158. Though the Tours Formulary dates from the early eighth century, its models are said to relate to a much earlier period. Ganshof, *Feudalism*, pp. 6–7 quoted the Tours commendation formula in its entirety and made it a cornerstone in his argument about the origins of feudalism.
57   *Royal Frankish Annals*, s.a. 757, trans. B. Sholz, *Carolingian Chronicles* (Ann Arbor 1972), p. 42.
58   Ganshof, *Feudalism*, pp. 51–61.
59   Reynolds, *Fiefs and Vassals*, p. 86.

lords and followers did become more prominent, and that there was indeed a growing emphasis on military obligations owed to superiors. If so, it would still be unnecessary to resort to a notion of structural change in the nature of political power and authority in order to explain it. An increase in warfare could have meant that magnates wished to secure the services of warriors on a more permanent basis. Second, one can imagine that the decline of Merovingian authority, and a possible reluctance to swear loyalty to a king controlled by Charles Martel, might have meant a change in the way in which armed forces were recruited, that is to say, soldiers now swore oaths of loyalty to magnates rather than to the king, although the source material here does not allow us to demonstrate that the situation had actually changed since the late seventh century. Third, the appearance of vassals in the sources (still relatively uncommon in the mid-eighth century) might be linked to the decline of a class of men who had enjoyed the special protection of the Merovingian kings. These were the *antrustiones*, mentioned fairly often in the royal legislation of the sixth and early seventh centuries, but rare thereafter. The late-seventh-century *Formulary of Marculf* preserved the model of charter which recorded how someone became an *antrustio*.[60] The man to be so honoured would appear with his weapons before the king and, placing his hand in the king's, he would pledge fidelity and support in war. Here the making of *antrustiones* looks very like the way in which at a much later date vassals swore oaths of loyalty, pledged military service and were assured of their lord's protection. Only kings could make *antrustiones*. Magnates, however, might have imitated the practice by conferring special status upon their own followers in a similar, but specifically non-royal ceremony. In our period, the Carolingians are to be included among the magnates, which is why they too made 'vassals' of some of their followers. They continued to use the term even after they became kings, perhaps because the term *antrustiones* had been out of use for so long that it had effectively been forgotten, or alternatively, if it had been remembered for its particular association with the Merovingian kings, the Carolingians might not have wished to revive it.

If vassalage did indeed become more important at this time, and if these explanations for its 'rise' hold true, it follows that this development, which lay at the heart of Ganshof's conception of so-called 'Carolingian feudalism', might thus indicate little more than that some magnates appropriated military authority formerly reserved to the kings, and that they also imitated royal practice in having men swear a kind of super-fidelity to them.

---

60 *Marculfi Formularum Libri Duo*, ed. and French trans. A. Uddholm (Uppsala 1962), I, 19, pp. 86–7.

Far from transforming the nature of power in Francia, this process of acculturation to royal practice actually reinforced the existing structure. As we saw at the beginning of this study, political institutions, law, custom and policing machinery in Francia changed remarkably little from the seventh through to the ninth centuries. In this wider frame, any 'rising' that vassals did, had relatively little effect upon the way in which power was organised. The appearance in a few eighth-century sources of high-status vassals reflected, in other words, a shift in terminology rather than a redistribution of power itself.

The age of Charles Martel can be seen as marking the transition between Merovingian and Carolingian regimes in Francia. Although under Charles Martel some church leaders, and some churches and monasteries, were caught up in conflict and suffered as a result, the Frankish church in general was in this period expanding into new areas in Frisia, Thuringia, Hesse and Bavaria. New monasteries and churches continued to be founded, and we can document a wider social range of people giving gifts to the church. This we can see from an increasing number of charters, and these also reveal to us both the spread of precarial tenures and the organisation of land into farmsteads (*mansi*) grouped around the central holding of a lord. Estates organised in this way appear to have been more productive, or at least allowed lords to collect surplus production more efficiently. A result of the collection of more wealth in the countryside was a growth in the number of silver coins in circulation and the continuing expansion of specialist trading centres. It was reasoned earlier that increased wealth at the disposal of lords would have made it possible for a larger number of people to afford the horses and other costs of mounted warfare. We have seen that there was, at any rate, more warfare in this period than in the previous generations, so that however people fought, we can speak of a stronger military element in Francia.

The need to provide for armies may have stimulated some, or all, of the developments just outlined, but this is impossible to quantify, or to qualify except in theoretical terms. It is possible with greater certainty to demonstrate that these changes had their origins in an earlier period. There is evidence for the development of precarial tenures, the reorganisation of estates, the spread of a silver coinage and the use of *emporia* in the late seventh century. This evidence is centred on Neustria and western Austrasia, the regions which produced the bulk of the earliest charters, and in which there was a concentration of newly founded rural monasteries. If we describe this area as the core of the Frankish kingdom, we can say that one effect of increased military and missionary activity in the time of Charles Martel was to spread these developments from the core to the periphery of Francia. It is in this sense that the age of Charles Martel can be described

153

as transitional, for by the second generation of Carolingian kings there was in terms of religious and elite culture, and political and military organisation, very little to distinguish the former areas of core and periphery.

Charles Martel worked through traditional custom and existing political institutions. Above all, he retained the royal palace as the central political institution in Francia. It was, after all, through his tenure of the office of mayor of the palace that his power was made legitimate. The effect of his success was eventually to breathe new life into the palace, even though in the short term he himself forced the Merovingian king into the shadows, alienated many magnates from the palace, and finally ruled without a king. Later, under a dynamic Carolingian regime committed to expansion and to a programme of moral reform, the powers of the Frankish king would be massively enhanced. A growth in the power of the ruler and the success of Frankish culture and institutions went hand in hand. But the development of such a regime was by no means a foregone conclusion when Charles Martel died in 741. In the next and final chapter we shall look at the last years of Charles's career and assess his standing in Francia at the end of it. We shall also see how his sons had to fight hard to cling on to his legacy, for after his death, Pippin and Karloman faced a crisis nearly as severe as the one Charles had faced when his own father Pippin died in 714. This time the resolution of a 'succession crisis' would lead directly to the elevation of the Carolingian leader as king.

CHAPTER SIX

Mayor Without a King and
King Without a Mayor

In this chapter we shall look at the events of the last years of Charles Martel's career and assess his position and standing at the time of his death in 741. There are two closely related issues here which require careful thought. The first is how and why Charles was able to rule without a king from 737 to 741. The second is the question of what Charles hoped or intended should happen after his death. Both issues turn on the history of the Carolingian family itself. We shall then follow the narrative of Frankish history over the next decade to 754, that is, up to the moment at which it was declared that henceforth the kings of the Franks should be chosen only from among the descendants of Charles's son Pippin. From this vantage point we can then think about the significance of Martel's career against the unfolding background of developments across the whole period we have examined, from the mid-seventh to the mid-eighth century.

So far we have either talked in general terms about the political and cultural background to Charles Martel's career, or we have discussed in some detail the particular campaigns and events which charted his rise to power. If little has been said about his government, this is for the simple reason that we can learn next to nothing about it. As we know, very few of Charles Martel's charters have survived, and, crucially, no charters at all survive from the years 727–40 when he was at the height of his power. No more than a handful of royal charters are preserved from the period after 717. What material there is includes only one *placitum*, and this document reveals nothing about those who took part in the judgement concerned.[1] This is unfortunate as, for the decades before 717, it is the charters issued

---

1 *MGH DD*, ed. G. Pertz (Hanover 1872), no. 94, p. 84.

from the palace, and especially those *placita* which list the members of the judgement tribunal, that can tell us most about the personnel, offices, and procedures of the royal court. Nor do the narrative sources for our period cast much light on the court. In contrast to the *LHF*, the *Continuations of Fredegar* seem to have been little interested in the affairs of the palace as opposed to events in the field, and since hagiography and episcopal histories tend to record complaints about the damage Charles did to churches and churchmen in the provinces, these sources too tell us little about what went on at the centre.

At the beginning of this study, when discussing the background to Charles Martel's career, we gave strong emphasis to the importance of the royal palace as the hub of Frankish politics and government. It was argued that though particular kings may have been in a personally weak position, government remained essentially royal in that legitimate power was seen to derive from royal authority. It was, moreover, through the annual assemblies in which king and magnates together discussed the 'well-being of the realm' that the different elements of the Frankish kingdom came together as one political community. Should we infer from the near silence on matters concerning the king and the court in the years 724–41 that Charles Martel broke with the traditional means of governing through the palace? Or since we know that the royal palace was central to Frankish politics under the Merovingian kings before 724, and after 751 under the Carolingian kings, should we assume that it was equally important in the intervening years under Charles Martel, even though we hear so little about it? One of the few things we do know, although no source tells us this directly, is that when King Theuderic IV died in 737, Charles Martel ruled until his death without a king. What significance should we attach to this turn of events, which must be seen as truly extraordinary, for this was the only interregnum the Franks ever experienced?

Charles Martel was referred to by a variety of terms intended to reflect his power. He was thus called 'leader' (*dux*), 'prince' (*princeps*), 'viceroy' (*subregulus*), 'mayor of the palace' (*major domus*), 'patrician' (*patricius*) or, more exotically, 'exarch'. It was, however, through his tenure of the position of mayor of the palace that he formally exercised power. It was as mayor that he styled himself in the few charters that we have, and we may recall that his rise to power hinged on the capture of this post. We saw how it was necessary for Charles to have control over the palace in order to stamp his authority on the Austrasian and Neustrian magnates in the period 717–24, and how he found that it was essential to rule through a king. Denied access to King Chilperic II by Ragamfred and the Neustrians, Charles had in 717 set up his own king, Clothar IV, and then after Clothar's death he had made strenuous efforts to capture Chilperic from Ragamfred. After

Chilperic's death in 721, the *LHF* closed its narrative with the report that Theuderic IV was made king in his place, but, as we have just seen, after this we hear very little about Theuderic and his palace. It is nevertheless clear that Charles continued to govern in the name of the king. One indication of this is his use of the title 'mayor'. Another is the citing of Theuderic's authority in charters. When Abbo received property confiscated from the rebels in Provence in 736, for example, this land was, according to his will, granted to him through Theuderic's authority.[2] The Etichonid leaders of Alsace called upon Theuderic to guarantee the grants they made to the church, and they may have seen Theuderic as a protector of their interests against Charles Martel.[3] Charles himself seems to have continued to operate from the traditional centres of Merovingian government in the Oise valley, and he likewise made efforts to associate himself with the monastery of St Denis which had special links with the Merovingian court.[4] In fact he spent his last days at the palace of Queirzy on the Oise, he was buried in St Denis and his son Pippin was said to have been brought up there.[5] In the light of these indications that Charles Martel did continue the traditions of late Merovingian government to a significant degree, the fact that Theuderic IV was not replaced as king in 737 seems all the more surprising. To seek an explanation for this phenomenon of rule without a king but in the name of the king, we must look more closely at the situation in the last years of Charles's life.

No narrative source tells us that Theuderic IV died in 737. We know that he did die then only because charters, including the last one issued by Charles himself, were now dated according to the number of years after his death. That is to say, contemporaries were very much aware that there was no king on the throne and yet they clung to the notion that documents should properly be dated with reference to the Merovingian ruler. There may have been some confusion about the situation, perhaps revealed by two charters from the monastery of St Gallen which were dated from the death of King Dagobert III (d. 715), the name Dagobert being synonymous with traditional Merovingian authority.[6] The fact that the pro-Carolingian

---

2 P. Geary, *Aristocracy in Provence: The Rhône Basin at the Dawn of the Carolingian Age* (Stuttgart 1985), p. 74.

3 Above, ch. 4, p. 106.

4 E. Ewig, 'Résidence et Capitale Pendant le Haut Moyen Age', *Revue Historique*, 230 (1963), 25–72, reprinted in *Spätantikes und Fränkisches Gallien. Gesammelten Schriften (1952–1973)* I (Zurich and Munich 1976), pp. 363–408, at p. 390.

5 *Fred. Contin.*, ed. and trans. J.M. Wallace Hadrill (London 1960), ch. 24, p. 97. For Pippin and the monastery of St Denis, *ubi enotriti fuimus*, MGH, *Diplomata Karolinorum* I, ed. E. Mühlbacher (Hanover 1906), no. 8, p. 13.

6 *Urkundenbuch der Abtei St Gallen I, 700–848*, ed. W. Wartmann (Zurich 1863), nos 8 and 9.

sources, starting with the *Continuations of Fredegar*, ignored the interregnum makes it even more difficult for the modern historian to gauge how contemporaries reacted to the situation, or what Charles Martel's intentions were in ruling without a king. One possibility is, of course, that Charles intended to make himself or one of his sons king, but that he faced too much opposition to put this plan into operation. He would have been aware of what had happened to his ancestor Grimoald, who had been overthrown and brutally slain as a result of making his son king. As we have just seen, the way in which charters continued to be dated with reference to the Merovingians suggests continuing loyalty to the old dynasty. We know too that after Charles's death, his sons Karloman and Pippin were forced to raise another Merovingian to the throne in order to counter opposition to their rule. But there is simply no clear indication that Charles did intend to replace the old dynasty, and what makes speculation about his plans for the future yet more difficult is the fact that we cannot determine his attitude towards members of his own family, for this is another area in which the pro-Carolingian sources have effectively rewritten history.[7] By damning the memory of Charles's second wife Swanahild and her son Grifo, they make it look as if Charles had only two sons, Karloman and Pippin, who were in the running for power.

It is the knowledge that Pippin did become king in 751 that tempts us to imagine that this was what Charles had intended all along. A passage in Paul the Deacon's *Historia* seems at first sight to lend support to this view. It tells us that in 737, the year that Theuderic died, Charles sent his son to King Liutprand in Italy. Liutprand had Pippin's hair cut in customary Lombard fashion, adopted him as his son and then sent him back to Francia with rich gifts.[8] Liutprand already had a co-ruler and designated successor, so it cannot be the case that Pippin was by this action being offered the Lombard throne. It might, however, be true that by acquiring a royal foster-father Pippin was being groomed for Frankish kingship. If so, one must wonder why Charles intended this for his second son, rather than for his first born, Karloman. One explanation of this curious episode could be that it was Pippin who was chosen for the adoption because, unlike his older brother, he was unmarried, and that the adoption itself was intended to seal an alliance with the Lombards rather than to prepare Pippin for the throne in Francia.[9] We know of Liutprand's close ties to the Agilolfings in

---

7 R. Schieffer, 'Karl Martell und seine Familie', in J. Jarnut, U. Nonn and M. Richter (eds), *Karl Martell in Seiner Zeit*, Beihefte der Francia, 37 (Sigmaringen 1994), pp. 305–15.

8 Paul the Deacon, *Historia Langobardorum*, ed. G. Waitz, *MGH SRG* (Hanover 1878), VI, ch. 53, p. 237.

9 T. Jarnut, 'Die Adoption Pippins durch König Liutprand', in Jarnut, Nonn and Richter (eds), *Karl Martell in Seiner Zeit*, pp. 217–26.

Bavaria. A Franco-Lombard pact is likely to have been aimed primarily at neutralising those ties and securing an ally against Arab incursions into Provence, for as we saw in an earlier chapter, Liutprand came to Provence with the Lombard army at Charles's request in 739 to help meet an Arab invasion.

Charles Martel's closeness to Liutprand was surely what prompted Pope Gregory III's overtures to the Frankish leader at this time. Fredegar's Continuator reported that in 739 Gregory twice sent embassies to Charles with the keys of St Peter's tomb and a link from his chains. It was proposed that the pope abandon the Byzantine emperor and form a pact with Charles instead.[10] The implication is that this unprecedented honour for the Franks marked the heights to which their power had risen under Charles Martel. It may do, but two surviving letters from Gregory to Charles show that what was more immediately at stake was the Franco-Lombard alliance.[11] Gregory was desperate for Charles to give up his support for Liutprand and to come to Rome's aid because Liutprand had attacked papal property and interests in Italy. The Lombards, said Gregory, had even stolen the lamps which Charles and his 'parents' had given to St Peter's. We also know that in reality, Rome's decisive break with Byzantium had come over a decade earlier, and that once Liutprand had driven the last Byzantine forces out of their enclave around Ravenna, the Byzantine Empire in Italy was no longer a force able to protect the papacy.[12] That Charles Martel could not be persuaded to turn against Liutprand underlines the importance to him of the Lombard alliance, and it strengthens the impression that what lay behind Pippin's adoption was a desire to outflank the Bavarian Agilolfings, rather than any intention of making Pippin royal by association.

In 737 Pippin would have been about 23 years old. It is curious that he was not married. He did not in fact marry until 744, nor have a son, the future Charlemagne, until 748. First his unmarried state and then his childlessness could have meant that far from being groomed as a future king, Pippin was in dynastic terms behind in the running until his son was born. It must, however, remain an open question whether or not his father prevented him from marrying in order to favour his older brother Karloman. Karloman was aged about 29 in 737. He was married and he did have at least one son, called Drogo. To his wife there is only one reference, and it

---

10 *Fred. Contin.*, ch. 22, p. 96.
11 *Codex Carolinus*, in *MGH Epistolae* III, ed. W. Grundlach (Berlin 1892), pp. 476–653, nos 1 and 2, pp. 476–9.
12 Jarnut, 'Adoption', pp. 21–6. For a thorough discussion of the position of the papacy within Italy at this time, and of its relations with other peoples, T. Noble, *The Republic of St Peter. The Birth of the Papal State 680–825* (Philadelphia 1984), esp. pp. 45–66.

does not name her.[13] We know that Charles had three other sons by a concubine named Ruodhaid.[14] They were Bernhard, Jerome and Remedius. It seems clear that these were not intended to rule alongside their half-brothers. Two of them, Jerome and Remedius, entered the church, although Bernhard and his sons Adalard and Wala later appear as important leaders in the reign of Charlemagne. Charles also had a half-brother, Childebrand, who, as we have seen, commissioned the first *Continuation of Fredegar*, a work which his son Nibelung would carry on. Childebrand was a count and military leader in Burgundy. In addition there was Charles's nephew Hugo, whom we have already met as the holder of a string of key ecclesiastical positions in Neustria. He died in 730. Then there was Theudoald, Plectrude's last surviving grandson, who had briefly been mayor of the palace in 714/15. The early Carolingian annals tell us that he was killed in the same year that Charles died, which might suggest that in 741 he was still a contender for power. Another relative, Wido, became abbot of the monastery of St Wandrille. The St Wandrille *Gesta* tell us that Wido was involved in a conspiracy against Charles, who had him executed.[15] This work, though, is one which ignored the interregnum after the death of King Theuderic. It thus had the reign of King Childeric III follow on directly in 737. Therefore when we hear that Wido was executed in the 'first year of King Childeric', we cannot be sure that this took place in 738, rather than in 743/44 which was really the first year of Childeric's reign. Wido was also bishop of Rouen, and since we know that his successor as bishop there was installed *c.* 744, it looks as if the conspiracy in which Wido was involved was mounted against Karloman and Pippin in about 742 rather than against Charles in 738.[16] If so, Wido may have been a supporter of Charles's youngest son, Grifo.

The strong impression is that Charles Martel was able to call upon the support of members of his wider family, but that after his death he wished power to be concentrated in the hands of his sons by his wives Chrotrude and Swanahild. If his exact intentions appear unclear in the period 737–41, this may be because one son, Pippin, had not married, and another, Grifo, was still a minor, and none of them seem to have been given any formal position of responsibility in their father's lifetime, even though in 741 Karloman was aged about 33 and Pippin 27. That Theudoald was still in

---

13   The reference comes in the *Vita Hugoberti*, ed. W. Levison, *MGH SRM* VI (Hanover and Leipzig 1913), pp. 482–96, ch. 20, p. 495, in which Karloman and his wife visited the tomb of the saint.

14   Schieffer, 'Karl Martell und seine Familie', p. 312.

15   *Gesta Sanctorum Patrum Fontanellensis Coenobii*, ed. F. Lohier and J. Laporte (Rouen 1936), VIII, ch. 1, pp. 56–8.

16   See *Gesta Fontanellensis*, pp. 56–7, n. 134.

the picture in 741, and that Wido was preparing to revolt soon after, suggests that it was far from clear who would emerge as leader. Charles Martel's failure to raise another king to the throne in 737 might relate to this uncertainty about the family succession, with Charles as it were keeping the political order in a state of suspended animation. This he could do because he had established a personal following and a military supremacy which was not at this time dependent upon the figure of the king. Our seventh-century sources made it clear that kings were particularly valued when they held the ring between different factions of magnates. By 737 Charles had crushed all his Frankish opponents and had built up his personal authority to an unprecedented degree. He could manage without a king, at least in the short term. On the other hand, the raising of a new king would have required a gathering of magnates who might conceivably have rallied around a new figurehead in opposition to the old mayor. With members of his own family jockeying for position, and ready to bid for the support of other magnates, this might have been a danger simply too great to risk.

After the death of Theuderic and after Pippin's return from Italy, Charles mounted two final major campaigns into Saxony and Provence in 738 and 739 respectively. Only in 740, with his health already in decline, did he finally make provisions for how Francia should be divided after his death. The way in which the *Continuations of Fredegar* describe this division, in a passage following directly upon the account of Gregory III's legation, makes Charles look like a king. He divided the Frankish kingdoms (*regna*) as if they were his to bestow, and Karloman he 'raised up' (*sublimavit*) over Austrasia, Alemannia and Thuringia.[17] The term 'raise up' (*sublimare*) is one hitherto used only for the succession of kings, and, more rarely, for the elevation of bishops. A different verb was used to describe Pippin's inheritance: Charles 'sent him out' (*praemisit*) to Burgundy, Neustria and Provence. It is possible that this difference of terminology reflects a difference in the status of the two sons. Missing from the Continuator's account is any reference to Charles's other son Grifo, but his position and that of his mother Swanahild may in fact hold the key to understanding the situation at the end of Charles Martel's life.

Swanahild, remember, was the wife Charles had brought back from Bavaria in 725. Unlike Charles's first wife Chrotrude, we know a little bit about her. As we saw in an earlier chapter, she was related to the dukes of both Bavaria and Alemannia and probably also had more distant ties with Plectrude's family.[18] Grifo was born probably in 726 or 727. According to

---

17 *Fred. Contin.*, ch. 23, p. 97.
18 Above, ch. 4, p. 108.

the so-called 'Revised' version of the *Royal Frankish Annals* (composed shortly after the death of Charlemagne (814)) and to the *Earlier Annals of Metz*, Swanahild lobbied for Grifo to be given a share of the 'kingdom'.[19] The *Earlier Annals of Metz* say that as Charles lay dying Swanahild persuaded him to give 'the middle part of his lands' to Grifo. This portion was to be made up of parts of his brothers' inheritance taken from Neustria, Burgundy and Austrasia. If this plan had been put into effect, then he would have received the very core of the Frankish kingdom. Though still a minor, Grifo may have been in a favoured position because he had the prospect of commanding loyalty in Bavaria and Alemannia. Bavaria at this time was still independent. Along with Aquitaine it was not included in the division of the kingdom as reported in the *Continuations of Fredegar* and we have just seen how keen Charles Martel had been in 737 to counterbalance Agilolfing power in Bavaria by forming an alliance with King Liutprand in Italy. Promoting Grifo to a powerful position may have been another part of a strategy of containment.

In 740 the duke of Bavaria, Odilo, who was Swanahild's kinsman, was driven out and took refuge at Charles's court. There he became the lover of Charles's daughter Chiltrude, before returning to power in Bavaria. On Martel's death, the Continuator tells us, Chiltrude, 'taking the advice of her wicked stepmother' Swanahild, fled to Odilo where she married him 'against the will and advice of her brothers'.[20] This act would be remembered in the ninth century as a terrible scandal. It seems obvious to connect Grifo's exclusion from power in 741 with Swanahild's advice and Chiltrude's flight. Swanahild herself was forced to enter the convent of Chelles, near Paris. Grifo was imprisoned. From these events we can infer that Swanahild was a powerful figure as long as Charles Martel lived. Indeed she was remembered at the monastery of Reichenau as a 'queen', although the *Earlier Annals of Metz* insisted that she was a mere concubine.[21] It was she and Grifo, not Karloman or Pippin, who witnessed the last charter Charles Martel issued in September 741, about five weeks before his death.[22] In this charter Swanahild was styled *inlustris matrona*, a term of great respect used in the past of Plectrude. This was indeed the term which described Plectrude in 714 as she, like Swanahild in 741, witnessed a charter at the bedside of her ailing husband. No concubine was ever called *inlustris matrona*. The *Earlier Annals of Metz* are therefore wrong about Swanahild's status but right when

---

19   *Royal Frankish Annals*, s.a. 741, trans. B. Sholz, *Carolingian Chronicles* (Ann Arbor 1972), p. 37. *AMP*, ed. B. von Simson, *MGH SRG* (Hanover and Leipzig 1905), p. 32.
20   *Fred. Contin.*, ch. 25, p. 95.
21   H. Schüssler, 'Die fränkische Reichsteilung von Vieux-Poitiers (742) und die Reform der Kirche in den Teilreichen Karlmanns und Pippins', *Francia*, 13 (1985), 45–111, at 54.
22   *MGH DD, Diplomata Maiorum Domus*, no. 14, pp. 101–2.

they tell us that she exercised great influence over Charles at the end. She clearly had similar influence over Chiltrude, and with Odilo at court there must have been a powerful lobby in favour of Grifo. The success of this lobby could suggest that Karloman and Pippin had less influence on the court circle. Certainly the first thing they did after Charles's death was to break it up, sending Chiltrude fleeing and Swanahild to a convent.

One important piece of evidence, an original royal charter issued in the year 753, has sometimes been taken to show that Swanahild was so powerful that sometime before Charles's death she even forced him out of the Paris region.[23] It does not actually show this, but it does cast light on Swanahild's power, and contains a great deal of information which is interesting in its own right. The charter was concerned with the rights of toll which the monastery of St Denis levied at the annual fair of St Denis. At the monastery's request King Pippin confirmed these rights, which earlier rulers had granted, but which had from time to time been usurped. Pippin's uncle, Grimoald, had in fact taken the tolls for himself, and was forced to acknowledge that he should not have done so in another original charter from the year 710. The problem seems to have been that the count of Paris was wont to demand a proportion of the toll on behalf of the treasury. In the 753 charter we are told that once again the toll revenues had been diverted, and this time it was Swanahild and the count of Paris, Gairefred, who were to blame. This had come about through a combination of Swanahild's greed and Gairefred's guile and together they agreed to extract four *denarii* from each free merchant who came to the fair. Then a later count, Gairhard, continued the practice, and extended it to unfree merchants who were each forced to pay five *denarii*. The merchants were now so heavily taxed, said the monks of St Denis, that they were no longer coming to the fair, much to the detriment of the monastery's coffers. In court Gairhard defended himself by saying that as count he was merely levying the customary toll that had been put in place by Swanahild and Gairefred, but that in future he would be happy to do whatever the king decided on the matter.

Let us begin with two general points of interest here before turning to what this charter tells us in particular about the regime of Charles Martel and about Swanahild's position within it. Firstly we should note the continuing importance of the St Denis fair. This is precious information from a time in which we hear almost nothing about markets and trade. It in turn tells us something about the monastery of St Denis and the Paris region: they were a source of cash in what historians generally regard as a cash-starved economy. No wonder the region remained important to rulers whose

---

23 *MGH Diplomata Karolinorum* I, no. 6, pp. 9–11.

lands and followers were now mostly elsewhere. The very reason that these tolls had so long been disputed was that the royal fisc, or treasury, had particularly strong interests in the region. Secondly, and even more generally, it is very interesting to note the reference to *servi*, unfree people, visiting the fair who were tolled even more heavily than the free merchants. Again, without this information, we would not know that the unfree were involved in trade. Finally, because this is an original document we can see that Pippin made his mark on it. That he did not sign it as the Merovingian kings had signed their documents suggests that he could not write, even though he had been brought up in the monastery of St Denis itself.[24] Whether or not his father could read and write we do not know.

Of more particular interest for our purposes is the similarity between the names of the two counts of Paris, Gairefred and Gairhard, mentioned in the charter. It suggests that they were related to each other. An earlier count, who had been killed by the mayor Ebroin *c.* 678, was called Gairenus. It is reasonable to suppose on the grounds of name-form that he was an ancestor of the two counts named in 753. If so, it looks as if there was something of a dynasty of Parisian counts. Gairenus, we know, was the brother of Bishop Leudegar of Autun, and thus a member of one of the leading families of the old Neustro-Burgundian regime which had so fiercely opposed Charles Martel's father Pippin. If the later counts were indeed his descendants, this would suggest that at least one leading family in the Paris region had survived in power all through the upheavals of the age of Charles Martel. If more of these old families remained in positions of influence in the area, we might see another reason why government itself continued in traditional form and why it was as yet still not possible to think in terms of non-Merovingian kings, for this was the Seine–Oise region which contained those palaces from which Charles Martel's regime continued to operate.

That Swanahild and Gairefred worked together to secure a part of the St Denis fair tolls for the fisc does not necessarily suggest that they were somehow conspiring against Charles Martel. This is the interpretation put on the case through the notion that Swanahild was simply being greedy, but we should remember that Pippin was hostile towards his stepmother. The idea that she had actually excluded Charles from the regions is, moreover, a modern one. It rests on a guess as to the form of one word which is illegible in this 1,246-year-old parchment document. The word, which begins with the letter 'e' and ends with the letter 's', completes the phrase 'when Charles was' (*quando Carlus fuit*) and in early printed editions of the

---

24   I. Heidrich, 'Titular und Urkunden der arnulfingischen Hausmeier', *Archiv für Diplomatik*, 11/12 (1965–66), 17–279, at 146–7.

charter it was rendered as *eiectus*, 'thrown out'.[25] Another guess, which would make better sense in the context of defraud by greed and guile, is *elusus*, 'deceived'.[26] The passage would then read, 'when Charles was deceived by the greed of Swanahild and the guile of Gairefred'. If this was Pippin blaming Swanahild for something for which his father was ultimately responsible, then far from conspiring against Charles, we may see Swanahild governing on his behalf, perhaps in his absence. We have seen that Swanahild was certainly not alienated from her husband a month before his death, and the charter in which they appeared together was one in which land was donated to St Denis. Were they, one wonders, now making amends for the toll alienation with a view to securing Charles's burial in the monastery?

The charter of donation from September 741 also provides another indication that the bureaucratic machinery of royal government remained in place after the death of Theuderic. In it we read that one Crothgangus, 'having been ordered, recognised this letter of donation'. This phrase is used in the final protocol of Merovingian royal charters in which an officer called the 'referendary' checked the document before the king signed it. Paul the Deacon in his 'History of the Bishops of Metz' tells us that the later bishop of Metz, Chrodegang, had been referendary to Charles Martel.[27] Here he is at work. In this context the 753 charter thus suggests that Swanahild may have played an important part in government through the palace. There may no longer have been a king in the palace, but it continued to function. Given that Charles Martel went on campaign virtually every year up to his final illness, Swanahild may have been required to act as a kind of regent in his absence. This scenario could explain why she had great influence in the Paris region, and could mount such a successful lobby for her son's interests.

The St Denis donation of 741 gives us a kind of snapshot of Charles Martel's standing at the end of his career. As we have just seen, he was in control of the machinery of the palace, and he even used protocol formerly reserved for royal documents. In his donation he gave the *villa* of Clichy, a favourite residence of the Merovingian kings, to St Denis, formerly their special monastery. Saint Denis was now the Carolingian family's 'special patron', and the monastery promised to become their necropolis. Having used force to install his followers in Neustria, Burgundy and Provence and to demand loyalty from those nobles who remained in place, Charles Martel could now rule without a king, he could raise armies without a king, and he

---

25 Schüssler, 'Reichsteilung', 54–6.

26 Heidrich, 'Titular', 202–3, n. 611 also offers *exitatus*, *excessus*, *eversus* and *elicitus*, none of which makes as much sense in this context as *elusus*.

27 Paul the Deacon, *Gesta Episcoporum Mettensium*, ed. G. Pertz, *MGH SS* II (Hanover 1829), pp. 262–8, at p. 267.

had his own treasure. The pope addressed him as leader of the Franks who was able to deliver the Frankish army at will, and Liutprand, king of the Lombards, had honoured him by adopting his son. In 741 he nevertheless remained the mayor of the palace, as he had been since 718. Nominally, therefore, he remained subject to a king, even when the king was dead. This, his last document, was dated 'in the fifth year after the death of King Theuderic', and apart from the end-protocol it was in the form of a private document.

Charles Martel had reached the position of unchallenged power that the *Earlier Annals of Metz* would attribute to his father half a century earlier, that is, he was a mayor who paid lip-service to the idea of Merovingian kingship but who in practice ran the country entirely on his own. Why, then, did he not take the next step and make himself king? One reason must be that it would have been difficult for Charles to raise himself up as king in 737 after having spent nearly twenty years as mayor. In 737 he still faced opposition in Burgundy, Provence, Aquitaine and southern Germany. Had Charles Martel made himself king, leaders in all of these regions would have found further cause to resist, for this meant that he would be their king too, and thus be able to claim direct authority over them. Another reason why Charles might not have wished to become king in 737 was his age. He was already 50 years old in 737, and we have seen that it was highly likely that there was great uncertainty about what would happen after his death. His own experience would have taught him to expect problems and even conflict, not just within the family, but also pressed upon the family by outsiders. It was possible to make all his three sons mayors of the palace, for in the past there had been separate mayors of Austrasia, Burgundy and Neustria, but dividing the kingship into three so soon after taking the throne would have been far more hazardous. In the event, one son, Pippin, would finally emerge as the undisputed leader of the whole family, having excluded his brothers or their offspring from power. When he had a son of his own and had, with the exception of Aquitaine, crushed his opponents in the south, Pippin could then take the step of making himself king. It is to the events leading up to this final act that we now turn.

Charles Martel died on 22 October 741, aged about 55.[28] Soon there was strife within the family. The *Earlier Annals of Metz* tell us that the 'Franks' (that is, the nobles) could not tolerate the idea of Grifo being given part of his brothers' legitimate inheritance 'on the advice of a monstrous woman' (Swanahild), and so they urged Karloman and Pippin to attack him.[29] The

---

28   *Fred. Contin.*, ch. 24, p. 97.
29   *AMP*, ed. von Simson, *MGH SRG*, p. 32.

Revised version of the *Royal Frankish Annals* adds that Swanahild had raised in Grifo the hope of taking the whole kingdom, and that it was he who declared war on his brothers.[30] Things may in fact have been in the balance for a little while after Charles's death, for we have a letter which the missionary Boniface wrote to Grifo asking him to protect the Christians of Thuringia, 'if Christ shall have given you the power'.[31] Boniface may have written similar letters to Karloman and Pippin.[32] In the event, Grifo fled to the stronghold of Laon, where he was attacked and captured. It may be no coincidence that Pippin later married the daughter of the count of Laon. Perhaps he had played some part in Grifo's capture. Grifo was then imprisoned for the next six years at Neufchâteau in the Ardennes, thus in Karloman's portion of the kingdom. The *Earlier Annals of Metz* and the *Royal Frankish Annals*, in what become strongly pro-Pippin narratives, both imply that it was Karloman's rather than Pippin's wish to imprison him.[33] It was now that Chiltrude fled to Odilo, Swanahild was sent to Chelles, and Theudoald was killed. This upheaval at the centre was matched by revolt on the periphery. The conjunction reinforces the impression that Charles Martel had not so much invented a new order as terrified his opponents into quiescent loyalty to him personally. Such a loyalty dissolved as soon as he was dead.

According to the *Earlier Annals of Metz*, which are, it must be emphasised, strongly anti-Agilolfing, it was Odilo of Bavaria who articulated opposition to Karlomann and Pippin, sending out his agents to the Aquitanians, Alemans, Saxons and Slavs to incite them to rebellion.[34] We also learn from the *Annales Guelferbytani*, one of the early sets of Carolingian annals, that Charles Martel's old adversary Theudebald, the former duke of Alemannia, returned to (or perhaps 'from') Alsace and rebelled along with the *Wascones* (which no doubt means the Aquitanians), the Bavarians and the Saxons.[35] For the next five years Karloman and Pippin fought almost non-stop to overcome this opposition. They began in early 742 with a campaign against Hunoald, duke of Aquitaine and the son of the late Eudo. In the course of this campaign they agreed to divide up Grifo's territories between them,

---

30   *Royal Frankish Annals*, trans. Sholz, *Carolingian Chronicles*, p. 37.
31   *Bonifatii Epistolae*, no. 48, trans. E. Emerton, *The Letters of St Boniface* (New York 1940), pp. 76–7.
32   This is the view of the letters' editor Tangl, in *Bonifatii Epistolae*, pp. 76–7, n. 1.
33   *AMP*, ed. von Simson, *MGH SRG* pp. 32–3, *Royal Frankish Annals*, trans. Sholz, *Carolingian Chronicles*, p. 37.
34   J. Jahn, *Ducatus Baiwariorum. Das Bairische Herzogtum des Agilolfinger*, Monographien zur Geschichte des Mittelalters, 35 (Stuttgart 1991), p. 178.
35   J. Jarnut, 'Untersuchungen zu den fränkisch-alemannische Beziehungen in der ersten Hälfte des 8 Jahrhunderts', *Schweizerische Zeitschrift für Geschichte*, 30 (1980), 7–28, at 22–3.

and came up with a division of Francia very much like that made between Charlemagne and his brother in 768.[36] Then in autumn of the same year they fought the Alemans on the Danube. In either February or early March of the next year, 743, a new Merovingian king, Childeric III, was raised to the throne. As with the death of Theuderic in 737, this must be deduced from charter material, for no narrative source mentions Childeric's elevation.

The ending of the six-year interregnum must be seen in the context of the widespread revolt against the Carolingians: the brothers clearly needed to draw upon residual loyalty to the Merovingians in order to rally support against their opponents, and this can be interpreted as a sign of their weakness. It has been argued, however, that it was Karloman who brought Childeric to the throne, and that he was prepared to serve as mayor to a Merovingian whereas Pippin was not. One obvious basis for this argument is that eventually it was indeed Pippin, not Karloman, who deposed Childeric and made himself king. Another reason for the suggestion is that in one of the two surviving charters issued by Childeric, dated to July 744, the king addressed Karloman as 'the distinguished Karloman, mayor of the palace, ruler of our palace, who placed us upon the throne of the kingdom'.[37] This, of course, is not to say that Childeric might not have addressed Pippin in a similar manner in charters which have not survived, but there are good grounds for thinking that Karloman might have had a particular interest in reconstituting the Merovingian palace. We know that at least as early as 746 Karloman was contemplating abandoning secular life to go to Rome. If this idea had been in his mind even earlier, he might also have thought that by raising a new king he could strengthen the palace community, which, in turn, might afford some protection for his wife and children in his absence.[38] When Pippin did eventually depose Childeric and take the throne for himself, he did this after Karloman had retired and after he had removed his nephew Drogo, Karloman's son, from power. This putative motive for Childeric's installation is not in conflict with the idea that the Carolingians needed a king in 743 because they were weak. No doubt motives were as mixed as the outcome was uncertain.

In 743 the two brothers fought against Odilo and the combined forces of the Bavarians, Alemans, Saxons and Slavs on the River Lech, that is, on the northernmost edge of Bavaria, where they were victorious despite suffering heavy losses.[39] According to the *Earlier Annals of Metz*, the papal legate

---

36   Schüssler, 'Reichsteilung', explores this division in detail.
37   *MGH DD, Diplomata Maiorum Domus*, no. 97, pp. 87–8.
38   M. Becher, 'Drogo und die Königserhebung Pippins', *Frühmittelalterliche Studien*, 23 (1989), 131–53, at 138.
39   *Fred. Contin.*, ch. 26, p. 99; *AMP*, ed. von Simson, *MGH SRG*, p. 33.

Sergius was captured in this battle. He had been trying to make peace between the Franks and the Bavarians. The author here returns to a device not employed since he or she told of the events leading up to the battle of Tertry in 687, namely the reporting of a speech by the leader. In this speech Pippin lectured Sergius on the justice of the Frankish cause which God had just revealed through their victory.[40] The detail of the speech, which is surely fictional, is another reflection of how sensitive the Carolingians were about the extinction of the Agilolfing dukedom. It is fair to say that they spent more time justifying this than any other conquest they ever made. It is also significant that it was Pippin alone who was given the speech, for in this work Pippin now becomes the sole hero of the Carolingian cause, rather as Charles Martel had been portrayed earlier. We also learn from this source that during the campaign Hunoald and the Aquitanians raided into Francia and burned down the town and church of Chartres. This was at Odilo's suggestion. In the same year, or the next, according to the Continuator of Fredegar, Karloman fought the Saxons on the Frankish frontier, and in 744 Pippin fought and defeated the Aleman leader Theudebald in the Alps.[41] In the same year both brothers fought in Saxony, and the next year they crossed the Loire to punish Hunoald. Finally, in 746 Karloman returned to Alemannia where he destroyed the Aleman forces at the battle of Canstatt (modern Stuttgart). This last conflict was remembered in the *Continuations of Fredegar* as particularly bloody.[42] The *Annales Petaviani*, another set of early Carolingian annals, reported that 'many thousands of men died, they say' and that it was this slaughter which prompted Karloman to turn his back on life as a warrior. For the latter idea there is no corroboration, but circumstantial evidence from the next generation, namely the wide-spread distribution of Aleman property among the Franks, does suggest that a substantial section of the Aleman nobility perished in the Canstatt campaign. Timothy Reuter has recently remarked that 'Canstatt did for Alemannic land-holding what Hastings did for Anglo-Saxon land-holding'.[43]

The pace of this campaigning was frenetic even by Carolingian standards. But even as they fought for survival, Karloman and Pippin, like their father a generation earlier, were building up a military following which would continue to sustain the family in power thereafter. At the same time they went further than Charles Martel in unifying Francia by summoning a series of church councils. This began with the holding of a council in

---

40   *AMP*, ed. von Simson, *MGH SRG*, pp. 34–5.
41   *Fred. Contin.*, ch. 27, pp. 99–100.
42   *Fred. Contin.*, ch. 29, p. 100.
43   T. Reuter, *Germany in the Early Middle Ages 800–1056* (London 1991), p. 60.

Karloman's territory in 742.[44] It was followed in 743 by the Council of Estinnes, the provisions of which we discussed in the last chapter when we looked at the question of church property.[45] Then it was pointed out that it was in the context of military crisis that land should be retained 'for the use of the army'. There were at least two more church councils in this period. In 744 Pippin held a council at Soissons[46] and in the Boniface letter collection there are references to a further council held probably in 747.[47] It is clear that Boniface was intimately involved in this conciliar activity, through which he urged the reform of the Frankish church. It has often been suggested that Boniface had made little headway with reform in the time of Charles Martel because the mayor was basically unsympathetic to a project which might alienate important supporters such as Milo and Gewilib, bishops whom Boniface regarded as corrupt. It has also been argued that of the two sons, Karloman was more supportive towards Boniface than Pippin.[48] The fact, frequency and agenda of church meetings after 741 all offer support for the first suggestion, but the notion that Karloman was keener on church reform than his brother finds no support in the missionary's letters. Boniface did indeed have more contact with Karloman in the period 742–45, but this is because his sphere of activity lay in the latter's territory. Pippin may have been personally less close to Boniface, but he did promote reform throughout his career, and he was the ruler who first began to borrow the language of church councils and of the Bible in his charters when he emphasised the moral duty of the ruler to succour the poor and the needy.[49] Care for the weak would become one of the most important ways in which Carolingian rule was justified. The fact that Karloman did abdicate and go to Rome must nevertheless mean that he was unusually pious, although he may, of course, have intended to return but was prevented from doing so. Close contact with Boniface may well have been an important factor in his decision to go to Rome, for thus far it had been only Anglo-Saxon rulers who had abdicated in order to spend their last days in the city of their hero, Pope Gregory the Great. Hunoald, duke of Aquitaine, did, however, at this time also leave power and enter a monastery on the Isle de Ré off

---

44   *Concilum Germanicum*, ed. A. Werminghoff, *MGH Concilia* II, i (Hanover and Leipzig 1906), pp. 2–4.

45   Above, ch, 5, p. 139 and n. 36.

46   *Concilium Suessionense*, ed. A. Werminghoff, *MGH Concilia* II, i, pp. 33–6.

47   *Bonifatii Epistolae*, nos 78 and 80, trans. Emerton, *Letters of St Boniface*, pp. 136–41 and 142–9.

48   Schüssler, 'Reichsteilung', 88–103.

49   See, for instance, the first part of a donation Pippin made to the monastery of Prüm in 762, *MGH Diplomata Karolinorum* I, no. 16, p. 20. I am grateful to M. Innes for drawing my attention to this charter.

the western coast.[50] It has recently been argued by the German historian Matthias Becher that the politics of the rest of the decade were governed by Karloman's decision and that this led indirectly to Pippin's seizure of the throne in 751.[51] Let us briefly examine this important argument as a way of thinking about the family's transition from mayoralty to royalty.

When Karloman left Francia in 747 he no doubt expected that his son Drogo would follow him as mayor of the palace to King Childeric in Austrasia. Pippin, we know, was not married until 744 and remained childless until 748, as Becher convincingly argues.[52] According to a letter written by Pope Stephen III in 770, he had actually tried to separate from his wife Bertrada, in order, presumably, to remedy the problem.[53] Drogo was very likely of majority age when he gave his consent to a charter Karloman issued in August 747.[54] He was, as Becher puts it, the only heir Karloman and Pippin had, and thus Karloman could depart for Rome confident in the knowledge that his son would remain in power. The birth of a son (Charlemagne) to Pippin and Bertrada on 2 April 748 changed the situation and now Pippin began to squeeze Drogo out. A letter from the Boniface collection, written in 748, expresses doubt about which leader Boniface should follow.[55] At the same time, Pippin released Grifo in order, argues Becher, to destabilise Drogo's territory. Karloman, now in Rome, became alarmed at the deteriorating situation but was made a monk by the pope and sent off to the monastery of Monte Cassino. This helpful act on the part of Pope Zacharias took place in the context of an alliance newly formed with Pippin. Pippin, famously, sought papal approval for his ousting

50 C. Stancliffe, 'Kings Who Opted Out', in P. Wormald (ed.), *Ideal and Reality in Frankish and Anglo-Saxon Society* (Oxford 1983), pp. 154–76, on Karloman, and probable Anglo-Saxon influence, p. 159. On Hunoald's 'abdication', *AMP*, ed. von Simson, *MGH SRG*, p. 36. M. Rouche, *L'Aquitaine des Wisigoths aux Arabes 418–781. Naissance d'une Region* (Paris 1979), p. 119, took the phrases *coma capitis deposita, et monachi voto promisso in monasterium . . . intravit*, to mean that Hunoald laid down his crown, and thus argued that he had been a king. It is much more likely to mean simply that Hunoald received the tonsure, vowed to become a monk, and entered a monastery.

51 Becher, 'Drogo'.

52 Becher first suggested this date (2 April 748) in 'Drogo', 143–5. He argues the case in greater detail in M. Becher, 'Neue Überlieferungen zum Geburtsdatum Karls des Grossen', *Francia*, 19 (1992), 37–60.

53 *Codex Carolinus*, no. 45, trans. P. King, *Charlemagne. Translated Sources* (Lambrigg 1986), pp. 270–3. There is also a possible reference to Pippin's marital problems in *Bonifatii Epistolae*, no. 77, trans. Emerton, *Letters of St Boniface*, pp. 134–5, a letter from Pope Zacharias to Boniface, written in 747. Zacharias refers to Pippin's urgent request for church canons on unlawful marriage, which might suggest that he was sounding out the possibility of divorce from the still childless Bertrada, perhaps on the grounds of consanguinity.

54 *MGH DD, Diplomata Maiorum Domus*, no. 15, p. 102.

55 *Bonifatii Epistolae*, no. 79, trans. Emerton, *Letters of St Boniface*, pp. 141–2.

of Childeric III, and by the end of 751 had enough support to declare himself king. In return for the pope's help, he agreed to break the Frankish alliance with the Lombards. But this worried many of his followers, and Drogo and Grifo were still at large. Pope Stephen III wrote in 753 telling the magnates to start supporting Pippin or suffer perdition,[56] and he then came in person to Francia. Karloman followed him. This was, most sources imply, to try and dissuade Pippin from attacking the Lombards, but Becher argues that it was to try to save Drogo. It failed on both counts. That year, say no fewer than three early sets of Carolingian annals, Karloman's sons (Drogo and an unnamed brother) were tonsured and sent to a monastery and Grifo was killed. Karloman was detained under the care of Queen Bertrada, and died in 755, according to the 'Revised' version of the *Royal Frankish Annals*.[57] In 754 Pippin, Bertrada and their sons were anointed by Pope Stephen, who solemnly declared that in future only the descendants of Pippin should be the kings of the Franks. Subsequently, sources from the reign of Charlemagne onwards locked this family skeleton firmly in the cupboard by presenting Pippin's coup as the long overdue and necessary solution to the powerlessness of the Merovingian kings, mounted in the name of good order, rather than revealing it as the coup within the family which it really was.

This scenario is attractive in several ways. It is very useful to show how these sources (letters, charters and some early Carolingian annals), which are either contemporary, or later but less influenced by the views prevailing in the court of Charlemagne, reveal that events leading up to 754 took place within the context of family politics. This in turn serves to challenge head-on the later tradition that the Carolingians had a moral obligation to take power in the way they did. It is also very useful to think in terms of the events of 753–54, rather than 751–52, as the final playing out of that succession struggle which began with the death of Charles Martel.[58] Becher's insistence on the importance of Drogo after 747 does, however, rely on a great deal of conjecture, simply because no source gives us any idea of what he was doing after 748. A more obvious rival to Pippin was Grifo, and Becher's most speculative and least convincing argument is that Pippin released Grifo in 747 in order to damage Drogo's prospects. Whatever the reason he was released, and it is a possibility that he actually escaped, Grifo

---

56 *Codex Carolinus*, no. 5, ed. Grundlach, *MGH Epistolae* III, p. 488.
57 *Royal Frankish Annals*, trans. Sholz, *Carolingian Chronicles*, p. 40.
58 On how the *Royal Frankish Annals* dealt with this period, see R. McKitterick, 'The Illusion of Royal Power in the Carolingian Annals', *English Historical Review* (forthcoming).

immediately began to seek power.[59] He first went to Saxony, taking some of the young nobles with him. It took an extended campaign in Saxony, fought with the help of the Slavs, before Grifo was defeated there. He then fled to Bavaria where Odilo had recently died. There, in 748, he took hold of Chiltrude and her young son Tassilo, and seems to have made himself duke with the help of one Suidger (a Bavarian count) and Lantfrid of the Aleman ducal family. Pippin came after him again, captured him, and made Tassilo duke, but this time under his own patronage. Grifo was given twelve counties in western Neustria, but soon fled to Aquitaine, which suggests that he was intent upon gaining much more than Pippin was prepared to offer him. Finally, in 753, Grifo left Aquitaine and was on his way to Italy when he was met in the Alps by a Frankish force led by counts Frederic and Theodoenus.[60] In the battle that followed, many were killed on both sides, including Frederic, Theodoenus and Grifo himself. To the end, it seems, he had a substantial following. It was only now, say the *Earlier Metz Annals*, that all the land of the Franks was at peace under Pippin's rule.

It was also now, and for the first time, a land without a mayor of the palace. In 749, according to later tradition, the papacy supported Pippin's desire to become king because he already had the power of a king.[61] But prior to his elevation, this power he had exercised as mayor of the palace, as Charles Martel had done before him. After he had become king, Pippin wielded much the same power as before. There was no longer any need for a mayor of the palace, for Pippin's role as warleader and leader of the palace had not changed. Not only had the post of mayor been made redundant, it was also too closely associated with the Merovingian kings, and with the Carolingians as their subjects, to be continued. Few major offices in European history have been dropped so suddenly and so finally. It came to an end not just because it had become an embarrassment, but also because unlike the Merovingians, the Carolingians did not hold the ring between different factions of magnates, and so did not have to deal with the leading

---

59   G. Wolf, 'Grifos Erbe, die Einsetzung König Childerics III und der Kampf um die Macht – zugleich Bemerkungen zur karolingische "Hofhistoriographie"', *Archiv für Diplomatik*, 38 (1992), 1–16. Wolf argues that it was Grifo, rather than Drogo, who was at the centre of events.

60   The narrative of Grifo's fight for power comes from the *Royal Frankish Annals*, trans. Sholz, *Carolingian Chronicles*, pp. 37–40, and the *AMP*, ed. von Simson, *MGH SRG*, pp. 39–43. The Continuator of Fredegar tells only of his death: *Fred. Contin.*, ch. 35, p. 103.

61   *Royal Frankish Annals*, s.a. 749, trans. Sholz, *Carolingian Chronicles*, p. 39; Einhard, *Life of Charlemagne*, ch. 3, ed. and trans. P. Dutton, *Charlemagne's Courtier. The Complete Einhard* (Ontario 1999), p. 18.

faction through a power-broking figure such as the mayor. But if they came to rule their magnates more directly than their predecessors, this was in large part because Charles Martel had taken the first step in smashing the opposing factions. With this in mind, let us now look back upon the age of Charles Martel as a whole.

Conclusion: The Age of Charles Martel

We began this study with general observations on the background to Charles Martel's career, but we have just ended it by discussing political history in terms of a single family. This is because, whatever can be said about the economic, institutional and cultural aspects of power in Francia, it remains true that in this period politics comes down to the relations between, and within, a few leading families. In this, our review of the career of Charles Martel in the context of his age, we shall focus on the relationship between the general background and particular events and people.

The importance of family is reflected in the prominence of women in political history. We have seen that at crucial moments in the career of Charles Martel women were key players. First Plectrude and then Swanahild, one 'cruel', the other 'monstrous', were poised to channel power through their descendants. It is because they failed, losing out to the offspring of other women, that they would be remembered as pushy stepmothers rather than kindly mothers. Ansfled, grandmother of Charles's nephew Hugo, Pilitrude of Bavaria and Charles's own daughter Chiltrude were three more women around whom the history of this period turned. Their roles were crucial because it was through them that leading families could be united and strengthened, and this was especially important where the alternative to alliance was conflict. This is not to say that the age of Charles Martel was a 'Golden Age' for women, even though some charters show women like Plectrude and her sisters inheriting land alongside male siblings. For these women were from exceptionally rich and powerful families, and their lives are likely to have been equally exceptional. It is nevertheless the case that after the age of Charles Martel the sequence of power-wielding women seems to end, or, to put it another way, they disappear from the sources.

Their disappearance can be explained in two closely related ways. First, the pre-eminence of the Carolingian family from the second half of the eighth century onwards meant that it became less dependent upon alliances with other families, and women became less important as mediators between it and other families. This is, in fact, the same context in which the office of mayor of the palace disappeared, for the mayor too was a figure of mediation. Second, after the Carolingian family had become a royal family and the writing of history had come to be centred on the royal court, the narrative sources concentrated on the ruling branch of this single family to the exclusion of all others. We thus hear of Carolingian queens, but few other women appear in the various annals. A narrowing down of the narrative focus to one branch of the family, which was then treated with a degree of adulation hitherto found only in hagiography, was one consequence of Carolingian success, but it also affects our view of how that success was achieved. We have just seen, for instance, how difficult it was to wrest from the sources an alternative view of how and why Pippin became king. It is in the age of Charles Martel that we find the conditions which not only made possible the rise of the Carolingian family to the pinnacle of power, but which also led to that concentration of power and exclusive sense of right which gave rise to the rewriting of history in the Carolingians' favour. A study of the career of Charles Martel thus points the way to the Carolingian future.

Both for medieval and for modern historians Charles Martel may stand as the personification of change. A more fundamental change came more than a generation after him, however, with the development of the Carolingian regime proper as a theocratic royal government which had ambitions to rule a Christian empire and which aspired to a programme of moral and cultural reform. We began this study with a brief examination of the so-called Edict of Paris which King Clothar II had issued in 614, and we noted that this kind of legislation was essentially similar to that which the Carolingian kings later promulgated through their capitularies. In the reign of Charlemagne (768–814) capitularies would be issued from places widely spaced across the Frankish lands, from Saxony to Lombardy and from Aquitaine to Bavaria. Such widespread distribution reflects the spread of Frankish culture and institutions across much of Western Europe. By contrast, the Frankish background we discussed in relation to the Edict of Paris was one which had as its heartland the much more restricted area of the region between the rivers Loire and Meuse, with the Paris basin being very much at the centre of the Merovingian world of the seventh century. A brief review of the essential political, social and cultural characteristics of this world can reveal what changed over the seventh and eighth centuries.

The heartland of later Merovingian Francia had been dominated by a small lay and ecclesiastical elite which drew its resources from widespread landed estates. There existed a social hierarchy which was strongly marked by the possession of wealth and that holding of office through which power was legitimated. The increasing use of charters by this elite to consolidate property relations, and its use of law courts to defend its interests, both indicate a formal aspect to social and political power. We have seen from charters how the existence of a stable and dependent peasant labour force made it possible for land to provide income with immediate effect, and that it was this factor which allowed land to be divided and redistributed. Control of the income from land, and the desire to channel it into the hands of clients or selected groups within families, also lay behind the making of precarial grants, and the process of 'manorialisation' with which the age of Charles Martel has been strongly associated. It was the same guaranteed income which enabled monasticism to spread from the towns to the countryside in the course of the seventh century. And the growth in the number of monasteries founded and controlled by the leading families marked the rise of the Frankish elite into the ranks of spiritual leaders, with abbots and especially bishops coming to occupy benchmark positions in the social hierarchy. Sanctity came to be associated with power as leading families and institutions produced saints or acquired relics.

We may, in short, describe a culture of power in which were united force, faith, wealth, law and custom. None of these elements was of course limited to the Frankish heartland, for they can be found in some measure in Aquitaine, Provence and Rhaetia, those other areas which had also once been part of the Roman Empire. It was nevertheless in the core region, at the centre of the Merovingian polity, that the long period of Neustrian domination had given firmest shape to this culture of power. Here the gathering of magnates at the royal palaces had played a particularly significant role in the growing cultural solidarity of the ruling elite. Both Charles Martel and before him his father had fought to enjoy the benefits of this culture by taking control of the Neustrian palace. But what counts as a new departure in this age is the fact that Charles Martel's victories had the effect of exporting this core culture to the lands beyond the Rhine. Two generations later, Charlemagne's ability to address with one voice the common concerns of an elite which was spread throughout most of Western Europe was both a consequence of his grandfather's victories and a mark of how warmly the conquered had embraced Frankish culture. For, as we have just seen, it was a culture which tended to reinforce the power of the elite. It was, in other words, a dual process of conquest and acculturation which made the Frankish empire.

The conventional picture of Francia in the late Merovingian period is that the Neustrian-based kings steadily lost control of the kingdom's peripheral duchies, which slipped into a kind of semi-independence. It took first Pippin and then his son Charles Martel, drawing upon their Austrasian power base, to bring the duchies to heel and to prepare for their reintegration into the Frankish kingdom. This is in fact a Carolingian viewpoint, cogently presented, for instance in the *Earlier Annals of Metz*. An alternative reading of the history of this period, viewed strictly in terms of its own contemporary sources, suggests that the age of Charles Martel saw the decisive step in the integration of the peripheral duchies, rather than their *re*integration, for they had hitherto not shared the culture of the Frankish heartland, nor had they broken away in the late Merovingian period. Here we may recall the case of Radulf, duke of Thuringia, who had rebelled against the Merovingians in 639. Though seemingly in an excellent position to form a separate kingdom, he did not do so, continuing to acknowledge the overlordship of the Merovingian king.

The headache for Charles Martel was not that the 'peripheral' regions of Thuringia, Bavaria, Alemannia, Alsace, Provence and Aquitaine had 'broken away', but that they continued to be loyal to the Merovingian kings and provided the greatest opposition to his rule. They were the last refuges of families linked to the old Neustrian regime. Bavaria was particularly dangerous because its ruling family, the Agilolfings, had links not only with Charles's opponents in Austrasia, but also with members of his stepmother Plectrude's family. We have seen that Charles's marriage to Swanahild helped temporarily to neutralise the Agilolfing threat, but the threat reappeared in even more dangerous form in the next generation after Charles Martel's daughter Chiltrude had run off with Duke Odilo of Bavaria, and the pair had produced a son, Tassilo. Tassilo was thus both a grandson of Charles Martel and an Agilolfing. Charlemagne, another of Charles Martel's grandsons, could not feel secure until he had destroyed this cousin. He set about the business with great care, exiling the duke to a monastery in 788, and eventually in 794 having Tassilo renounce his position as duke of Bavaria in a show trial which was recorded in triplicate. He was then sent one copy of his renunciation to keep with him in his monastery, forever. Aquitaine, the region culturally closest to the heartland, also posed a great threat in the early part of Charles's career because its ruler Eudo was prepared to make common cause with the Neustrians. It was hugely to Charles's advantage that Eudo was distracted by Arab raids from 721 onwards. Charles's own victories against the Arabs were, of course, massively important in allowing him to extend his influence further into Aquitaine, Burgundy, Provence and Septimania. Of all these regions it was surely Provence and Septimania which were most affected by the turmoil. For Provence the age of Charles Martel was a disaster as rebellion, followed by invasion from both the Frankish north and the Arab south-west, destroyed what was left of its once lucrative trade in Mediterranean produce. Provence, minus this trade, was a poor backwater.

It is no accident that for Bavaria and Frisia, the age of Charles Martel was both a time of conflict with the Franks and of 'conversion' to Christianity. It was the 'conversion period' for Hesse and Thuringia too, although these regions did not fight against Charles. We saw how conversion should be understood as the organisation of already nominally Christian communities into regional churches, rather than the persuasion of 'pagan' peoples to accept new beliefs. Christianisation was in these terms a lengthy cultural development which was accompanied by the emergence of new settlement patterns in which the population was regrouped around churches founded by families which came to dominate the local community. Following the establishment of monasteries and bishoprics, we have seen the growing use of charters which reveal these families defining and reinforcing their control of rights and property. It is in this sense that conversion marks the extension of the core culture to the periphery. It was a process which prepared the way for these regions to become fully integrated into the Frankish kingdom, but at the same time the development of better-organised elites in Frisia and in southern Germany gave them the resources to resist Carolingian control. This is why we see a period of fierce conflict in the first half of the eighth century, followed by rapid assimilation in the second half. The exception to this model is the case of the Saxons, among whom the twin processes of Christianisation and elite formation had made little headway by the time of Charles Martel. Why the Saxons should have been so resistant to some aspects of Frankish culture while in other respects (material culture, dress and language, for instance) they were basically similar to other trans-Rhine peoples is a question which has never been satisfactorily answered, and is probably unanswerable, for one feature of Saxony's cultural difference was that it produced no writing before the late Carolingian period. Upon the Saxons, therefore, the age of Charles Martel seems to have had little impact, even though the Saxons fought against Charles just as much as any other people did. But overall this period can be said to see the erasure of the Rhine as one of the major cultural boundaries in Europe, that is, as the dividing line between areas more or less influenced by the religion, social structure and bureaucratic traditions of the later Roman Empire.

If the cultural balance was tipped more firmly in favour of the Frankish heartlands in our period, this was in part because the power of Neustria and Austrasia combined would always outweigh that of the other regions. Whoever could draw upon the resources of Neustria–Austrasia would be able to dominate the rest of Francia, despite the fact that the peripheral duchies were fast catching up in terms of organisation. Not only did Neustria and Austrasia have a long tradition of fighting campaigns in distant regions, they were at the centre of a political system which had long carefully nurtured contacts and alliances with leading families in the outlying regions. Charles Martel could everywhere find allies to whom the notion of cooperating with the palace would have been perfectly familiar. The leaders of the peripheral duchies may have maintained their loyalty to the Merovingian kings, but Charles Martel was mayor of the palace, and he acted in the name of the king, even, as we saw earlier, when there was no king. It was a tribute to the coherence of this political arrangement that it did not fall apart in the age of Charles Martel, although it came close when Charles died in 741. It was, remember, the raising of a new Merovingian king in 743 which was an important step in pulling it together again. By 751 the palace had lost none of its power, although the Merovingian kings had lost theirs. This loss was not so gradual, complete or simple as Carolingian tradition would have it, because residual loyalty to the dynasty was strong and the Carolingian family less united and less secure than its propaganda leads us to believe. The fact that Carolingian kingship was not challenged except in Aquitaine and Bavaria suggests that the Franks' traditional respect for their kings soon passed to the new dynasty, and one key reason for this is that royal authority was necessary for the legitimation of magnate power, and the legal processes which protected property and privilege ultimately drew upon the authority of the king. We saw, for example, how the descendant of one bitter opponent of Charles Martel called upon the authority of Charlemagne in his attempt to recover property lost in our period. This was the case of Bishop Maurontus of Marseilles and it is revealed to us through the record of a lawsuit and in a report sent back to the king by one of his agents, the *missi*. It is therefore true to say that whoever controlled the palace in Neustria and Austrasia not only had access to the best organised resources in Francia, they also controlled a vital source of authority.

In these conditions, and in particular after a series of royal minorities, bitter factional fighting and war between Neustria and Austrasia had forced the magnates into different armed camps, it was very likely that a strongman would emerge. Charles Martel was not the first of these, and it was by no means the case that his family had reached an unassailable position by the time he came on the scene in 714. There were in fact several people who might have dominated Francia at this time, had they managed to take and hold the mayoralty, just as the Neustrian mayor Ebroin (c. 658–c. 680) had done two generations earlier. There was of course Ragamfred, who in alliance with the leader of the Frisians, Radbod, nearly succeeded in uniting Neustria and Austrasia in the years 715–16. Theudoald, grandson of Plectrude and Pippin, also briefly held the mayoralty. Had he been older and luckier we might now be talking of his line (Theudoaldingians?) rather than Carolingians. Eudo, duke of Aquitaine, was also in a favourable position when he had control of King Chilperic II and his treasure and enjoyed the support of many Neustrians. But, as we have just seen, Eudo was soon attacked by Arab raiders from the south and was forced to concentrate on the defence of Aquitaine. Perhaps other Austrasian families such as the Gundoinings might have picked up the baton had Charles Martel not rescued his own family in 716, and the Agilolfings seem to have had friends and relatives throughout Francia, which put them in a strong position too. In other words, when Charles Martel's father Pippin died in 714, the situation was wide open. But if the background shows us how conditions would favour the victor, it is to particular circumstances and events that we must look to understand why it was Charles Martel, rather than someone else, who emerged on top.

Throughout this study it has been emphasised that we know very little about Charles Martel the man. Not only are we completely ignorant about his life before the age of 26, his personality is hidden from us under layers of conventional, often biblical, language and further obscured by Carolingian propaganda. But we can deduce some elements of personality from the circumstances in which his career unfolded. We can observe that his exclusion from power and influence prior to his father's death must mean that he had occupied an inferior position in the Pippinid family. It was the exceptional crisis following Pippin's death which had catapulted him to prominence, and then in the years 715–16 he had to fight for survival not just against the Neustrians, Frisians and Saxons, but also against Plectrude and her supporters. That he could come from so far behind and win against the odds must mean that Charles was an exceptional fighter, strategist and political operator. We can also infer that his ruthlessness towards opponents, not least towards members of his own family, probably relates to the struggles of the early part of his career. His *curriculum vitae* after 716 reads as a long list of military campaigns, all of which were successful. We must therefore accept that Charles Martel was a brilliant military leader. To this conclusion we should add the earlier observation that whoever controlled the combined resources of Neustria and Austrasia would be more than a match for any other grouping in Francia, and also note an element of good fortune in the way that the Arabs in effect opened up Aquitaine and Burgundy to Charles. There is, therefore, no need to resort to special explanations, such as the introduction of the stirrup, the development of cavalry, the secularisation of church land and the invention of 'feudalism', to account for his success.

It is clear that this was a time of great turmoil in which violence played a major role in the reconfiguration of Frankish politics. There must have been a militarisation of the nobility as the incidence of warfare became much greater. It is quite sensible to associate the spread of precarial tenures with this militarisation if we reason that precarial tenure strengthened the position of some nobles and by stabilising their resources gave them the wherewithal to fight as mounted warriors. It is also obvious that some churches and some churchmen did suffer in the violence. But it is wrong to see Charles Martel as the author of a structural change in military and social organisation and as the prime mover in the secularisation of the church. It has been possible to demonstrate that this was not the case by examining each aspect of the Brunner thesis and showing how the sources have been misread or misinterpreted time after time, even down to the details of the description of the battle of Poitiers in the *Continuations of Fredegar*. It is never-theless possible to argue that developments in the age of Charles Martel did in important respects provide a basis for later Carolingian successes, as long, that is, as we understand the essential continuities between the Merovingian and Carolingian worlds. The yearly campaigning by which Charles Martel and his sons subdued Francia followed on into the Carolingian period to become yearly expeditions against peoples beyond Francia's borders. The spoils of war had now become an expected, rather than exceptional, part of the ruler's income. Precarial tenure continued to spread, and rulers did now make use of it to endow some followers, as Charles Martel had not. The papacy continued where it had left off in 740 in trying to persuade the Carolingians to abandon the Lombards and to back Rome. The spiritual alliance which resulted when Pippin did eventually switch sides went hand in hand with the church reform begun in the 740s to present the ruler as a protector of the church and of the weak. The development of a rhetoric of justice and moral authority centring upon the person of the ruler accom-panied that cultural assimilation of the peripheral duchies we have just been discussing, and both worked to reinforce the position of the king and the role of the palace as a cultural centre.

From the 760s onwards manuscript production in Francia began to increase dramatically, and there followed a revival of learning which has justifiably been termed a 'Renaissance'. This we cannot attribute to Charles Martel, for his age is said to have witnessed a decline in written culture. The effect of this decline, and the result of the Carolingian revival of learn-ing, are the root of the problems of evidence so often encountered in this study. Because we are faced with a dearth of writing from the age of Charles Martel itself, we are often forced to rely on a later Carolingian view of this period which is full of hindsight and opinion, whether written from the point of view of the ruling family itself, like the *Earlier Annals of Metz*, or, like the various *Gesta*, written in the interests of a particular abbey or bishopric. The former tend to see Charles Martel as a hero in biblical mould, the latter as the villain who stole church land. We began this study by explaining that it was the wish to reconcile these contradictory positions which gave rise to Brunner's overarching thesis. We now end it with an appreciation of the relationship between them which is both more subtle and casts a truer light on the age of Charles Martel.

We know that the death of Charles Martel's father in 714 triggered a struggle for power which lasted throughout his son's career. Charles Martel of course had many enemies and had to fight every inch of the way to gain control of Francia. He left many victims and much bitterness in his wake. His best remembered victim would be Eucherius, bishop of Orléans, whose fate was recorded in a near contemporary work. This period produced very little history and hagiography, but what little was produced was sufficient to preserve a tradition that it was a time of violence and suffering for the church. The letters of Boniface also gave the impression that the Frankish church was in a bad way. In the generation after Charles's death the struggle for power finally ended with complete Carolingian domination. Beginning with the *Continuations of Fredegar* we see the writing of history which ignored the victims of the Carolingians: Eucherius of Orléans, for instance, is quite absent from the *Continuations*. With the composition of the *Vita Eucherii* we also see the end of a long sequence of hagiographical works in which church leaders who were the victims of political violence were sometimes recognised as saints and their 'Lives' quickly written up. The Carolingians preferred more ancient saints, not least because this shift in attitude precluded the chance of any of the Carolingians' own victims being celebrated as heroes. By the end of the eighth century, there was very little reference to internal opposition to the ruling house. On the other hand there was a much more sophisticated justification of the ruler's actions. It was in history written from this cultural and political standpoint that Charles Martel appears as a hero of Christendom whose vigour and purpose made it clear that the powerless Merovingian dynasty should be replaced.

By the mid-ninth century there was clearly a revival of opposition to the Carolingians, or at least divisions within the family fragmented the sense of solidarity which had characterised the reign of Charlemagne and the first part of that of his son Louis the Pious. When in the mid-ninth century Hincmar of Rheims wished to criticise present kings for their misuse of church property, he was faced with a recent tradition which extolled the kings as protectors of the church, and which presented their authority as unquestioned and unopposed. In order to find a 'bad' Carolingian whose example and fate could serve as a warning to the dynasty, he went back to those much earlier sources which preserved the memory of Carolingian injustice, and to a time when the church was said to be being harmed by laymen. He thus went back to the *Vita Eucherii* and to the letters of Boniface, and argued that it was Charles Martel who was ultimately responsible for the secularisation of church property. To this he added the legendary vision of Charles being tortured in hell. That other writers and institutions keenly followed Hincmar's example in making Charles Martel the personification of injustice towards the church shows how successful his descendants had been in identifying themselves with justice and moral rectitude. In this sense the explanation of Charles Martel's contrasting reputations is to be found not in the fact that painful measures had to be taken to save Christendom from the Arabs, but in the evolution of ecclesiastical attitudes towards the Carolingian dynasty in later generations. First, as past and present complaint against the dynasty was excised from history, Charles was constructed as the eponymous hero, but then when opposition to the rulers resurfaced and earlier complaints were rediscovered, he became the original villain. But this later opposition was not of the kind Charles Martel himself had faced, that is, from people who were prepared to resist him by force. For, unlike the resistance to Charles, critics like Hincmar did not challenge the right of the Carolingians to rule, so much as the way in which they ruled. By and large, it was a challenge made with the pen rather than the sword. By contrast, the age of Charles Martel was an age of swords and of warlords, rather than kings.

BIBLIOGRAPHY

Primary Sources

Actus Pontificum Cenomannis in Urbe Degentium, ed. G. Busson and L. Ledru, Le Mans, 1901–2.

Adalelm, *Vita Opportunae, Acta Sanctorum*, Aprilis III, Antwerp, 1675, pp. 62–5.

Alcuin, *Vita Willibrordi Archiepiscopi Traiectensis*, ed. W. Levison, *MGH SRM* VII, Hanover and Leipzig, 1920, pp. 113–41.

Annales Alamannici, ed. G. Pertz, *MGH SS* I, Hanover, 1826, pp. 22–30.

Annales Guelferbtytani, ed. G. Pertz, *MGH* SS I, Hanover, 1826, pp. 22–30.

Annales Laubacenses, ed. G. Pertz, *MGH SS* I, Hanover, 1826, pp. 6–12.

Annales Laureshamenses, ed. G. Pertz, *MGH SS* I, Hanover, 1826, pp. 22–30.

Annales Mettenses Priores, ed. B. von Simson, *MGH SRG*, Hanover and Leipzig, 1905.

Annales Nazariani, ed. G. Pertz, *MGH SS* I, Hanover, 1826, pp. 22–30.

Annales Petaviani, ed. G. Pertz, *MGH SS* I, Hanover, 1826, pp. 6–12.

Annales Sancti Amandi, ed. G. Pertz, *MGH SS* I, Hanover, 1826, pp. 6–12.

Annales Tiliani, ed. G. Pertz, *MGH SS* I, Hanover, 1826, pp. 6–12.

Arbeo, *Vitae Sanctorum Haimhrammi et Corbiniani*, ed. B. Krusch, *MGH SRG*, Hanover 1920.

Bede's Ecclesiastical History of the English People, ed. and trans. B. Colgrave and R. Mynors, Oxford, 1969.

Chartae Latinae Antiquiores, ed. A. Bruckner and R. Marichal, vols 13, 14, ed. H. Atsma and J. Vezin, Zurich, 1981, 1982.

Chronicle of Ado, ex Chronicon Adonis, ed. G. Pertz, *MGH SS* II, Hanover, 1829, p. 318.

Chronicon Herimanni Augiensis, ed. G. Pertz, *MGH SS* V, Hanover, 1844.

Clotharii Edictum, Capitularia Regum Francorum I, ed. A. Boretius, *MGH Legum*, sectio II, 1, Hanover, 1883, pp. 20–3.

Codex Carolinus, ed. W. Grundlach, *MGH Epistolae* III, Berlin, 1892, pp. 476–653.

Concilium Liftinense, ed. A. Werminghoff, *MGH Concilia* II, i, Hanover and Leipzig, 1906, pp. 6–7.

Concilium Parisiense, ed. C. de Clercq, *Concilia Galliae a 511–695, Corpus Christianorum*, series Latina 148A, Turnhout, 1963, pp. 275–82.

Concilium Suessionense, ed. A. Werminghoff, *MGH Concilia* II, i, Hanover and Leipzig, 1906, pp. 33–6.

Concilum Germanicum, ed. A. Werminghoff, *MGH Concilia* II, i, Hanover and Leipzig, 1906, pp. 2–4.

Descriptio Mancipiorum Ecclesie Massiliensis, ed. B. Guérard, *Cartulaire de l'Abbaye de Saint-Victor de Marseille* II, Paris, 1857, pp. 633–54.
Diplomata Belgica ante Annum Millesimum Centesimum Scripta I, ed. M. Gysseling and A. Koch, Brussels, 1950.

Edictum Pistense, Capitularia Regum Francorum II, ed. A. Boretius and V. Krause, *MGH Legum*, sectio II, 2, Hanover, 1897, pp. 311–28.
Edictus Chilperici, Capitularia Regum Francorum I, ed. A. Boretius, *MGH Legum*, sectio II, 1, Hanover, 1883, pp. 8–10.
Eigil, *Vita Sturmi*, ed. G. Pertz, *MGH SS* II, Hanover, 1829, pp. 365–77.
Einhard, *The Life of Charlemagne* ed. and trans. P. Dutton, *Charlemagne's Courtier. The Complete Einhard*, Ontario, 1999, pp. 15–39.
Emerton, E. (trans.), *The Letters of St Boniface*, New York, 1940.
Erchanbert, *Breviarum Regum Francorum*, ed. G. Pertz, *MGH SS* II, Hanover, 1829, a 715–827, p. 328.

Flodoard, *Historia Remensis Ecclesiae*, ed. I. Heller and G. Waitz, *MGH SS* XIII, Hanover, 1881, pp. 405–599.
Formulae Turonenses, ed. K. Zeumer, *MGH Formulae Merovingici et Karoli Aevi*, Hanover,1886, no. 43, p. 158.

Gesta Episcoporum Autissiodorensium, extracts ed. G. Waitz, *MGH SS* XIII, Hanover, 1881, pp. 394–400.
Gesta Episcopum Virdunensium, ed. G. Waitz, *MGH SS* IV, Hanover, 1841, pp. 39–51.
Gesta Sanctorum Patrum Fontanellensis Coenobii, ed. F. Lohier and J. Laporte, Rouen, 1936.
Gregory of Tours, *Decem Libri Historiarum*, ed. B. Krusch and W. Levison, *MGH SRM* II, Hanover, 1951.

Halkin, J. and Roland, C. *Recueil des Chartes de l'Abbaye de Stavelot-Malmedy*, Brussels, 1909.
Hincmar, *Epistola Synodali Carisiacensis ad Hludowicem Regem Germaniae Directa, MGH Capitularia Regum Francorum* II, ed. A. Boretius and V. Krause, Hanover, 1897, pp. 427–41.

John of Worcester, *The Chronicle of John of Worcester, II, The Annals from 450–1066*, ed. R. Darlington and P. McGurk, trans. P. Bray and P. McGurk, Oxford, 1998.

King, P. *Charlemagne. Translated Sources*, Lambrigg, 1986.

Leges Alamannorum, ed. K. Lehman, *MGH Legum*, sectio I, 5, Hanover, 1888.
Leges Baiwariorum, ed. E. de Schwind, *MGH Legum*, sectio I, 5, Hanover, 1888.
Liber Historiae Francorum, ed. B. Krusch, *MGH SRM* II, Hanover, 1888.
Liber Pontificalis, trans. R. Davis, *The Lives of the Eighth-Century Popes*, Liverpool, 1992.
Liber Traditionum of St Peter's, Ghent, ed. Gyselling and Koch, *Diplomata Belgica*, no. 49, p. 125.

Liudger, *Vita Gregorii Abbatis Traiectensis*, ed. A. Holder-Egger, *MGH SS* XVI, Hanover, 1887, pp. 66–79.

Marculfi Formularum Libri Duo, ed. and French trans. A. Uddholm, Uppsala, 1962.
MGH Diplomata Karolinorum I, ed. E. Mühlbacher, Hanover, 1906.
Miracula Austregisili, ed. B. Krusch, *MGH SRM* IV, Hanover and Leipzig, 1902, pp. 200–8.

Pardessus, J. (ed.), *Diplomata, Chartae, Epistolae, Leges, Aliaque Instrumenta ad Res Gallo-Francicas Spectantia*, 2 vols, Paris 1843, 1849, reprinted, Aalen, 1969.
Passio Kiliani, ed. W. Levison, *MGH SRM* V, Hanover, 1910, pp. 722–8.
Passio Leudegarii, ed. B. Krusch, *MGH SRM* V, Hanover, 1910, pp. 282–322, trans. with commentary in Fouracre and Gerberding, *Late Merovingian France*, pp. 191–253.
Passio Praejecti, ed. B. Krusch, *MGH SRM* V, Hanover 1910, pp. 225–48, trans. with commentary in Fouracre and Gerberding, *Late Merovingian France*, pp. 254–300.
Passio Sancti Salvii, ed. M. Coens, 'La Passion de Saint Sauve, Martyr à Valenciennes', *Analecta Bollandiana*, 87 (1967), commentary 131–63, text 164–87.
Paul the Deacon, *Gesta Episcoporum Mettensium*, ed. G. Pertz, *MGH SS* II, Hanover, 1829, pp. 262–8.
Paul the Deacon, *Historia Langobardorum*, ed. G. Waitz, *MGH SRG*, Hanover, 1878.

Revised Annals of the Kingdom of the Franks, trans. King, *Charlemagne. Translated Sources*, pp. 108–31.
Royal Frankish Annals, trans. B. Sholz, *Carolingian Chronicles*, Ann Arbor, 1972.

Sancti Bonifatii et Lulli Epistolae, ed. M. Tangl, *MGH Epistolae Selectae* I, Berlin, 1955.

Talbot, C. *The Anglo-Saxon Missionaries in Germany*, London, 1954.
Tardif, J. 'Les Chartes Mérovingiens de Noirmoutier', *Nouvelle Revue Historique de Droit Francais et Étranger*, 22 (1899), 763–90.
The Cartulary of Flavigny, ed. C. Bouchard, Cambridge Mass., 1991.
The Fourth Book of the Chronicle of Fredegar with its Continuations, ed. and trans. J.M. Wallace-Hadrill, London, 1960.
The Laws of the Salian Franks, trans. K. Fischer-Drew, Philadelphia, 1991.
The Life of St Wilfrid by Eddius Stephanus, ed. and trans. B. Colgrave, Cambridge, 1927, reprinted New York, 1985.
Thegan, *Gesta Hludowici Imperatoris*, ed. G. Pertz, *MGH SS* II, Hanover, 1829, pp. 585–605.
Thorpe, L. (trans.), *Gregory of Tours. The History of the Franks*, Harmondsworth, 1974.
Traditiones Wizenburgenses, ed. L. Glöckner and A. Doll, Darmstadt, 1979.

Urkundenbuch der Abtei St Gallen I, 700–848, ed. W. Wartmann, Zurich, 1863.

Vita Ermenlandi, ed. W. Levison, *MGH SRM* V, Hanover and Leipzig, 1910, pp. 682–710.
Vita Erminonis Abbatis Lobbiensis, ed. W. Levison, *MGH SRM* VI, Hanover and Leipzig, 1913, pp. 461–70.

Vita Eucherii, ed. W. Levison, *MGH SRM* VII, Hanover and Leipzig, 1920, pp. 46–53.

Vita Galli, auctore Walafrido, ed. B. Krusch, *MGH SRM* IV, Hanover and Leipzig, 1902, pp. 280–337.

Vita Geretrudis, ed. B. Krusch, *MGH SRM* II, Hanover 1888, pp. 464–71, trans. with commentary in Fouracre and Gerberding, *Late Merovingian France*, pp. 301–26.

Vita Hugoberti, ed. W. Levison, *MGH SRM* VI, Hanover and Leipzig, 1913, pp. 482–96.

Vita Landiberti auctore Sigeberto, ed. B. Krusch, *MGH SRM* VI, Hanover and Leipzig, 1913, pp. 393–406.

Vita Landiberti Vetustissima, ed. B. Krusch, *MGH SRM* VI, Hanover and Leipzig, 1913, pp. 353–84.

Vita Lebuini, ed. A. Hofmeister, *MGH SS* XXX, ii, Hanover, 1926–34, pp. 789–95.

Vita Pardulfi, ed. W. Levison, *MGH SRM* VII, Hanover and Leipzig, 1920, pp. 24–40.

Vita Rigoberti, ed. W. Levison, *MGH SRM* VII, Hanover and Leipzig, 1920, pp. 58–80.

Wampach, C. *Geschichte der Grundherrschaft Echternach im Frühmittelalter* I, pt 2, Luxembourg, 1930.

William of Malmesbury, *Gesta Regum Anglorum, The History of the English Kings* I, eds. and trans. R. Mynors, R. Thomson and M. Winterbottom, Oxford, 1998.

Willibald, *Vita Bonifatii*, ed. W. Levison, *MGH SRG*, Hanover, 1905.

Secondary Works

Angenendt, A. 'Willibrord im Dienste der Karolinger', *Annalen des historisches Vereins für den Niederrhein inbesondere das alte Erzbistum Köln*, 175 (1973), 63–113.

Bachrach, B. *Merovingian Military Organisation*, Minneapolis, 1972.

Bachrach, B. 'Military Organisation in Aquitaine under the Early Carolingians', *Speculum*, 49 (1974), 1–33.

Bachrach, B. 'Was Marchfield Part of the Frankish Constitution?', *Medieval Studies*, 36 (1974), 178–85.

Barnwell, P. *Kings, Courtiers and Imperium. The Barbarian West, 565–725*, London, 1997.

Baudot, M. 'Localisation et Datation de la Première Victoire Remportée contre les Musulmans', *Memoires et Documents Publiées par la Société de l'Ecole des Chartes*, 12, i (1955), 93–105.

Becher, M. 'Drogo und die Königserhebung Pippins', *Frühmittelalterliche Studien*, 23 (1989), 131–53.

Becher, M. 'Neue Überlieferungen zum Geburtsdatum Karls des Grossen', *Francia*, 19 (1992), 37–60.

Becher, M. 'Der sogenannte Staatsstreich Grimoalds. Versuch einer Neubewertung', in Jarnut, Nonn and Richter (eds), *Karl Martell in Seiner Zeit*, pp. 119–47.

Bergengruen, A. *Adel und Grundherrschaft im Merrowingerreich*, Wiesbaden, 1958.

Borgolte, M. *Geschichte der Grafschaften Alemanniens in fränkishe Zeit*, Vorträge und Forschungen, 31, Sigmaringen, 1984.

Brett, M. 'John of Worcester and His Contemporaries', in R.H.C. Davis and J. Wallace-Hadrill (eds), *The Writing of History in the Middle Ages. Essays Presented to Sir Richard Southern*, Oxford, 1981, pp. 101–26.

Brunner, H. 'Der Reiterdienst und die Anfänge des Lehnwesens', *Zeitschrift der Savigny-Stiftung für Rechtsgeschichte, Germanistische Abteilung*, 8 (1887), 1–38.

Chaume, M. *Les Origines du Duché de Bourgogone*, Dijon, 1926.

Collins, R. *The Arab Conquest of Spain*, Oxford, 1989.

Collins, R. 'Deception and Misrepresentation in Early Eighth-Century Frankish Historiography: Two Case Studies', in Jarnut, Nonn and Richter (eds), *Karl Martell in Seiner Zeit*, pp. 227–47.

Collins, R. *Fredegar*, Authors of the Middle Ages, 13, Aldershot, 1996.

Costambeys, M. 'An Aristocratic Community on the Northern Frankish Frontier 690–726', *Early Medieval Europe*, 3 (1994), 39–62.

Damminger, F. 'Dwellings, Settlements and Settlement Patterns in Merovingian Southwest Germany and Adjacent Areas', in Wood (ed.), *Franks and Alemanni*, pp. 33–89.

Davies, W. and Fouracre, P. (eds), *Property and Power in the Early Middle Ages*, Cambridge, 1995.

Depeyrot, G. *Richesse et Société chez les Mérovingiens et Carolingiens*, Paris, 1994.

Deviosse, J. *Charles Martel*, Paris, 1978.

Devroey, J-P. 'Réflexions sur l'Économie des Premiers Temps Carolingiens: Grands Domaines et Action Politique entre Seine et Rhin', *Francia*, 13 (1985), 475–88.

Dierkens, A. *Abbayes et Chapitres entre Sambre et Meuse (VIIe–Xie siècles)*, Beihefte der Francia, 14, Sigmaringen, 1985.

Duchesne, L. *Fastes Episcopaux de l'Ancienne Gaule*, 3 vols, Paris, 1894–1915.

Dutton, P. *The Politics of Dreaming in the Carolingian Empire*, Lincoln and London, 1994.

Ebling, H. *Prosopographie der Amtsträger des Merrowingerreiches*, Beihefte der Francia, 2, Munich, 1974.

Ebling, H. 'Die inneraustrasische Opposition', in Jarnut, Nonn and Richter (eds), *Karl Martell in Seiner Zeit*, pp. 295–304.

Effros, B. '*De Partibus Saxoniae* and the Regulation of Mortuary Custom: A Carolingian Campaign of Christianization or the Suppression of Saxon Identity?', *Revue Belge de Philologie et d'Histoire*, 75 (1997), 267–86.

Ewig, E. 'Milo et eiusmodi similes', in *Sankt Bonifatius Gedenkengabe zum zwölfhundertsten Todestag*, Fulda, 1954, pp. 412–20, also in *Spätantikes und Fränkisches Gallien II*, pp. 189–219.

Ewig, E. 'L'Aquitaine et les Pays Rhénans au Haut Moyen Age', *Cahiers de Civilization Médiévale*, 1 (1958), 37–54, also in *Spätantikes und Fränkisches Gallien I*, pp. 553–72.

Ewig, E. 'Résidence et Capitale Pendant le Haut Moyen Age', *Revue Historique*, 230 (1963), 25–72, also in *Spätantikes und Fränkisches Gallien I*, pp. 363–408.

Ewig, E. 'Noch einmal zum "Staatsstreich" Grimoalds', in C. Bauer, L. Böhm and M. Müller (eds), *Speculum Historiale: Geschichte im Spiegel von Geschichtsschreibung und Geschichtsdenkung*, Freiburg and Munich, 1965, pp. 454–57.

Ewig, E. 'Studien zur merowingische Dynastie', *Frühmittelalterliche Studien*, 8 (1974), 15–59.

Ewig, E. 'Die Civitas Ubiorum, die Francia Rinensis und das Land Ribuarien', in *Spätantikes und Fränkisches Gallien* I, pp. 472–502.

Ewig, E. *Spätantikes und Fränkisches Gallien. Gesammelten Schriften (1952–1973)*, Beihefte der Francia, 3, pts 1 and 2, 2 vols, Zurich and Munich, 1976, 1979.

Fletcher, R. *The Conversion of Europe. From Paganism to Christianity 371–1368 A.D.*, London, 1997.

Fouracre, P. 'Observations on the Outgrowth of Pippinid Influence in the "Regnum Francorum" After the Battle of Tertry (687–715)', *Medieval Prosopography*, 5 (1984), 1–31.

Fouracre, P. 'Merovingian History and Merovingian Hagiography', *Past and Present*, 127 (1990), 3–38.

Fouracre, P. 'Carolingian Justice: The Rhetoric of Improvement and Contexts of Abuse', *La Giustizia nell 'alto Medieovo (Secole V–VIII)*, Settimane di Studio del Centro Italiano di Studi sull'alto Medieovo, 42, Spoleto, 1995, pp. 771–803.

Fouracre, P. 'Eternal Light and Earthly Needs: Practical Aspects of the Development of Frankish Immunities', in Davies and Fouracre (eds), *Property and Power*, pp. 53–81.

Fouracre, P. 'The Nature of Frankish Political Institutions in the Seventh Century', in Wood (ed.), *Franks and Alemanni*, pp. 285–316.

Fouracre, P. 'The Origins of the Carolingian Attempt to Regulate the Cult of Saints', in J. Howard-Johnston and P. Hayward (eds), *The Cult of Saints in Late Antiquity and the Early Middle Ages*, Oxford, 2000, pp. 143–65.

Fouracre, P. and Gerberding, R. *Late Merovingian France. History and Hagiography 640–720*, Manchester, 1996.

Fritze, W. 'Zur Entstehungsgeschichte des Bistums Utrecht. Franken und Friesen 690–734', *Rheinische Vierteljahrsblätter*, 35 (1971), 107–51.

Ganshof, F. *Feudalism*, trans. P. Grierson, London, 1964.

Ganz, D. 'The Ideology of Sharing: Apostolic Community and Ecclesiastical Property in the Early Middle Ages', in Davies and Fouracre (eds), *Property and Power*, pp. 17–30.

Geary, P. *Aristocracy in Provence: The Rhône Basin at the Dawn of the Carolingian Age*, Stuttgart, 1985.

Geary, P. 'Die Provenz zur Zeit Karl Martells', in Jarnut, Nonn and Richter (eds), *Karl Martell in Seiner Zeit*, pp. 381–92.

Geary, P. 'Extra-judicial Means of Conflict Resolution', *La Giustizia nell 'alto Medieovo (Secole V–VIII)*, Settimane di Studio del Centro Italiano di Studi sull'alto Medieovo, 42 , Spoleto, 1995, pp. 569–601.

Gerberding, R. *The Rise of the Carolingians and the Liber Historiae Francorum*, Oxford, 1987.

Gerberding, R. '716: A Crucial Year for Charles Martel', in Jarnut, Nonn and Richter (eds), *Karl Martell in Seiner Zeit*, pp. 203–16.

Goffart, W. *The Le Mans Forgeries*, Cambridge Mass., 1966.

Goffart, W. 'From Roman Taxation to Medieval Seigneurie: Three Notes', *Speculum*, 47 (1972), 165–87 and 373–94.

Goffart, W. 'Old and New in Merovingian Taxation', *Past and Present*, 96 (1982), 3–21.

Goody, J. *The Family and Marriage in Europe*, Cambridge, 1982.

Grahn-Hoek, H. *Die fränkische Oberschicht im 6 Jahrhundert. Studien über ihre rechtliche und politische Stellung*, Sigmaringen, 1976.

Halsall, G. *Settlement and Social Organization. The Merovingian Region of Metz*, Cambridge, 1995.

Hammer, C. 'Land Sales in Eighth- and Ninth-Century Bavaria: Legal, Social and Economic Aspects', *Early Medieval Europe*, 6 (1997), 47–76.

Hartung, W. 'Adel, Erbrecht, Schenkung: Die strukturellen Ursachen der frühmittelalterlichen Besitzübertragungen und die Kirche', in Seibt (ed.), *Gesellschaftsgeshicthte*, I, pp. 417–38.

Hartung, W. 'Tradition und Namengebung im frühen Mittelalter', in I. Eberl, W. Hartung and J. Jahn (eds), *Früh- und hochmittelalterlicher Adel in Schwaben und Bayern*, *Regio*, Forschungen zur schwäbischen Regionalgeschichte, 1, Sigmaringen, 1988, pp. 21–79.

Haselbach, I. 'Aufstieg und Herrschaft der Karolinger in der Darstellung des sogenannten *Annales Mettenses Priores*', *Historischen Studien*, 406 (1970), 1–208.

Heidrich, I. 'Titular und Urkunden der arnulfingischen Hausmeier', *Archiv für Diplomatik*, 11/12 (1965–66), 17–279.

Heidrich, I. 'Die Gründungsausstatung der elsässischen Klöster St Gallen und Reichenau in der ersten Hälfte des 8 Jahrhunderts', in P. Classen (ed.), *Die Gründungsurkunden der Reichenau*, Vorträge und Forschungen, 24, Sigmaringen, 1977, pp. 31–62.

Heinzelmann, M. ' "Sanctitas" und "Tugendadel". Zur Konzeptionen von "Heiligkeit" in 5 und 10 Jahrhundert', *Francia* 5 (1977), 741–52.

Higounet, C. 'L'Occupation du Sol du Pays entre Tarn et Garonne au Moyen Age', *Annales du Midi*, 65 (1953), 301–30.

Hlawitscha, E. 'Die Vorfahren Karls des Grossen', in W. Braunfels (ed.), *Karl der Grosse. Lebenswerk und Nachleben*, I, Düsseldorf, 1965, pp. 51–82.

Hodges, R. and Hobley, B. (eds), *The Rebirth of Towns in the West, 700–1050*, London, 1988.

Hodges, R. and Whitehouse, D. *Mohammed, Charlemagne and the Origins of Europe*, London, 1983.

Innes, M. *State and Society in the Early Middle Ages: The Middle Rhine Valley 400–1000*, Cambridge, 2000.

Irsigler, F. *Untersuchungen zur Geschichte des frühfränkischen Adels*, Bonn, 1969.

Jahn, J. 'Tradere ad Sanctum: Politische und gesellschaftliche Aspekte der Traditionspraxis im agilolfingischen Bayern', in Seibt (ed.), *Gesellschaftsgeschichte*, I, pp. 400–16.

Jahn, J. *Ducatus Baiwariorum. Das Bairische Herzogtum des Agilolfinger*, Monographien zur Geschichte des Mittelalters, 35, Stuttgart, 1991.

James, E. *The Origins of France*, London 1982.

Jarnut, J. 'Untersuchungen zur Herkunft Swanahilds, der Gattin Karl Martells', *Zeitschrift für bayerische Landesgeschichte*, 40 (1977), 254–9.

Jarnut, J. 'Untersuchungen zu den fränkisch-alemmanische Beziehungen in der ersten Hälfte des 8 Jahrhunderts', *Schweizerische Zeitschrift für Geschichte*, 30 (1980), 7–28.

Jarnut, J. 'Die Adoption Pippins durch König Liutprand', in Jarnut, Nonn and Richter (eds), *Karl Martell in Seiner Zeit*, pp. 217–26.

Jarnut, J., Nonn, U. and Richter, M. (eds), *Karl Martell in Seiner Zeit*, Beihefte der Francia, 37, Sigmaringen, 1994.

Joch, W. 'Karl Martell – ein minderberechtiger Erbe Pippins?', in Jarnut, Nonn and Richter (eds), *Karl Martell in Seiner Zeit*, pp. 149–69.

Krusch, B. 'Der Staatsstreich des fränkischen Hausmeiers Grimoald', in *Festgäbe für Karl Hampe*, Weimar, 1910, pp. 411–38.

Le Jan, R. *Famille et Pouvoir dans le Monde Franc (VIIe–Xe siècle). Essai d'Anthropologie Sociale*, Paris, 1995.

Lesne, E. *Histoire de la Propriété Ecclésiastique en France*, 6 vols, Lille, 1910–38.

Levillain, L. 'Encore la Succession d'Austrasie', *Bibliothèque de l'Ecole des Chartes*, 106 (1945–46), 5–63.

Lifshitz, F. *The Norman Conquest of Pious Neustria: Historiographic Discourse and Saintly Relics 684–1090*, Toronto, 1995.

Loseby, S. 'Marseille: A Late Antique Success Story', *Journal of Roman Studies*, 82 (1992), 165–85.

McKitterick, R. *The Carolingians and the Written Word*, Cambridge, 1989.

McKitterick, R. 'Constructing the Past in the Early Middle Ages: The Case of the Royal Frankish Annals', *Transactions of the Royal Historical Society*, 6th series, 7 (1997), 101–29.

McKitterick, R. 'The Illusion of Royal Power in the Carolingian Annals', *English Historical Review* (forthcoming).

Mitteis, H. *The State in the Middle Ages*, trans. H. Orton, Amsterdam, 1975.

Mordek, H. 'Die Hedenen als politische Kraft im Austrasischen Frankenreich', in Jarnut, Nonn and Richter (eds), *Karl Martell in Seiner Zeit*, pp. 343–66.

Nehlsen, H. 'Zur Aktualität und Effectivität germanische Rechtsaufzeichnungen', in P. Classen (ed.), *Recht und Schrift im Mittelalter*, Vorträge und Forschungen, 23, Sigmaringen, 1977, pp. 451–83.

Nelson, J. 'Dispute Settlement in Carolingian West Francia', in W. Davies and P. Fouracre (eds), *The Settlement of Disputes in Early Medieval Europe*, Cambridge, 1986, pp. 45–64.

Niermeyer, J. *Mediae Latinae Lexicon Minus*, Leiden, 1984.

Noble, T. *The Republic of St Peter. The Birth of the Papal State 680–825*, Philadelphia, 1984.

Nonn, U. 'Das Bild Karl Martells in Mittelalterliche Quellen', in Jarnut, Nonn and Richter (eds), *Karl Martell in Seiner Zeit*, pp. 9–21.

Prinz, F. *Frühes Mönchtum im Frankenreich*, Munich, 1965.

Prinz, F. 'Frühes Mönchtum in Südwestdeutschland und die Anfänge der Reichenau', in A. Borst (ed.), *Mönchtum Episkopat und Adel zur Gründungszeit des Klosters Reichenau*, Vorträge und Forschungen, 20, Sigmaringen, 1974, pp. 37–76.

Prinz, F. 'Die Bischöfliche Stadtherrschaft im Frankenreich vom 5 bis 7 Jahrhundert', *Historische Zeitschrift*, 217 (1974), 1–35.

Reuter, T. *The Early Medieval Nobility*, Amsterdam, 1978.

Reuter, T. 'Plunder and Tribute in the Carolingian Empire', *Transactions of the Royal Historical Society*, 5th series, 35 (1985), 75–94.

Reuter, T. 'The End of Carolingian Military Expansion', in P. Godman and R. Collins (eds), *Charlemagne's Heir*, Oxford, 1990, pp. 391–405.

Reuter, T. *Germany in the Early Middle Ages 800–1056*, London, 1991.

Reuter, T. '"Kirchenreform" und "Kirchenpolitik" im Zeitalter Karl Martells: Begriffe und Wirklichkeit', in Jarnut, Nonn and Richter (eds), *Karl Martell in Seiner Zeit*, pp. 35–59.

Reuter, T. 'Property Transactions and Social Relations between Rulers, Bishops and Nobles in Early Eleventh-century Saxony: The Evidence of the *Vita Meinwerci*', in Davies and Fouracre (eds), *Property and Power*, pp. 165–99.

Reynolds, S. *Fiefs and Vassals. The Medieval Evidence Reinterpreted*, Oxford, 1994.

Ridé, J. *L'Image du German dans la Pensée*, Lille and Paris, 1977.

Rouche, M. *L'Aquitaine des Wisigoths aux Arabes 418–781. Naissance d'une Region*, Paris, 1979.

Samson, R. 'The Merovingian Nobleman's House: Castle or Villa?', *Journal of Medieval History*, 13 (1987), 287–315.

Schieffer, R. 'Karl Martell und seine Familie', in Jarnut, Nonn and Richter (eds), *Karl Martell in Seiner Zeit*, pp. 305–15.

Schlesinger, W. 'Das Frühmittelalter', in H. Patze and W. Schlesinger (eds), *Geschichte Thüringens I. Grundlagen und frühes Mittelalter*. Mitteldeutsche Forschungen, 48, I, Cologne and Graz, 1968.

Schüssler, H. 'Die fränkische Reichtsteilung von Vieux-Poitiers (742) und die Reform der Kirche in den Teilreichen Karlmanns und Pippins', *Francia*, 13 (1985), 45–111.

Scull, C. 'Urban Centres in Pre-Viking England?', in J. Hines (ed.), *The Anglo-Saxons from the Migration Period to the Eighth Century. An Ethnographic Perspective*, Woodbridge, 1997, pp. 269–310.

Seibt, F. (ed.), *Gesellschaftsgeschichte. Festschrift für Karl Bosl zum 80. Geburtstag*, 2 vols, Munich 1988.

Semmler, J. 'Pippin und die Fränkische Klöster', *Francia*, 3 (1975), 87–146.

Semmler, J. 'Zur pippinidisch-karolingische Zuksessionskrise 714–723', *Deutsches Archiv für Erforschung des Mittelalters*, 33 (1977), 1–36.

Stadt-Lauer, A. 'Carlus Princeps Regionem Burgundie Sagaciter Penetravit. Zur Schlacht von Tours und Poitiers und die Eingreifen Karl Martells in Burgund', in Jarnut, Nonn and Richter (eds), *Karl Martell in Seiner Zeit*, pp. 79–100.

Stancliffe, C. 'Kings Who Opted Out', in P. Wormald (ed.), *Ideal and Reality in Frankish and Anglo-Saxon Society*, Oxford 1983, pp. 154–76.

Steuer, H. 'Archäeologie und die Erforschung des germanischen Sozialgeschichte', in D. Simon (ed.), *Akten des 26 Deutschen Rechtshistorikertages*, Studien zur Europäischen Rechtsgeschichtes, 30, Frankfurt, 1987, pp. 443–53.

Thacker, A. 'Memorialising Gregory the Great: The Origins and Transmission of a Papal Cult in the Seventh and Early Eighth Centuries', *Early Medieval Europe*, 7 (1998), 59–84.

Theuws, F. 'Centre and Periphery in Northern Austrasia (6th–8th centuries). An Archaeological Perspective', in J. Besteman, J. Bos and H. Heidinga (eds), *Medieval Archaeology in the Netherlands. Studies Presented to H.H. van Regteren Altena*, Aasen and Maastricht, 1990, pp. 41–69.

Theuws, F. 'Landed Property and Manorial Organisation in Northern Austrasia: Some Considerations and a Case Study', in N. Roymans and F. Theuws (eds), *Images of the Past. Studies on Ancient Societies in Northwestern Europe*, Amsterdam, 1991, pp. 299–407.

Thomson, R. 'William of Malmesbury's Carolingian Sources', *Journal of Medieval History*, 7 (1981), 321–38.

Wallace-Hadrill, J. *The Frankish Church*, Oxford, 1983.

Weidemann, M. *Das Testament des Bischofs Bertramn von Le Mans von 27 März 616*, Mainz, 1986.

Werner, K-F. 'Faire Revivre le Souvenir d'un Pays Oublié', in H. Atsma (ed.), *La Neustrie. Les Pays au Nord de la Loire de 650 à 850*, Beihefte der Francia, 16, 2 vols, Sigmaringen, 1989, pp. xiii–xxxi.

Werner, M. *Adelsfamilien im Umkreis der frühen Karolinger. Die Verwandtschaft Irminas von Oeren und Adelas von Pfalzel*, Vorträge und Forschungen, 28, Sigmaringen, 1982.

Werner, M. *Der Lütticher Raum in frühkarolingischer Zeit*, Veröffentlichungen des Max-Planck Instituts für Geschichte, 62, Göttingen, 1980.

White, L. Junior. *Medieval Technology and Social Change*, Oxford, 1962.

Wilsdorf, C. 'Le Monasterium Scottorum de Honau et la Famille des Ducs d'Alsace à VIIe Siècle. Vestiges d'un Cartulaire Perdu', *Francia*, 3 (1975), 1–87.

Wolf, G. 'Grifos Erbe, die Einsetzung König Childerics III und der Kampf um die Macht – zugleich Bemerkungen zur karolingische "Hofhistoriographie"', *Archiv für Diplomatik*, 38 (1992), 1–16.

Wolfram, H. 'Der heilige Rupert und die antikarolingische Adelsopposition', *Mitteilungen des Instituts für österreichische Geschichtsforschung*, 80 (1972), 4–34.

Wolfram, H. *Die Geburt Mitteleuropas. Geschichte Österreichs vor seiner Entstehung*, Vienna, 1987.

Wolfram, H. 'Karl Martell und das fränkische Lehenswesen', in Jarnut, Nonn and Richter (eds), *Karl Martell in Seiner Zeit*, pp. 61–78.

Wood, I. *The Merovingian North Sea*, Alsingås, 1983.

Wood, I. *The Merovingian Kingdoms*, London 1994.

Wood, I. 'Teutsind, Witlaic and the history of Merovingian *precaria*', in Davies and Fouracre (eds), *Property and Power*, pp. 31–52.

Wood, I. 'Boniface', *The New Dictionary of National Biography*, Oxford, forthcoming.

Wood, I. (ed.), *Franks and Alemanni in the Merovingian Period. An Ethnographic Perspective*, Woodbridge, 1998.

The Later Merovingian Kings and Queen–regents 612–751

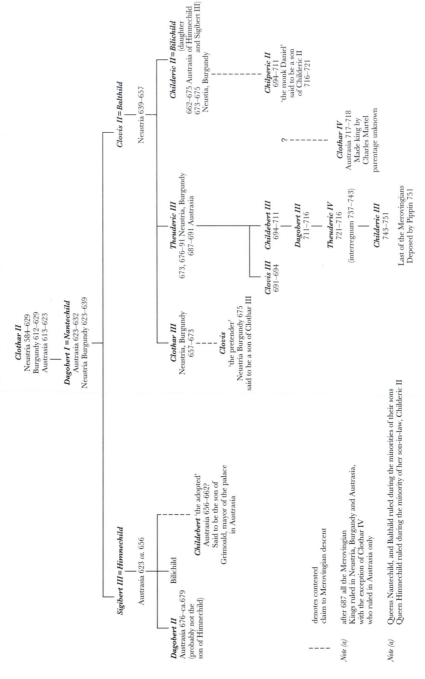

Plectrude, her sisters and their descendants

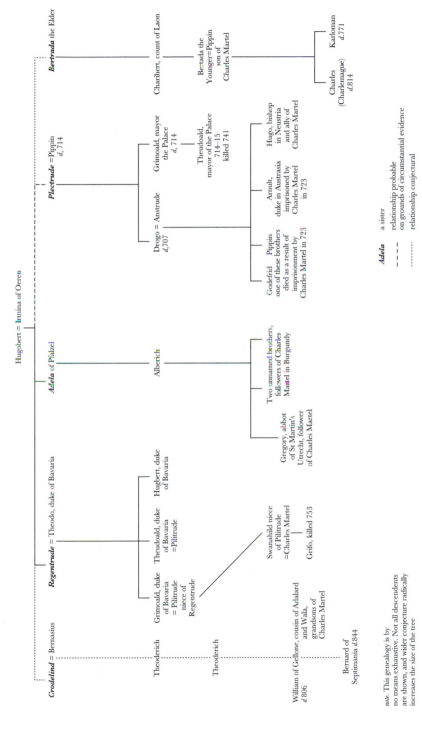

Hugobert = Irmina of Oeren

Crodelind = Bernasius   **Regentrude** = Theodo, duke of Bavaria   **Adela** of Pfalzel   **Plectrude** = Pippin *d. 714*   **Bertrada** the Elder

Theoderich

Theoderich

Bernard of Septimania *d. 844*

Grimoald, duke of Bavaria = Pilitrude niece of Regentrude

Theudoald, duke of Bavaria = Pilitrude

Hugbert, duke of Bavaria

Swanahild niece of Charles Martel = Charles Martel

Grifo, killed 753

William of Gellone, cousin of Adalard and Wala, grandsons of Charles Martel

Alberich

Gregory, abbot of St Martin's Utrecht, follower of Charles Martel

Two unnamed brothers, followers of Charles Martel in Burgundy

Drogo = Anstrude *d. 707*

Grimoald, mayor the Palace *d. 714*

Theudoald, mayor of the Palace 714–15 killed 741

Godefrid   Pippin one of these brothers died as a result of imprisonment by Charles Martel in 723

Arnult, duke in Austrasia imprisoned by Charles Martel in 723

Hugo, bishop in Neustria and ally of Charles Martel

Charibert, count of Laon

Bertrada the Younger = Pippin son of Charles Martel

Charles (Charlemagne) *d. 814*   Karloman *d. 771*

Adela   a sister

– – –   relationship probable on grounds of circumstantial evidence

....   relationship conjectural

note. This genealogy is by no means exhaustive. Not all descendents are shown, and wider conjecture radically increases the size of the tree

197

The descendents of Pippin and Alpaida

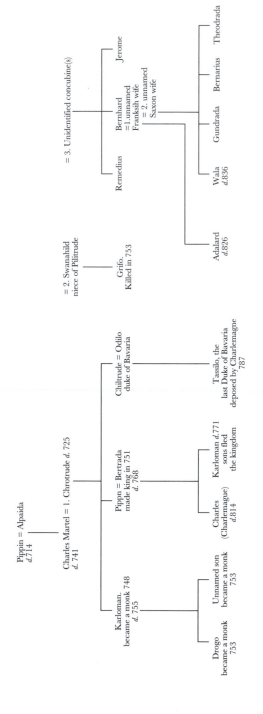

Note. Charles Martel also
had a half-brother, Count Childebrand
He was either the son of Pippin, mother unidentified
or the son of Alpaida, father unidentified

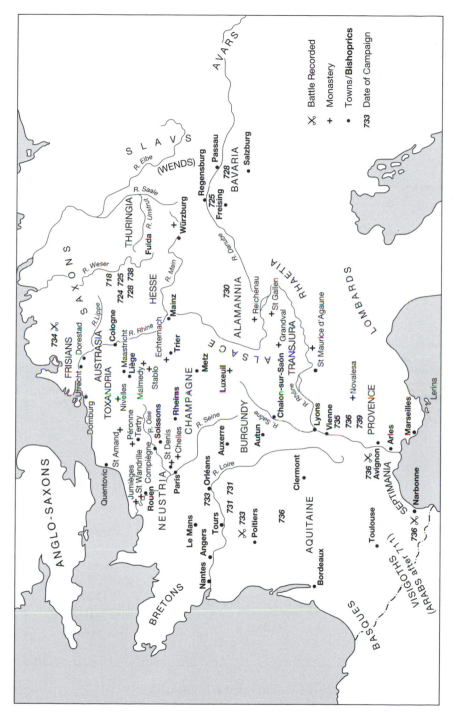

Francia, regions and neighbours in the seventh and early eighth centuries; and Charles Martel's campaigns in the outlying regions.

199

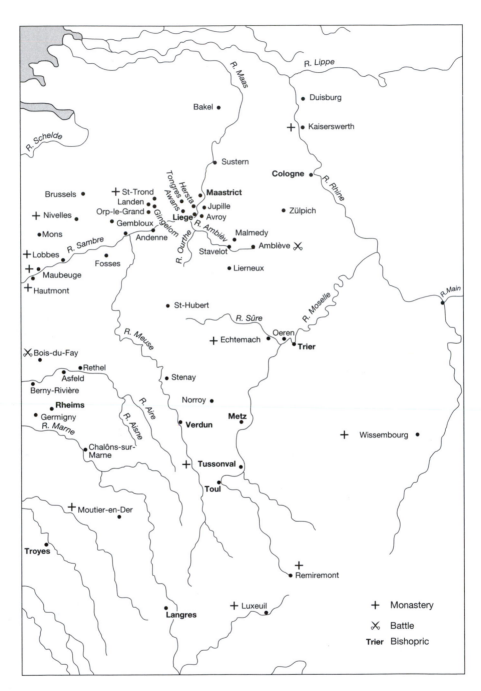

The Carolingian heartlands in the early eighth century.

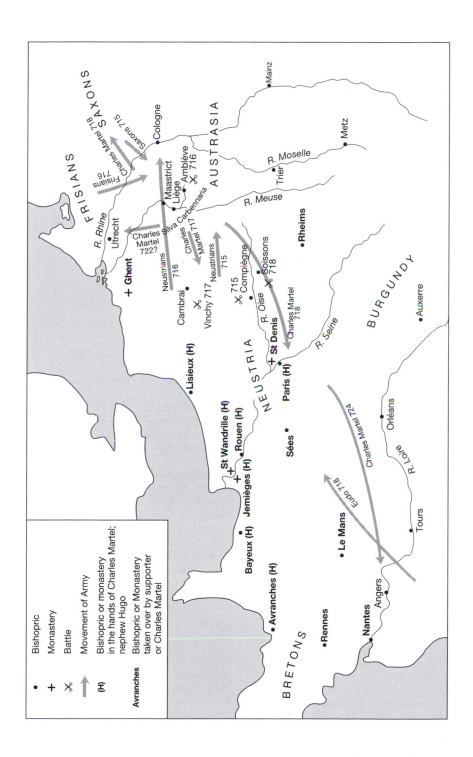

FRISIANS

SAXONS

AUSTRASIA

BURGUNDY

NEUSTRIA

BRETONS

• Mainz

• Metz

R. Moselle

Trier •

R. Meuse

• Cologne

Charles Martel 718

Saxons 715

Frisians 716

Maastrict
Liège
Amblève ✗ 716

R. Rhine

Utrecht •

Charles
Martel
722?

+ Ghent

Silva Carbennaria

Charles
Martel 717

Neustrians 716

Cambrai •

Vinchy 717

Neustrians 715

✗ 715

Compiègne •

Soissons 718
✗
R. Oise

Charles Martel
718

R. Seine

• Rheims

• Auxerre

• Lisieux (H)

St Denis
+

Paris (H)

St Wandrille (H)
+ Rouen (H)
+
• Jemièges (H)

Bayeux (H) •

Avranches (H) •

Sées •

Le Mans •

Eudo 718

Charles Martel 724

Orléans •

R. Loire

Tours •

Angers •

Nantes
•

• Rennes

INDEX

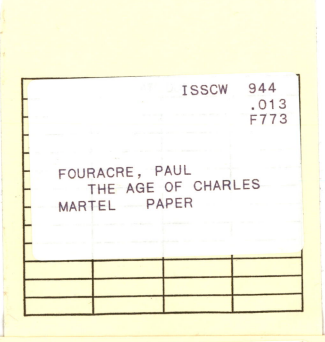